Designing World Class Corporate Strategies

Value-Creating Roles for Corporate Centres

Designing World Class Corporate Strategies

Value-Creating Roles for Corporate Centres

Keith Ward, Cliff Bowman and Andrew Kakabadse

ELSEVIER
BUTTERWORTH
HEINEMANN

AMSTERDAM BOSTON HEIDELBERG LONDON NEW YORK OXFORD
PARIS SAN DIEGO SAN FRANCISCO SINGAPORE SYDNEY TOKYO

Elsevier Butterworth-Heinemann
Linacre House, Jordan Hill, Oxford OX2 8DP
30, Corporate Drive, Burlington, MA 01803

First published 2005

British Library Cataloguing in Publication Data
A catalogue record for this book is available from the British Library

Library of Congress Cataloging in Publication Data
A catalog record for this book is available from the Library of Congress

ISBN 0 7506 6368 5

For information on all Elsevier Butterworth-Heinemann publications
visit our website at http://elsevierbooks.com

Printed and bound in Great Britain

Contents

Preface

This book focuses on the key value-adding role of corporate centres within large, primarily multi-business organisations. At present these corporate centres are frequently accused of not creating any value and merely adding cost to their groups. We have identified four ways in which corporate centres can have value-adding roles. These four value-creating roles have differing levels of sustainability and each can be more appropriate to specific types of external environment. However, they all require significantly different types of leadership and other key skills at the corporate centre.

Our objective in starting the research that has resulted in this book was to consider the challenges facing corporate centres in an integrated and multi-functional way. Many leading management books and the supporting academic literature are becoming increasingly narrowly focused, even when they address the overall strategic management of organisations. This approach can create problems for practising managers as, in many cases, they face a broad range of issues and challenges which affect their whole organisations. Each of the authors has therefore progressively been broadening their individual research initiatives from their own originally strongly focused areas of expertise. Working together on this project has enabled us to take a more holistic approach to the development of corporate strategies. Thus our resulting model incorporates leadership styles and cultural issues, as well as relevant control processes and appropriate performance measures, for our four value-adding corporate centre roles.

We wanted to write a book that is of direct relevance and value to practising managers, but not one which is so overfull of detailed case studies that there is no room for any structured arguments. Hence the book tries, in Part I, to set out the development of our corporate configurations model in a logically argued way; before, in Part II, discussing each of the four configurations in depth with a number of real company case studies. Part III then considers issues involved in applying the model in practice, as well as providing more background to the academic theories underpinning the model.

All the functional and process elements involved are integrated within each chapter, rather than considering each particular functional attribute separately. This means that the book, like the development of the corporate configurations model, has been a genuinely collaborative effort, unlike many similar ventures that are really a series of individual chapters bound together only physically by the outer covers.

We hope that you, the reader, feel that the efforts involved in producing the book have been worthwhile and that the ideas discussed can help to make corporate centres more effective and value creating.

We would like to thank Sheila Hart for typing the manuscript and Angela Ward and Hilary Browne for producing all the complicated figures.

Keith Ward
Cliff Bowman
Andrew Kakabadse

PART I

A corporate configurations framework

Chapter 1

Value-adding corporate centres

Introduction

Multi-business groups are under attack. In the major developed markets of the world not only is the truly diversified conglomerate seen as a dinosaur from a bygone corporate era, but also the corporate centres of very many other large corporations are seen as endangered species, facing ever increasing demands and challenges to justify their continued existence.

Corporate centres are seen as adding costs, not creating value. If this is true, the next logical argument is that these corporate centres actually destroy part of the value created by the underlying businesses within the group. Hence, if the group was to be broken apart, this destruction of value could be stopped by closing the corporate centre. Shareholders in the resulting separately constituted companies would be financially better off.

This helps to explain the recent trends towards refocusing initiatives, demergers, partial public listings, i.e. flotations, management buy-outs, private equity funded take-overs of parts of large groups, etc. At the opposite end of the spectrum, mergers and acquisition activity has been at an all-time record level within many global industries. Interestingly the impact on the corporate centres involved is remarkably similar: severe cost-cutting exercises and dramatic head-count reductions.

This shareholder value focused argument has been actively reinforced by the work of many of the major strategic consultancies and much of the academic research into the role and effectiveness of corporate centres. Consequently this theme is also frequently reflected in the media, which normally seems much more concerned with a small reduction in employment at any operating site within such a group than with the complete closure of a major corporate head office.

It is our contention in this book that value destruction is not the inevitable result of having a corporate centre. We do not disagree with the conclusions of much of the academic research that this is often the actual result, but we believe that this is caused by a lack of clarity about the role of the corporate centre in most large groups.

The corporate centre must first really understand its corporate philosophy, i.e. its reason for existing, and then adopt the consequently appropriate corporate configuration, of which, we argue, there are only four, if it is to add significant value to the various businesses making up the group.

Corporate philosophy is the combination of the nature of the relationship adopted by the centre with its divisions and the source of the corporate advantage developed by the group. These combinations represent the causal relationship that dictates the most appropriate corporate configuration for this group. Each of the resulting four possible corporate configurations has dramatic implications for the size, style, skills and expertise, culture, application of performance measures, etc. of the required corporate centre for the group, if that centre is to add significant value rather than adding cost and destroying value.

This may seem a bold claim with which to start this book, but each of our configurations is underpinned by a well-established economic rationale, which enables these combinations of corporate advantage and method of corporate centre involvement to add value sustainably over time. As is explained later, this does not mean that any group will need the same corporate configuration for ever. As the corporate philosophy should adjust to a changing external environment, so should the configuration of the corporate centre also change appropriately.

These underpinning economic rationales are explained in some detail at the end of this chapter, but first it is essential to develop these four value-adding corporate configurations. The model itself is deceptively simple but each configuration has significant consequences for the structure and culture of the group, the types of businesses it should contain, the way these businesses must be managed, and the types of managers required at the corporate centre.

The focus of the book

The research initiative that led to the development of the corporate configurations model that is at the heart of this book set out to consider the specific value-adding role of the corporate centre. Most existing publications on business strategy have focused on the underlying businesses (i.e. they have looked at the firm, the operating divisions or strategic business units) and their capacity to create value. In some cases, these studies have talked about the overall 'organisation' but without explicitly considering the role of the corporate centre. Yet, much research discusses the importance of the 'leadership role' of the top management team at the centre of the organisation. Our objective was to focus on the specific nature of the corporate centre in multi-business groups and to seek to identify ways in which this corporate centre could add sustainable value to its underlying businesses.

In many large groups, the corporate centres carry out a wide range of activities and often get involved in quite diverse business processes. However, it is now well accepted that the totality of business activities and processes can be separated into *a few* that actually contribute to value creation, *the majority* that need to be done but which do not in themselves create value (often referred to as hygiene factors), and possibly some that actually destroy value. Identifying the key value-adding processes of corporate centres is the focus of the book. These are called different things by different people (e.g. core competences, dynamic capabilities, critical resources or, as we shall normally be referring to them, sources of sustainable advantage). We shall also discuss whether, by carrying out other non value-adding activities that could be done outside the corporate centre, these centres risk reducing or totally destroying any potential value added by creating confusion among the underlying business units.

Given the varied backgrounds of the collaborators on this project, the most logical start point for the research was to try to synthesise, and then develop, the differing approaches to this issue from several academic and business disciplines. Thus the resulting model draws on corporate and competitive strategy; leadership, organisational development, and cultural issues; financial planning and control, performance measurement, and management information requirements.

Another key element in our approach was a desire to start from first principles to develop an overall framework as to how corporate centres can add value. This can be contrasted with the recently popular process of examining several successful companies and then drawing conclusions about the causes of their success. A major benefit of this alternative research methodology is that it should automatically generate some in-depth case studies that illustrate clearly the identified success criteria. The downsides are that it can be difficult to establish the essential cause and effect relationship or to draw predictive generalisations that can subsequently be applied by other companies. Our ambitious aim was to come up with a fairly prescriptive set of frameworks that could be applied by top management teams at the centre of complex organisations.

The basis of our framework was to use the well-tried and tested configurational approach, particularly building on Mintzberg's notion of configurations as is discussed in more detail in Chapter 10. The reason for adopting this configurational approach is rooted in our belief that corporate strategy and organisational structure should not be treated as separate phenomena. Any strategy will have distinct and particular organisational requirements if it is to be successfully implemented. Thus, realised strategies and structures should be viewed as inextricably connected. If our research was able to establish feasible links between our four corporate strategies and their required organisational structures and processes, this would lend considerable weight to the argument that these strategies are not merely theoretical concepts.

The methodology used was therefore an iterative process of framework and model development, testing against specific companies and with 'in-situ' management teams, review and modification of the framework and model, comparison with other published material in the area, and then more testing and development. Thus each element of the model has been subjected to rigorous analysis and scrutiny by a large number of practising managers. However, as the model was initially developed from the first principles of value creation, rather than by directly observing corporate practice, we cannot give neatly packaged, classic examples of companies that exactly comply with every nuance of the corporate configurations model. This means that we strongly believe that even the very good examples of the application of the model that we do include in the book can add even more value to their groups if they comply more fully with the recommendations of the model!

Relevance to 'single' business 'groups'

Although the initial focus of our research was on corporate centres in multi-business groups (e.g. diversified multinationals), we rapidly realised that this was an unnecessary restriction on the applicability of the corporate configurations model. The resulting model has direct relevance to any group that has a corporate centre that is separately structured from its underlying business units, whether those business units are selling the same or highly diverse goods and services to similar or very different groups of customers.

Indeed, the more closely related nature of the underlying businesses places even greater pressure on any 'separated' corporate centre to justify its existence. In practice, the development of such a corporate centre is the almost inevitable result of the success of the initial single business division. As the business becomes geographically more spread out, particularly if the terms 'international' or 'global' become relevant to the business, there is an increasing need for some co-ordination of the business' activities and critically of the resource allocation priorities within this single business. Many large single businesses have created very complex regional and area structures and/or utilise significant separately constituted centralised support functions. These separate support areas have often been given their own strategic objectives and their own performance measurements, and they report against these, not to the regional sub-businesses that they support, but to the centre of the organisation. A corporate centre has been created.

Thus the corporate centres of large-scale retailers, financial services groups, and 'single' product manufacturers and service providers can all be analysed using the model. It is also possible to apply this analytical framework to the 'not-for-profit' sector. This is achieved by considering the true value-adding role of the corporate centre of, for example, government controlled entities such as the Health Service, rather than restricting the definition of value adding to the normal commercially orientated view of shareholder value. Indeed, as will become clear as the model is developed, a broad view of how corporate centres add value is critical to applying the model. Some of the issues involved in applying the model in these areas are considered in Chapter 3.

The what and how of the model

Many large groups have spent considerable time and money in seeking to justify their continued existence by developing group-wide vision or mission statements. Unfortunately many of these do not indicate how remaining as a 'group' will create more value than can be generated by the component businesses comprising the group. Any such difference in value creation (whether positive or negative) is attributable to the influence of the corporate centre.

Corporate centres differ both in what they try to do and how they try to do it. The 'how' dimension refers to the nature of the involvement of the centre and the type and degree of intervention that the corporate centre makes in the operations of the group's businesses. At its very simplest, the corporate centre can intervene directly by doing things

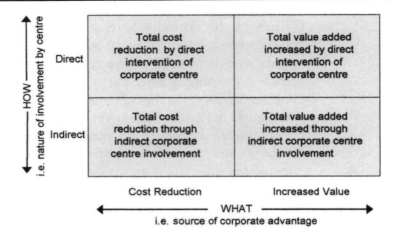

Figure I.I
Causal relationship of
the model—the what
and how.

for the businesses within the group, or it develops an indirect method of involvement by influencing how these businesses behave, i.e. more 'showing and telling' than actually 'doing'.

Similarly, a corporate centre can only justify its own central cost levels in one of two ways: either it somehow reduces the total costs of the group or it does something that adds more value to the group than the centre itself costs.

As shown in Figure 1.1, combining these alternative types of involvement with these two ways of adding value generates four potentially value-adding roles for any corporate centre. Our research indicates that these four combinations really do represent the only ways in which corporate centres can consistently and sustainably create value, as opposed to adding costs.

However, in order to realise this potential added value, each corporate centre has to ensure that it is operating within the appropriate configuration for its group. The appropriate configuration depends on the specific external environment that the group is facing and the mix of businesses in the group. The issues of transitioning from one configuration to another are initially discussed in Chapter 3, once each dimension has been fully explained and refined into the complete model.

Sources of corporate advantage

In many multi-business groups, the different businesses comprising the group have developed their individual, appropriately tailored sources of sustainable competitive advantage, or areas of core competence. These should be tailored to suit the specific environment that they face in the markets where they operate. As no other businesses within the group may operate in these markets or face these specific circumstances, there is no certainty that any of these competitive advantages will be common across the group. This of itself does not, however, destroy the economic rationale for the businesses staying together as a group.

Our interest is at the corporate centre of the group, and how this corporate centre can develop its own, equally appropriately tailored, sustainable core competence, which will allow it to enhance the overall value of the businesses within the group.

One potential approach is for the corporate centre to find a way in which *it* can reduce the total costs of the group, even after allowing for *its* own costs. This requires the centre to generate some form of scale economy for the group, either directly by doing things centrally, or, more indirectly, by 'showing' the constituent businesses how to reduce their costs.

The only other alternative is, as already stated, for the centre to add more value to the businesses in the group than the centre itself costs to run. To do this, the corporate centre must have some particular skills or knowledge that are relevant and applicable to all of the businesses within the group. This relevance and applicability may, for any specific business, be current or may be expected to occur in the foreseeable future; but, if it is already in the past, there is no extra value created by retaining that specific business within the group.

These skills may not be directly to do with the specific operations or customers of any individual business, because the centre may possess knowledge or appropriate process skills which enable any specific business unit's competitive advantage to be exploited more widely within the group.

It should be noted that the source of corporate advantage does not need to have the same fundamental basis as the individual competitive advantages that have been developed by the group's various business units. Indeed, in many cases, it is their very differences that increases the value added by the corporate centre, as is discussed in Chapter 8. Thus, it is by no means unusual to find a corporate centre focusing on reducing total group costs, in a group where the main business unit strategies are based on enhancing customer service, product differentiation, technology advantages, etc.

This can be very important because the corporate centre often competes at a different level, on a different basis, against different competitors than the underlying business units within the group. In many cases, the group, through its corporate centre, competes primarily for the attention of investors in its relevant capital market; thus 'the competition' is made up of all the alternative investments that are available. These may not be direct competitors of the underlying businesses in terms of products and customers in any specific market, but may represent a broader category of investment.

For example, Procter & Gamble's largest global direct competitor would undoubtedly be Unilever, as they compete in many markets around the world for the same consumers with relatively similar products; e.g. washing powders. However, at the group level, investors considering purchasing Procter & Gamble's shares on the USA stock market would probably compare this investment against the expected returns from alternative investments in other leading USA based, branded, fast moving consumer products companies. Thus other groups, such as Coca-Cola, Altria, Pepsi-Cola, Kelloggs, etc, become competitors at the group level, despite the absence of directly competing products. Despite the trend towards global capital markets, most of Unilever's investors are still based in Europe, and consequently they will tend to have a different list of potential alternative investments. Competition at the corporate strategy level can therefore significantly differ from the competitive strategy basis, which has been the focus of most of the research and publications to date.

Creating or capturing value

When considering strategies that seek to increase shareholder value, it is very important to understand where this increased value is coming from. Some strategies seek *to create* completely *new* value that would not otherwise have existed, while other strategies try *to capture* more of the already *existing* value available within an industry; this create or capture value concept is very important in the application of game theory to shareholder value analysis. It also can be applied to our sources of corporate advantage.

The focus on cost reduction by the corporate centre can be regarded as unlocking existing potential value from the underlying businesses. In some cases, the increased value comes quite directly from external suppliers by centralising the sourcing of support activities or even core business processes. This is really increased value capture by the centre, because the impact of this corporate strategy is unseen by the customers of the underlying businesses. This cost reducing corporate centre changes the way that the businesses do things, not what they do. These businesses operate more efficiently due to the presence of the corporate centre but, from their customer's perspective, they do not operate differently.

Where the corporate centre applies its skills or knowledge to increase value, the result is much more likely to be the creation of new value by the underlying businesses. The whole purpose of this type of centre is to change what the businesses do and these changes are normally clearly visible to their external customers. Thus new products may be created and launched by the businesses, existing products may be sold in innovative ways or to new market segments. This emphasis on transforming the underlying businesses, rather than improving their efficiency, has important implications for the leadership role required at the corporate centre, as is discussed in Chapter 2.

Nature of corporate involvement

The two sources of corporate advantage that we refer to as economies of scale and knowledge can be implemented within a group in significantly different ways. In some groups, the corporate centre actually carries out certain key activities on behalf of the individual business units. This centralisation may involve only support activities that are common across the group. Typical examples are accounting processes such as accounts payable processing which may be done globally, information technology, recruitment, management development and training. However, centralisation may extend to some of the core processes of component group businesses, e.g. sourcing, procurement, logistics, production, sales, and even marketing.

The critical issue is the justification for this centralisation and the resulting direct interference in the affairs of individual group businesses. Many of these individual businesses will resent any such direct meddling by the corporate centre. One obvious economic justification is that it is significantly cheaper to carry out these activities for the group as a whole, rather than to duplicate them within each of the businesses. Thus this direct style of intervention may be done to reduce the total costs of the group, through achieving economies of scale in these centralised activities. (There are examples of centralisation, particularly of the core processes of a group, where the economic rationale is not to reduce costs and these are considered below.)

Alternatively the corporate centre can seek to reduce the total costs of the group via a more indirect method of involvement. This normally involves setting financial targets and other performance measures for each business. The corporate centre therefore generates an economy of scale for the group in this important area of management planning and control. The individual businesses rely upon the governance processes established by the centre, rather than needing to develop their own.

This type of corporate centre sometimes provides 'advice and guidance' (quite often in the form of a 'large stick') to those businesses that are not performing well enough, i.e. they have not responded to the 'carrot' of the financial incentives associated with achieving the centre's targets. However, this type of corporate centre does not normally get involved either in 'doing' things on behalf of the businesses or directly running the businesses within the group.

Indeed this type of corporate centre is more likely to sell or close down non-performing business units within the group's portfolio. Thus, although the corporate centre has an indirect method of involvement in terms of managing its businesses, it may actively and directly intervene in order to manage the portfolio of businesses within the group. Acquisitions and divestments often form a significant part of the role carried out by these indirect cost reduction focused corporate centres.

A very different indirect nature of involvement can also be value adding. The main focus of this type of corporate centre is in creating new know-how within the group, rather than reducing costs across the group. As a key part of this role the corporate centre establishes a clear vision for the group as a whole and states a set of values (often referred to as guiding principles, etc.) that all group businesses must subscribe to. This type of corporate centre is creating a sense of belonging and trust within the group. Consequently the unquestioning adherence to short-term financial targets reinforced by the threat of a 'big stick' or,

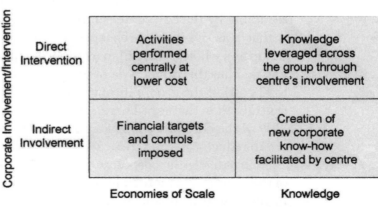

Figure I.2
The 'value added' by the corporate centre.

Register for eNews, the free email service from Elsevier Science and Technology Books, to receive:

- specially written author articles
- free sample chapters
- advance news of our latest publications
- regular offers
- related event information
- ...and more

Go to **http://books.elsevier.com**, select a subject, register and the eNews will soon be arriving on your desktop!

If you would prefer to register by post, complete and return this card to the address overleaf.

http://books.elsevier.com

Select the subjects you'd like to receive information about, enter your email and mail address and freepost this card back to us.

ARCHITECTURE AND THE BUILT ENVIRONMENT
☐ General Architecture
☐ Architectural Practice Management
☐ History of Architecture
☐ Landscape
☐ Urban design
☐ Sustainable Architecture
☐ Planning and Design

BUILDING AND CONSTRUCTION

BUSINESS & MANAGEMENT
☐ Accounting/CIMA Publishing
☐ Finance
☐ Hospitality, Leisure and Tourism
☐ Human Resources and Training
☐ Pergamon Flexible Learning
☐ Knowledge Management
☐ Sales and Marketing
☐ IT Management/Computer Weekly

COMPUTING & COMPUTER SCIENCES
Computer Weekly:
☐ Management and Business Computing
Made Simple Computing:
☐ Introduction to computing and programming

Computer Science:
☐ Computer Sciences
☐ Artificial Intelligence
☐ Computer Graphics
☐ Human Computer Interaction
☐ Information Security
☐ Information Systems/Databases
☐ Networking
☐ Operating Systems
☐ Software Development
☐ Information systems

Professional Computing:
☐ Data Management
☐ Information Security
☐ IT Management
☐ Networking
☐ Operating Systems
☐ Software Engineering
☐ MCSE Certification
☐ Security

☐ **CONSERVATION AND MUSEOLOGY**

ELECTRONICS AND ELECTRICAL ENGINEERING
☐ Communications
☐ Control and Instrumentation
☐ Electrical Power Engineering
☐ Electronics and Computer Engineering

ENGINEERING
☐ Bioengineering
☐ Environmental Engineering
☐ Industrial Engineering
☐ Materials Engineering
☐ Mechanical Engineering
☐ Optical Engineering
☐ Petroleum and Petrochemical Processing

☐ **FORENSICS**

MEDIA TECHNOLOGY
☐ Film/TV/Video Production
☐ Postproduction
☐ Scriptwriting
☐ Lighting
☐ Computer Graphics and Animation /Gaming
☐ Photography/Imaging
☐ Audio
☐ Radio
☐ Broadcast and Communication Technology
☐ Broadcast Management and Theory
☐ Journalism
☐ Theatre and Live Performance
☐ Special effects/Make-up

☐ **SECURITY**

Name:

Job title:

Email address:

Mail address:

Postcode:

Signature: **Date:**

☐ I would like to receive information by Email ☐ Post ☐ Both ☐

Science and Technology Books, Elsevier Ltd. Registered office: The Boulevard, Langford Lane, Kidlington, Oxon OX5 1GB. Registered number 1982084

Jo Blackford
Data Co-ordinator
Elsevier
FREEPOST - SCE5435
Oxford
OX2 8BR
UK

even worse, divestment from the group or outright closure have no place within this corporate configuration.

As these corporate centres have only an indirect involvement in the operations of the group's businesses, their own key role is facilitating the creation of new corporate know-how. This quite commonly requires collaboration across the boundaries of the existing organisation structure. Hence the importance of trust within the group, so that two or more business units can willingly work together to develop a new potential group source of added value, without destructive and delaying arguments about who pays for what and who gets what share of the potential return. This type of corporate centre may therefore increase the total costs incurred by the group, but it tries to create far more added value from the creative stimulus and values leadership that it gives to the businesses.

However, there are many other groups where knowledge (as opposed to generating economies of scale to reduce group costs) is also the key source of corporate advantage but where a more direct intervention by the corporate centre is required. The individual businesses within this type of group may have developed individually strong, knowledge based, sustainable competitive advantages; such as brands, customer service processes, differentiated products or process advantages. However, either the group structure or the management capabilities/resources of the individual business units are restricting the exploitation of this knowledge. For example, a business unit may be focused on a specific geographic region of the world, while its technology advantage or brand may have far broader applicability.

The value-adding role of the corporate centre is not therefore to facilitate the development of new knowledge as this already appears to be happening around the group, but to ensure that the existing knowledge is fully exploited across the group. This may simply involve ensuring total global availability within the group, so that the full economic potential of each such competitive advantage is realised. Normally, however, real life is not that simple. Merely telling all the other business units about the 'great new product' available from Division X does not make anything change. Indeed, in many cases, this total global availability can be achieved more easily without any interference from a corporate centre. If a business unit does not possess the management capabilities or resources to exploit fully any new knowledge based competitive advantage, it can enter into licensing agreements with other business units within the group or, failing that, with external third parties.

The corporate centre should be looking more deeply at the sources of competitive advantage that exist within the group. Such a corporate centre may identify a particular business unit that has successfully developed and is currently exploiting a range of strong brands in its own markets. This business unit may well possess brand development and exploitation expertise, which could have great value if it could be utilised elsewhere within the group. This knowledge may be far more valuable to the group than simply transferring the business unit's specific brands globally, as they may have been tailored to suit its particular competitive environment.

Therefore the corporate centre can intervene directly in spreading this brand development know-how to those other parts of the group where it should be of value. This requires a great deal of information at the corporate centre concerning the particular circumstances of the various businesses in the group. It also needs managers at the corporate centre with leading edge skills in systems and process management to ensure that this knowledge transfer is successfully achieved. In a number of such groups, this has resulted in the centralisation of certain core processes (such as brand management, new product development and launch) in an attempt to control directly the group-wide exploitation of such critical knowledge based assets. As mentioned above, this form of centralisation is not done in order to reduce costs; it is done to speed up and optimise the exploitation of existing knowledge across the group.

The different roles for corporate centres

The four possible value-adding combinations indicate significantly different roles for the corporate centre in each of these configurations. In addition, these differing roles mean that significantly different key skills are needed at the centre. These distinguishing features have led us to come up with generalised descriptions for each style of corporate centre.

The primary role for an indirect type of involvement combined with a cost-reducing, economies of scale based source of corporate advantage is to establish appropriate control processes for the businesses within the groups, as shown in Figure 1.3. An important part of these control processes is the setting of financial targets, but how these financial targets are actually achieved is delegated to the individual businesses. However, the corporate centre must have the skills to identify what is achievable by the underlying business units, albeit with

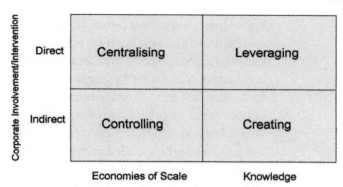

Figure 1.3
Primary role of
corporate centre.

some difficulty and stretch. Clearly, setting totally unreasonable and unrealistic financial targets will be counter-productive from a group perspective as the business unit management teams will rapidly become demotivated.

Thus the key skills needed at the corporate centre for the configuration are those of financial management, as shown in Figure 1.4. A relatively small group of highly skilled corporate financiers and financially oriented managers can control, and alter when necessary, a large portfolio of relatively diverse businesses, provided that the appropriate planning, control and reporting systems have been put in place. Thus a 'corporate governance' based economy of scale can be achieved.

However, the other type of indirect corporate involvement has a fundamentally different primary role, which requires an almost diametrically opposed set of skills in the corporate centre. Where the corporate advantage is based on knowledge and the value added by the corporate centre is facilitating the creation of new corporate

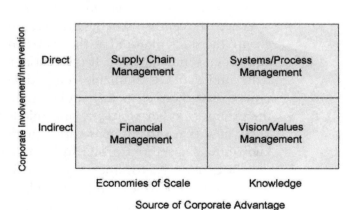

Figure 1.4
Key skills needed at the
corporate centre.

know-how, a focus on any individual business unit's adherence to its own financial targets may not be appropriate. The emphasis is on stimulating creativity and innovation across the group and, particularly, among separate business units. Corporate centre managers therefore must create an environment where the businesses not only feel encouraged to take controlled risks, but also to share their learning (from both their successes and, perhaps even more importantly, their failures) with their colleagues in other parts of the group.

This requires the establishment of a clear vision and an appropriate set of values for the group. However, it is essential that the centre's management is then seen to 'walk the talk' consistently in the way that it deals with the businesses in the group. The key skills of vision/values management are thus vital if a strong group identity is to be developed and a high degree of trust can be built up between both individual businesses and the centre and across the business units directly.

In the target oriented and financial management focused corporate centre these objectives would normally be unachievable. In many cases there is no group identity in the minds of the business units and they do not completely trust the centre, nor does the centre totally trust the business units. Further, the centre may discourage direct contact from one business unit to another, as it prefers to exercise tight control over the individual businesses in the group, creating a 'divide and rule' environment, albeit by an 'indirect' process.

The vision/values management oriented corporate centre also still has only an indirect influence on the actual business units within the group. Therefore its management team requires highly developed communication and counselling skills, if the group's vision and values are to be widely and accurately adopted. In the other two corporate centre configurations, there is a much more direct form of involvement; consequently the required skills are very different.

Where the centre is seeking to leverage existing knowledge across the group, the skills required at the centre are primarily those of systems and process management. It is essential to distil the key elements that truly underpin a sustainable competitive advantage in one business unit so that these elements can be applied in other businesses across the group. In other words, a vital role for the centre is to codify the know-how that already exists in a single business. By codifying this know-how, the centre transforms it into corporate knowledge that can then be exploited across the group. [We draw the now common distinction between know-how and knowledge. Know-how is more intuitive and hence people specific, whereas knowledge is codified know-how that can therefore be more widely shared. This difference has significant implications for the ease of imitation by competitors.]

The centre can ensure that this corporate knowledge is applied wherever relevant within the group through its direct intervention. This can be achieved with minimal disruption to the continued successful exploitation within the originating business unit. However, in order to do this, there will almost automatically be a significantly larger corporate centre than with either of the indirect styles of involvement. The value adding is, of course, not achieved by reducing total group costs and, accordingly, the key test is whether the centre can justify its size and costs.

If the group is to achieve the maximum value added from the corporate centre's attempts to leverage existing knowledge, there are three sets of key skills/knowledge needed within, or available to, the centre. Systems and process management skills are needed for the codification/ distillation of the existing knowledge prior to its being leveraged across the group. In addition, the corporate centre must have an excellent understanding of the businesses within the group, in order to identify those other businesses where this particular competitive advantage is applicable. The centre can also seek to add new business units to the group where this knowledge can also be leveraged to create substantial added value. A related but separable skill relates to the evaluation of this particular competitive advantage. The centre must be capable of understanding the relative strength and defendability of this advantage when it is taken out of its current specific competitive context. This evaluation must be done before the group invests substantial resources in first codifying the advantage and then attempting to leverage it elsewhere within the group. Many competitive advantages turn out to be so context specific that their leveraging potential is in reality very limited.

The remaining combination of type and source also involves direct intervention but with a focus on reducing total group costs. The resulting emphasis tends to be on the centre actually doing things for and on behalf of its business units. Thus the centre's primary role can be described as centralising, in order to achieve economies of scale for the group as a whole. These group savings are often achieved at some cost to the individual businesses, and it is clearly important that the financial justification properly takes these negative impacts into account. The costs often arise from the corporate centre's desire to standardise those processes and activities that it centralises, so as to maximise its apparent cost savings. The standardised process may significantly adversely affect the way in which particular units conduct their businesses. In some cases the adverse impact is so great that they opt out of

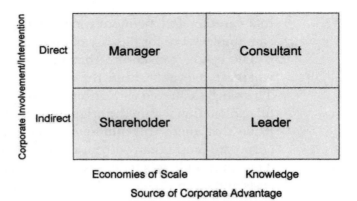

Figure 1.5
Descriptors of corporate
centre style.

the centralised activity, despite the increased costs to the group that result.

If these disfunctionalities are to be avoided, the corporate centre needs a high degree of supply chain management skills, so that it can centralise those processes that generate a high level of true net savings for the group. This may necessitate a lower level of centralisation or of using a more flexible centralised process that can accommodate the wide range of specific requirements of the business units.

This analysis of the primary roles of corporate centres and their consequently required key skills shows how different these corporate centres are in practice. We have found it helpful to use generic descriptions for each of these different styles, as shown in Figure 1.5.

As the centralising corporate centre is most heavily involved in doing things for the other parts of the group, our style descriptor is that of manager. This can be contrasted with the other direct intervention style where the centre focuses on ensuring that existing knowledge is fully leveraged across the group. Our descriptor for this corporate centre style is consultant, as the key involvement is to ensure that it can be, and is, done rather than totally taking over the activity on an ongoing basis.

The indirect style of involvement which relies on financial management skills in order to set targets and controls for the business units we describe as a shareholder. This is due partly to the almost exclusive focus on the financial returns generated by the business units but, even more fundamentally, because of the corporate centre's willingness to dispose of its investment in a subsidiary if this return is perceived as inadequate, or if a sufficiently high price is offered by a prospective purchaser.

The only corporate centre type that we feel demonstrates true overall leadership qualities is the one that focuses on creating new corporate know-how by emphasising the vision and values of the group. Hence its style descriptor is, unsurprisingly, leader.

The corporate configurations model

These descriptions will be used in the remainder of the book when referring to particular styles of corporate centres, but they are inadequate references to the four differing corporate configurations that are at the heart of this model.

Creative

In the creative configuration, the centre plays an indirect role in the creation of new know-how for the group. By bringing together people from different business units to work on specific projects, or through the encouragement of informal networks across the corporation, new corporate owned know-how is created. Individual business units could also separately be working on creating new know-how, which is specifically aimed at their own businesses; indeed, this can happen under any of the four configurations.

The key difference is that, in this configuration, the creative role of the centre and its establishment of the guiding values that permeate throughout the corporation are the reason for the group remaining as a group. Successful examples of this configuration normally exhibit internally a very strong group identity, i.e. in preference to identifying primarily with their individual business unit, through their shared vision and values. This leads to a high level of trust and mutual respect among the various business units within the group, even though they may be operating in very diverse end markets, employing widely varying technologies, producing and selling significantly different products.

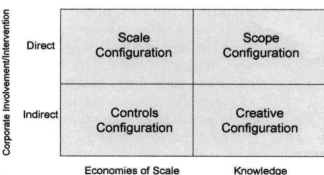

Figure 1.6
The corporate
configurations model.

Despite these differences, there is a discernible commonality across these businesses, which is normally perceptible even to an outsider.

This corporate configuration faces one very significant challenge to its continued existence, which is how does it exploit the newly created corporate know-how without destroying, or severely damaging, the strong group-wide culture which is its essential life-blood. This challenge is explored in detail in Chapter 7 but, in some cases, the very success of a creative configuration can bring about its transition into the scope configuration, with its very different role for the corporate centre.

Scope

Under the scope configuration, the key role of the centre is to ensure that existing knowledge is leveraged to its full potential across the whole group. The centre seeks to achieve this by direct intervention in appropriate business units. This direct intervention may take the form of centralising a key process or activity, not in order to reduce its cost by achieving economies of scale, but so as to ensure that the best practice available within the corporation is applied throughout the group. Whether centralised or not, a key role of the centre is to codify any such business unit developed know-how into generally available knowledge where this is possible, so that it can be applied by the other business units.

The codification process may make it easier for competitors to copy this specific competitive advantage, thus shortening its economic life during which it can generate true shareholder value. Consequently the really sustainable corporate advantage is the continuing ability to leverage across the group a succession of possibly short-lived specific competitive advantages. This means that the corporate centre does not itself necessarily need to develop any of these specific competitive advantages; this can be done by the business units. However, in all cases the corporate centre needs the in-depth knowledge of its businesses to know which of these new advantages have more widespread application within the group and where; plus the systems and process management skills to make this transfer as foolproof and value adding as possible. Where existing know-how is personal and tacit, the centre can re-deploy the individuals or team that have this expertise to other parts of the group.

There are significant implications for the type of businesses that should form part of this corporate configuration. The businesses, once again, may superficially appear quite diverse but, this time, they should share a common way of gaining competitive advantage. If this is not true, the centre will find it very difficult to leverage these advantages widely across the group. Interestingly it is quite possible for the common competitive advantage among the business units to be that of 'lowest cost' producer within their own competitive environments. In this case the corporate advantage is to leverage across the group all new knowledge developed about how to reduce costs. This group-wide leverage capability creates economies of scope for the group, as is discussed in a later section of this chapter and this explains the title given to this corporate configuration.

Scale

The other direct intervention configuration seeks to reduce total group costs, most frequently by centralising processes or activities. The aim is to generate economies of scale but, for these to create a sustainable corporate advantage, the group really needs to become the volume leader in this process or activity.

Which processes should be centralised is dictated by the businesses comprising the groups. If these businesses are particularly diverse, centralisation may be restricted to common support services such as HR, accounting, legal, etc. The more related the mix of businesses, the more opportunities there will be to gain scale economies and volume leadership in core processes such as manufacturing, procurement, distribution, research and development, and even sales and marketing.

A common problem with this corporate configuration is, as already mentioned, a tendency at the corporate centre to want to centralise processes that are currently performed differently across the group. In order to maximise the economies of scale benefits to the group, the centre imposes a standardised method or process. This can have detrimental impacts on the underlying businesses if there were sound economic rationales for their original differences.

Even without this problem, centralisation can reduce the level of trust between the business units and the centre. The centre now carries out certain processes on behalf of the business units, with the result that the business unit managers may no longer feel completely in control of their businesses. This may demotivate some of the business unit managers, but this problem can be resolved if the accountability/controllability issues are properly considered when establishing the performance measures used within both the business units and the centralised processes. This is discussed in detail in Chapter 5.

The corporate centre for this configuration may be very large, depending on the type of processes that are centralised, and will require a strong level of relevant technical expertise. However, there is always a need for high quality supply chain management skills in this type of corporate centre, as was highlighted in Figure 1.4 earlier, irrespective of the precise activities that have been centralised. The supply chain skills are needed not only to ensure that the process is correctly and appropriately centralised, but also to establish the service level agreements and transfer pricing methodologies that are essential to this corporate configuration, if it really is to reduce the total group costs on a sustainable basis.

The scale configuration is the one most commonly found in practice, but it can have a problem of sustainability over time. Once most common areas of activity have been centralised, there is little extra value that can be added by the corporate centre. At first sight, this does not necessarily seem to be an issue, so long as the group has achieved 'volume leader' status in its centralised activities. This should allow all its operating units to have sustainably the lowest cost possible for these centralised processes; unless and until their competitors find alternative strategies which achieve equally low or even lower costs. For many such centralised processes, particularly of support activities, much smaller competitors may be able to achieve this through outsourcing their activity to very large specialist suppliers, e.g. the big accounting firms, specialist IT outsourcing companies, third party distributors, etc. or by entering into strategic alliances with similar but non-competing companies. Thus the retention of volume leadership may require the corporation to continue to grow quite rapidly. This can result in the group acquiring businesses mainly because they will increase the economies of scale that can be achieved by the corporate centre; a case of the tail starting to wag the dog.

Controls

The remaining corporate configuration is also focused on reducing total group costs but through the indirect involvement of the corporate centre. The centre adds value to the business units through its financial management and governance skills, like targeting, financial planning, financial control disciplines, corporate finance and treasury expertise, tax planning and structuring. In some senses this can be viewed as another form of centralisation, because the group can afford a level of expertise that is not justifiable by any individual business unit. However, the key impact on the businesses is more indirect, as the centre achieves economies of scale in effective governance. The centre not only sets stretching financial targets for each of the businesses, but also develops appropriate control processes that monitor actual performance against these financial targets. The focus can tend to be on the short-term financial results, i.e. performance versus this year's budget.

In many such groups, there is consequently a very strong culture of delivering the required financial performance. Phrases such as 'the budget is a fixed contract between the business unit and the centre', 'non-achievement of your budget is career limiting' and 'the group rewards divisional managers who regularly achieve their budgets' are very common in the controls corporate configuration. A common outcome of such a short-term profit focus from the centre is that business units resort to cost cutting in order to achieve this year's target; even if these cost-cutting initiatives place in jeopardy the successful achievement of their longer term competitive strategies. The emphasis on cost reductions is often reinforced in the planning instructions issued from the corporate centre, as they set 'efficiency improvement' management tasks that require costs to fall, in real terms at least, over the planning period.

Not too surprisingly, this kind of planning process can motivate the business units to 'play a game' when proposing their budget. The planning target is negotiated to be as low as possible, thus making it more easily achievable. Further, if a business unit is doing well this year its management may be very tempted to try to disguise this year's outperformance in order to make achieving next year's target easier than it would otherwise be. The centre consequently may take on a further role of checking and testing the figures submitted by the business units. There is a resulting reduction in trust and potentially no over-riding group identity in this controls configuration, whereas in the creative configuration these were vital to the success of the group.

The controls configuration has a style descriptor of 'shareholder' because another key role for its centre is actively managing the portfolio of businesses within the group. Acquisitions and divestments are normally quite common in these groups, which often include the most diverse range of businesses found in any of the four configurations. (It should be clearly understood that acquisitions and divestments can play a role in each of the four corporate configurations.) Once again, however, there should be a common feature across attractive acquisitions for this configuration; the acquisition targets should benefit significantly from the clearly defined financial planning and control procedures applied within the group, i.e. they will benefit from and therefore add to the governance related economies of scale generated by the corporate centre.

This economy of scale can generate significant cost savings for the group. The establishment of structures and controls across the group, as well as setting tight financial targets, means that each separate business unit operates within a clearly defined set of parameters. Consequently they do not need to incur costs developing these processes for themselves. The centre focuses on developing appropriate targeting and monitoring processes and measures for the group, thereby achieving an economy of scale. Although the individual businesses within this type of group may look very different, they will normally share the attribute that the group's financial management processes are highly relevant to them, and hence are value adding for the group.

If and when this is no longer the case, the corporate centre may consider divesting itself of the business unit concerned. As with any commercially oriented shareholder, this corporate configuration only retains investments within its portfolio that it believes have value-adding potential. This is, of course, another reason for a low level of group identification by the business units within this type of group.

These descriptions of the four configurations can be used to categorise, albeit loosely for now, the types of corporations that often fit into each configuration. This may appear to describe a type of corporate lifecycle over time as groups could move from one configuration to another. This is discussed in Chapter 3, once the full model has been developed.

The underpinning economic rationales

Very early in the chapter, we claimed that each of the four corporate configurations had an underpinning economic rationale, which demonstrated why the corporate centre should be able to add value to the group on a sustainable basis.

The easiest configurations to justify are those where the corporate centre directly intervenes in the group's business units. The scale configuration seeks to exploit economies of scale through centralising certain processes and activities. An obvious form of this is the spreading of large, indivisible fixed costs across the group, where no individual business unit has sufficient scale to justify the cost on its own. Other sources of scale advantage may be technical (size of plant, minimum efficient level of output), power related (bargaining leverage with suppliers of goods, services and labour), or 'critical mass' related (size enables the group to employ more specialised skills, e.g. R&D, PR). Indeed economies of scale can relate to any activity that the group can economically justify but which would be prohibitively expensive for any individual business unit within the group.

Thus the buying power economy of scale may include access to capital markets that can reduce the overall cost of financing the group's operations. It may also reduce the cost of advertising to business units, through centralising media buying. Another potential economy of scale in the sales and marketing area would be a combined sales-force; some business units could gain access to customers/channels of distribution that otherwise they would not be able to justify financially.

Interestingly economies of scale may also justify the development of corporate brands and the use of group based public relations (now often referred to as corporate PR). The advantage to the individual business units is that they do not have to incur the cost of developing their own brand image or reputation.

The benefit and hence the underlying economic rationale is a cost saving for the group. The potential risk is that the resulting standardisation creates opportunity costs that more than offset the economies of scale.

Where knowledge, insight and expertise can be leveraged into other areas of business, the corporation is exploiting economies of scope. Thus, by extending the scope of its operations into different products and/or markets, these knowledge assets can be more extensively exploited. As with the economies of scale economic rationale, the

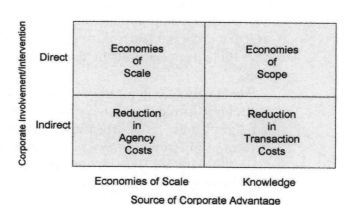

Figure I.7
The underpinning
economic rationales.

corporate centre will itself incur quite significant costs because of its direct intervention. The group must, therefore, gain benefits that more than outweigh these significant costs; the difference is that in the economies of scope configuration, the benefits are realised directly by the business units themselves through the exploitation of the knowledge advantage. This can create some problems that are explored in Chapter 6.

Knowledge advantages may take the form of enhanced systems or processes that reduce relative costs for the business units. Alternatively, the knowledge advantage may derive from expertise that enables other business units in the group to differentiate their goods or services so that they can be sold at higher prices with higher profit margins, or more volume can be sold at the existing price.

It is important to understand clearly which corporate advantage the group is trying to exploit. Brand management illustrates the difficulty well. Brand management may be centralised within the group for two very different reasons. Centralisation may be done to achieve buying power related economies of scale. These savings can be generated by all business units using the same advertising agency globally and from producing only one global series of advertisements for each product range (thus spreading the fixed advertising production costs more widely). As mentioned above, there may be significant issues involved with this form of global standardisation. Alternatively, brand management may be centralised in order to ensure that the excellent, competitive advantage enabling brand management processes that have been developed somewhere in the group are fully leveraged across the rest of the group. Here, the corporate centre is intervening to achieve economies of scope, which derive from its core competence in brand management. The role of the corporate centre is not therefore to do it 'more cheaply' but to do it more effectively across the group. This may mean more, rather than less, local discretion in developing and sourcing advertising, provided that the 'best practice' processes (such as using marketing research techniques to validate the effectiveness of the advertising) are applied by the business units.

The creative configuration seeks to establish a strong group identity and a high degree of trust within the group. If this is achieved the group can significantly reduce the transaction costs incurred in the high level of intra-group transactions which should occur if the group's objectives are to be achieved. Transaction costs occur in managing the relationships between economic entities, whether this is done through an external market transaction or within a group organisation. Within many multi-business groups, there are very extensive rules and procedures that dictate how formal service level agreements must be drafted, how transfer prices must be established, and complex, technical accounting rules as to which costs can be included, etc. Consequently there is normally an inverse relationship between transaction costs and trust.

These rules and procedures can result in a very high level of transaction costs for intra-group collaborations, particularly where the project is very nebulous and the benefits (and the beneficiaries within the group) are largely unknown. If the corporate centre can create an environment where business units are willing to collaborate together on the development of a new process, or on sharing their knowledge of particular customers or market segments, without the need for too much formality, the saving on transaction costs can be significant. It is, of course, also likely to speed up the project substantially as well.

In the controls configuration, the corporate centre primarily sees itself as the owner of the businesses currently within the group. The issues of ownership and control over businesses have led to the concept of agency costs becoming highly developed. As ownership of companies became more widely spread, shareholders delegated the control of the companies to professional management teams (i.e. acting as their agents). However, there has been a developing concern that some of these companies are being run more for the benefit of the managers than the actual owners. Thus there may be a cost to the owner of using agents, in the form of less than optimal returns for the shareholder.

As a consequence, many companies now incur significant governance related costs including communicating with their shareholders, checking on the actions of the managers, and designing incentive schemes for these managers. These costs can also be considered as an element of agency costs. If the corporate centre can act as an informed shareholder, it has an opportunity to reduce these agency costs significantly. This potential value added is increased if it also has the skills required to develop and implement appropriate financial structures and control systems (including incentive schemes) that remove the motivation for business units to act against the interests of their shareholders.

There have been theoretical developments in the strategy field that have focused on the internal resources of the firm. This 'resource-based view' rightly directs our attention to the idiosyncratic resources and capabilities that give a firm competitive advantage. These resources, which can be know-how, brands, patents, relationships, etc. are not only valuable, they are difficult for competitors to imitate; hence they can give *sustainable* advantage. From an investor perspective, these inimitable 'resources' are the source of superior profits, and hence a question that could be directed at the corporate centre would be 'how can the centre *create* inimitable "resources"?' More recently this issue has been taken up with attention being focused on the 'dynamic capabilities' of firms. These are the capabilities to create, re-deploy, reconfigure and dispose of resources, which, we would argue, are key capabilities that the corporate centre should perform. The essential differences between resources and dynamic capabilities are that resources are profit-generating assets, whereas dynamic capabilities are embedded routines or processes that *create* resources. Resources are *stocks* of valuable assets; dynamic capabilities are routines that change the asset stock.

So our configurations can be understood as combinations of structures, processes, values, and systems that deliver dynamic, resource creating and leveraging capabilities. Specifically, the creative configuration encourages corporate resource creation by facilitating the production of new knowledge. These knowledge resources may be exploited within existing business units, or they may require the establishment of new units. The centre would need to be involved in assembling the correct set of complementary assets that are required to effectively leverage the new know-how. The scope configuration is essentially leveraging existing resources. The resource may need to be codified, if it exists in the form of tacit knowledge, and the centre would need to be involved in determining where and how the resource should be deployed. The scale configuration aims to create resources by achieving scale advantages in support or core processes. The controls configuration acts indirectly to *provoke* business units to create their own resources, in order to meet stretching performance targets.

But each configuration entails a different combination of dynamic capabilities and resources. In the creative configuration there are unlikely to be any resources located at the centre, but the centre acts as a stimulus to resource creation within and between business units. Hence, in the creative configuration the centre provides a dynamic capability, not a *resource*. In the scale configuration the centre owns and operates the scale efficient resources, and insofar as these scale efficient resources can be continually extended, the centre is also delivering a form of dynamic capability. But at some point the efficient scale of operations will be reached, in which case the centre is merely managing the scale resources.

In the scope configuration, the centre is providing and delivering the dynamic capability that enables existing resources to be leveraged across the corporation. Thus the centre enacts the dynamic capability that can continue to add value as long as opportunities to leverage resources continue to emerge in the corporation. Finally, in the controls configuration again the centre is performing a dynamic governance capability that provokes the development of resources within the portfolio of businesses in the group.

For those readers particularly interested in the theoretical underpinnings for our model, we discuss these issues in more detail in Chapter 10.

Refining the model

So far we have not introduced any scales on the axes of the corporate configurations model, simply referring to corporate centre involvement as either direct or indirect. Similarly the source of corporate advantage is either economies of scale or knowledge based. Obviously there are relative degrees of direct or indirect involvement, as well as stronger or weaker economies of scale and knowledge based corporate advantages. These adjustments are shown in Figure 1.8, where scales are added to each separate dimension of the model.

We have deliberately made the scale for each segment increase away from the centre towards each corner of the matrix. This attempts to reflect the practical reality where both the type of corporate centre involvement and source of corporate advantage can be regarded as almost a continuum rather than exclusively one or the other. The consequences of this are developed in more detail in Chapter 3, but it does have an immediate impact on the model.

Figure 1.8
The corporate configurations model: refinements.

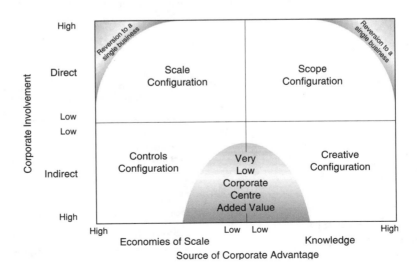

At the top left and top right-hand corners of the matrix, Figure 1.8 shows two shaded areas. Both of these areas should be removed from the model because the group has really reverted to being a single business, where the corporate advantage has taken over from the competitive advantages of the business units within the group.

A combination of a very high level of economy of scale corporate advantage with a very directly intervening corporate centre will result in all key processes within the group being centralised. In other words, substantially all the value added is generated by these centralised activities. For all practical analytical purposes, we can treat this group as being a single business.

Similarly, if the corporate centre completely dominates, through a very high level of direct intervention, the exploitation of a very high knowledge based corporate advantage, the centre is really generating the vast majority of the value added of the group. Once again, the group can be considered as a single business. This has led us to restate our original square matrix in the differently shaped format shown in Figure 1.9.

This scaling highlights a problem at the bottom of the model, in the middle of the horizontal axis. In this area the corporate centre not only has a very indirect method of involvement in its business units but also possesses a low level of corporate advantage, either economies of scale or knowledge based. This combination means that the corporate centre is unlikely to be adding any value to the businesses within the group. The low level of corporate advantage, highlighted by being near the central vertical line of the model, means that adding value will be a challenge for any corporate centre, but at least a directly intervening centre can take more specific actions to ensure that this is achieved.

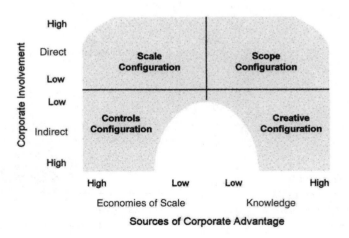

Figure 1.9
The corporate configurations model – restated.

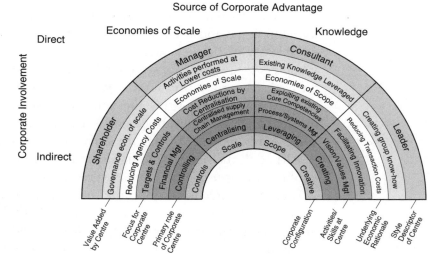

Figure 1.10
Corporate
configurations: The
Rainbow Diagram.

Another problem for corporate centres 'caught in the middle' in this way is that it is much more difficult for them to move rapidly to a more attractive, sustainable position. This is considered in Chapter 3, when we start to discuss transitioning around the model. This concern has resulted in the modified presentation of the model that is shown in Figure 1.9.

Introducing the rainbow diagram

Through the remainder of the book, we will be using the corporate configurations model shown in Figure 1.9, but we will also develop a further refinement of this presentation, which we have found helpful when applying the model within corporations. This is known as the Rainbow Diagram and is shown in Figure 1.10, as a summary of the model's development so far.

Conclusion

As discussed in this chapter, the corporate configurations model gives four ways for corporate centres to create value, rather than just add cost and consequently destroy value. However, there are many leadership challenges that arise from the implications of trying to implement this model. These are discussed in Chapter 2 before developing the model still further in Chapter 3. Each individual configuration is then examined in depth in Chapters 4–7.

Some readers may wish to get a more in-depth understanding of the four configurations before getting involved in the slightly increased complexity of the developments in the model that are dealt with in Chapters 2 and 3. If so, we recommend that you read the overviews for each configuration that are at the start of each chapter in Part II: namely, pages 97–100 for the controls configuration; pages 124–127 for the scale configuration; pages 153–157 for the scope configuration; and pages 177–179 for the creative configuration.

Although there are some significant developments in the corporate configurations model that are covered in these subsequent chapters, it is already possible to start to rank the different configurations in terms of their sustainable value-adding potential. The most limited value-adding configurations are on the left-hand side of the model as no group has ever 'cost-cut its way to sustained greatness'. While both the controls and the scale configurations can add value to any existing portfolio of businesses for some time, there eventually comes a point where the portfolio needs fairly radical change if more value is to be added by the corporate centre.

Similarly even the scope configuration can eventually run out of steam once the centre has comprehensively leveraged the existing value-adding knowledge across the group. Either the mix of businesses again needs changing or the centre has to identify a new source of advantage that can be widely applied across the existing business units. This can present, at best, a timing problem as the focus of the corporate centre is on applying existing knowledge rather than creating new knowledge for the group.

However, the generation of new corporate know-how is the main emphasis of the creative configuration and therefore this can be the most sustainable value-adding role for a corporate centre, particularly when allied to the problems faced by competitors in trying to copy such a values oriented, indirectly implemented, leadership role.

Chapter 2

Leading, managing and sustaining

Introduction

The basic corporate configurations model introduced in Chapter 1 raises some interesting challenges for chief executive officers and top management teams at the corporate centres of large organisations. This chapter considers these issues by adding in additional dimensions to the model.

The most obvious questions that are asked when managers first encounter the model are:

- Do we currently fit within any of the four value-adding configurations and, if so, which one?
- Which configuration should we ideally be in, given the style and skills at the corporate centre, the external environment in which we operate, and the businesses within the group?
- If where we should be differs from where we are now, how do we manage the required transition across the corporate configurations model?

For most organisations, discovering where they currently are is not too difficult. A very common result is that corporate centres appear to be trying to be everything at once; i.e. they can identify parts of themselves in each of the four configurations. It is, of course, almost inevitable that a corporate centre in a large group will have some activities that could be described as fitting into each configuration. For example, the corporate centre of even a very highly centralised cost focused group:

- will probably set performance targets for its business units;
- will receive plans from them;

- may have established a group vision and even a set of guiding principles;
- could even try to ensure that best practices are shared across the group.

However, the main focus of activity for this corporate centre is centralisation in order to reduce the total costs of the group. Whether this focus of activity creates added value for the group should be the criteria for judging the success of this corporate centre. If the centre fails to add value in its main area of focus, it is almost certain that it will not add value in its more peripheral activities.

Hence the current positioning of a corporate centre depends upon identifying the main focus of the centre in terms of enhancing the total value created by the group. If the centre is genuinely trying to be 'everything at once' then there is no such focus, and there probably will be no added value either, as is illustrated by an example at the end of Chapter 3.

The most interesting outcome of this analysis is that it frequently reveals substantial differences between the perceptions of managers within the corporate centre and those of managers at the business units. The first issue is, therefore, to resolve these differing perceptions as to the current role and focus of the corporate centre, and to agree whether the centre is actually adding value to the group through its current role. This raises the first leadership challenge facing the corporate centre.

For the corporate centre to add sustainable value, there needs to be complete agreement between the centre and the business units both on what the style of the relationship actually is and that this style is appropriate to the actual context and strategy of the group.

Even if, at present, the centre is adding cost, rather than value, the problem may be with the way the role of the centre is being carried out, rather than that the centre is trying to fulfil the wrong role. Consequently, we would recommend chief executives actually start by considering the ideal corporate configuration for their group. The way that this question is answered provides a lot of insight as to the overall style of the group and its corporate centre, and the way in which any required transitioning from one configuration to another should be managed.

The key is that each of the four corporate configurations can create shareholder value; although the most sustainable value creator is the creative configuration, as was already mentioned and is discussed later in this chapter and in Part II of the book. However, they are all significantly different and therefore each should be selected and implemented when their differences make them most relevant to the group. If any corporate centre continues to implement a previously very successful long-term configuration after the external competitive environment has changed significantly, the group's future performance will probably suffer, often dramatically and very rapidly.

Nevertheless, such a corporate centre may find it very difficult to change such a well-entrenched formula for success, which probably suits the personal style of the group's top management team. The group then has two significantly different options. It can either change the composition of the businesses within the group so that the existing corporate configuration is still relevant; or, it can change the top management team to one that can successfully implement the new, more appropriate corporate configuration.

There are examples of both of these dramatic changes, which are discussed in more detail later, and even of a combination of the two happening together. This combination can occur when a new group chief executive, or top team, is appointed, particularly if they come from outside the group. They probably already have a successful track record, which is why they have been brought in, but their success may have been achieved in a very different configuration from that currently in use by this corporate centre. It is by no means unknown for this individual, or team, very rapidly to change many, if not most, of the businesses within the group so that the revised composition is more suited to their preferred corporate configuration. Good examples of this are the USA based GE Corporation and its UK based namesake GEC, but the success levels of these changes were very different. Jack Welch took over as Chairman and Chief Executive Officer of General Electric in December 1980 and, in his first year, 71 businesses were sold and 118 businesses joined the group. This may sound dramatic, but it seems less so when put into the context of GE's around 1500 profit centres. He also significantly changed the style of the corporate centre and its then world-renowned planning processes. These changes are discussed in more detail in Chapters 3 and 7. More recently, in 1996, Lord Simpson replaced Lord Weinstock as Chief Executive of GEC plc (now called Marconi) and the impact was dramatic. The original core defence and electronics businesses of the old GEC group were sold (largely to BAE Systems, which also changed its name as a result) and a new telecoms focus was developed for the group by a completely reconfigured corporate centre.

These are extreme examples of corporate centres exercising very strong control over their groups, by radically changing the focus of the corporate centre and changing the businesses comprising the groups. It is important that the corporate centre should be in control because, if it is merely reactive to its external environment, the economic rationale for remaining as a group can be, and increasingly is being, questioned.

Leadership: Philosophy and role

This issue of control being exercised by the corporate centre is very often linked to the concept of the corporate centre providing leadership for the group as a whole. Hence, the vast majority of group chief executives see themselves as leaders but many are unsure as to the real implications of this leadership role.

We discuss the leadership implications of our model throughout the book, but it is important to clarify how leadership fits into the model before we develop the model any further. In the descriptors of corporate centres, introduced in Chapter 1, we deliberately only used 'leader' for one style, as shown in Figure 2.1. This was to highlight that the key value-adding roles of the corporate centres in the other configurations each have a more specific focus than is provided by the generic heading of leadership. Also, in the names given to the four corporate configurations, we have deliberately omitted any direct reference to leadership.

However, this is not meant to under-emphasise the important leadership roles played by the corporate centre in each of the four different corporate configurations. We want to focus attention on the specific nature of each associated leadership role, and the consequent implications for each style of corporate centre. In an attempt to achieve

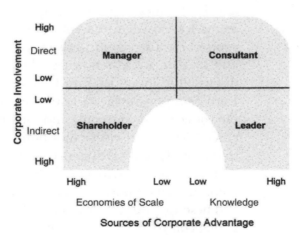

Figure 2.1
The corporate
configurations model:
Style descriptors of
corporate centres.

this we first distinguish between leadership philosophy and the more specific leadership role; major problems can be created when an inappropriate combination of philosophy and role are found within a corporate centre.

The leadership philosophy of a corporate centre relates to the belief that the top management team have about the nature and impact of their leadership within their group. This belief includes the relative importance of their leadership and also the style and manner in which this leadership activity should be carried out.

Hopefully, this philosophy completely matches the actual leadership role that is both required by the businesses in the group and is actually being fulfilled by the corporate centre. Unfortunately, there are many examples where there are significant gaps between the philosophy and the role. One such gap leads to many of the differing perceptions mentioned in the introduction to this chapter. The corporate centre may believe that its leadership philosophy and role are completely matched and totally appropriate for the group. However, the businesses may feel strongly that either the philosophy is inappropriate, or that it is not being properly delivered by the top managers at the corporate centre.

A common example of this is where the corporate centre believes that the businesses in the group require very strong leadership. Not surprisingly, the centre often believes it is the responsibility of the centre, because it is the corporate centre, to provide this leadership; irrespective of whether it actually possesses any relevant leadership skills. Even worse, this frequently misguided attempt at strong leadership from the centre can be very counter-productive if the individual business unit managers are already providing strong leadership for their own businesses. This is often the case in some of the highly decentralised businesses found as part of the controls configuration. It may be far more appropriate for the corporate centre to adopt a relatively low profile leadership philosophy in this style of group.

It is also quite common to find similar problems within the scope configuration, if the corporate centre misunderstands the specific nature of its leadership role with respect to the leverage of existing knowledge across the group. Examples of both of these issues are given later in the chapter. Therefore it is very important for the corporate centre to identify the appropriate type of leadership for its particular corporate configuration and external environment.

It is possible to distinguish between transactional leadership and transformational leadership. All leadership philosophies and roles involve both transactional and transformational elements, but it is the balance of time and effort spent on each and their relative importance that classifies leadership as one type or the other.

Transactional leadership seeks to make the workplace work better, whereas transformational leadership tries to make the business different. An over-simplistic comparison would be between efficiency gains and effectiveness improvements. Transactional leadership focuses on control processes and is often results oriented. It is frequently relatively formal and short-term in its time frames. By contrast, transformational leadership looks at the long-term direction of the business and is more informal as it focuses on the people in the business. Also it is more means oriented rather than concentrating on the results produced by the business. Transformational leadership establishes visions and values for the business and consequently influences the mind-sets and beliefs of employees.

If these attributes are applied to the corporate configurations model, there is clearly an increasing transformational leadership input on the right side of the model, as shown in Figure 2.2. The increasing emphasis on knowledge as the source of corporate advantage and the decreasingly direct style of involvement requires the corporate centre to get the businesses to do things differently, rather than it just doing things differently itself. Hence the direction of increase is diagonally downwards, as the main leadership requirement of the creative corporate centre is to establish the vision and values that create the strong group identity essential to the creation of new corporate know-how in these organisations.

On the left-hand side of the model there is an increasingly transactional leadership requirement but the direction is diagonally upwards.

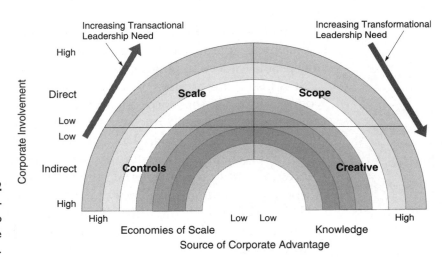

Figure 2.2
The corporate configurations model: Leadership implications for corporate centres.

The highly indirect style of an extreme controls configuration means that the corporate centre has to have a very limited and focused 'internal' leadership input. (They often have an externally oriented, capital markets focused leadership role that is discussed in Chapter 4.) As the nature of their involvement moves through being indirect to more direct, the corporate centre can increasingly lead from the front. First, by advising and counselling the businesses on what changes to make, and second, by centralising increasing areas of activity in order more rapidly to bring about the desired changes across the group.

As the economies of scale corporate advantage weakens (i.e. moving to the right along the horizontal axis), this transactional leadership apparently becomes increasingly important. It becomes vital that the group takes maximum advantage of any opportunity to reduce total group costs, and the corporate centre should demonstrate clear and strong leadership to achieve this. However, in centralising there is an increasing element of transformational leadership, because the centre is forcibly changing the way in which the business units function, but the leadership philosophy is still likely to be transactional. The centre still believes that it should be trying to make the existing group of businesses function more efficiently. It should not be trying to change the underlying businesses, in terms of the products they sell or the customers to which they sell them.

The challenge facing a corporate centre in this position (i.e. the shaded area in the scale segment of Figure 2.3) is whether it can continue to add value within its current configuration. It is already highly centralised but the economy of scale based corporate advantage

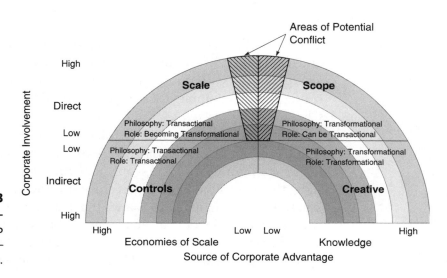

Figure 2.3
The corporate configurations model: Leadership philosophy & role – potential conflicts.

is reducing. It may need to change its focus away from cost reduction towards leveraging knowledge across the group. This requires a significant transformational leadership role from the corporate centre in order to change the way the businesses see the role of their corporate centre, but the leadership philosophy within the centre may well have a strongly entrenched transactional basis. As previously mentioned the centre may need to change the businesses comprising the group, so that the existing configuration and leadership philosophy are relevant. Alternatively the group may need to change the centre, so that the required transformational leadership role can be applied.

Our research demonstrates very strongly that it is much more difficult to achieve a strong transformational leadership role if the managers involved have a transactional leadership philosophy, than the other way round. This is somewhat good news for corporate centres in the top left hand part of the scope configuration (i.e. the other shaded area of Figure 2.3). They are likely to have a transformational philosophy because leadership to them is mainly about changing the ways in which the group does business and competes, e.g. by leveraging knowledge across the group. However, when this knowledge based corporate advantage is relatively weak but the centre has a high level of direct intervention, e.g. through centralisation of core processes, the actual leadership role is likely to be perceived by the businesses within the group as being primarily transactional.

Conversely, in the bottom right-hand part of the scope configuration, the leadership role will be perceived as very much more transformational in nature. The centre will be leveraging new knowledge across the group and even turning business unit developed know-how into corporate knowledge, so that it can be leveraged more widely within the group.

The conflict here between leadership philosophy (transformational) and leadership role (mainly transactional) does create problems for the group, but these are more easily managed than for the previous scale configuration example: these conflicts are discussed in more detail in Chapter 6.

These directional leadership roles indicate, as shown in Figure 2.4, a challenge for any corporate centre that wants to move from the scale leader configuration to the scope configuration, or vice versa. At first sight this transition does not seem too difficult because the style of involvement remains direct and the existing corporate advantage, whether economies of scale or knowledge based, is likely to be relatively low. However, the scale focused corporate centre may have developed a strong transactional leadership philosophy that is much less

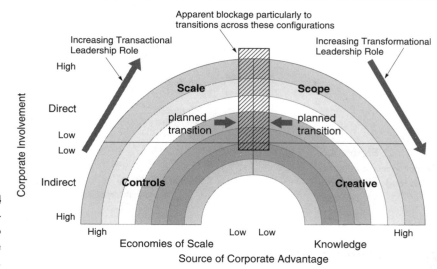

Figure 2.4
The corporate configura-
tions model: Leadership
roles for corporate
centres.

appropriate for the scope configuration to which it is trying to move. The reverse movement requires the ex-scope based corporate centre to rapidly acquire the transactional leadership skills that it previously did not require. These issues are developed in Chapter 3, where transitioning across the model is discussed, but the most detailed discussions of this aspect are left until Parts II and III of the book.

Leadership focus

These different types of leadership (i.e. transformational and transactional) help in providing some clarity to the leadership roles that are relevant to each corporate configuration. However, this clarity is greatly enhanced if we also consider another definition of leadership. As well as referring to the ability to lead, a related interpretation of leadership is of becoming pre-eminent in a particular field. It can be strongly argued that, if corporate centres are to optimise their value-adding role within particular areas of activity, the achievement of the appropriate pre-eminence should be the real focus of the leadership within these different corporate centres. Not surprisingly, therefore, this leadership focus should be based on the value-added role of the centre and this can be described as the basis of 'the leadership' for which the centre should be striving. In other words, if both the business units and the outside world are asked to describe what any particular corporate centre was best at doing (i.e. one specific area), this should be where its leadership effort is focused. These are shown in Figure 2.5.

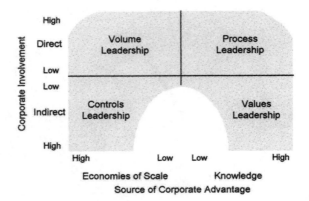

Figure 2.5
The corporate configurations model: Leadership focus.

Controls configuration

The corporate centre in the controls configuration reduces total group costs through achieving economies of scale by developing appropriate financial targets and controls for its business units. It is utilising its expertise in corporate governance and control to add value to the group. This expertise is therefore the basis of its leadership within the group but the potential value added can be increased if the corporate centre achieves true leadership in this area of expertise. Consequently this should provide the leadership focus for the corporate centre so that it strives to be the best in the world (or, at least, in its sphere of competition) in its chosen area of expertise. For our shareholder style of corporate centre, this entails focusing on achieving controls leadership; i.e. becoming the best corporate centre at developing tailored planning and control processes for its business units so that the governance processes implemented in its group add more value than in any comparable group. The companies discussed below and in Chapter 4, such as WPP and Hanson, are classic examples of such corporate centre leadership.

Interestingly, in order to achieve this level of leadership, the corporate centre may have to restrict (i.e. focus) its own activities either in terms of the range and spread of businesses within the group or in terms of the operations carried out by the centre. This may act as a constraint on the growth potential of the group, which is an issue we return to later in this chapter. There are a number of good examples of this leadership focus in the controls configuration as shareholder styles of corporate centre have been developed in several people based, service industries.

A number of these service industries largely comprise fast growing owner managed, high value-adding businesses. Individually one might be tempted to place many of these businesses in the creative configuration because they have very charismatic, strong leaders who possess very clear visions for their businesses. These are not therefore the sort of businesses that are immediately associated with the controls configuration and its focus on adding value through economies of scale. As already stated the corporate advantage must be separated from the competitive advantages of the businesses within the group. A common problem of these industries (which include advertising, software, employment agencies and travel companies) is that the high growth and potential for high added value never get translated into high actual profits and cash flows. Quite frequently this is caused by the emphasis placed on growth in the overall corporate vision (to be the biggest, etc.) by the strong leaders within the business. They are not focused on profit but on sales revenue growth and other non-financial measures of success, such as winning advertising awards or landing very prestigious, but potentially significantly unprofitable, clients.

Hence the introduction of a corporate centre with very strong expertise in financial planning and control can very rapidly improve the financial performance of these underlying businesses. This can sometimes even be done without significantly interfering with the previous way the businesses were being run; i.e. the existing management team is retained.

Perhaps the groups that best illustrate this were the original Saatchi & Saatchi and then, rapidly following them, WPP. WPP subsequently surpassed Saatchi & Saatchi, which is perhaps not too surprising as its Chief Executive, Martin Sorrell, was involved in the development of the corporate centre at Saatchi's where he had been finance director. The value-adding role of these corporate centres is to provide appropriately tailored planning, control and other governance processes to a wide range of creatively focused advertising and promotion companies. Thus both these groups grew very rapidly through acquisition, which is made easier when the corporate centre expertise extends to the structuring of the acquisition prices and methods of payment. These are frequently linked to the future performance of the acquired business, through what is known as an earn-out formula, which immediately motivates the management of the business unit to focus on and improve their subsequent financial performance.

A key skill required by such corporate centres is a very good understanding of the real economic value drivers of these underlying businesses. But they do not need to be able to write great advertising copy, develop brilliant consumer promotions, or design leading edge marketing research techniques. These skills need to be possessed by the managers of the business units, whereas recognising that advertising agencies should have substantial negative working capital (because clients can be made to pay the agency before the agency has to pay the media company) was one of several significant value-adding roles provided by Maurice Saatchi and Martin Sorrell.

These corporate centres acquired a reputation as true leaders in these control processes for this industry and this leadership position made it easier for them to continue to grow through acquisition. Their reputation attracted acquisition candidates and it also made it easier to raise the funding needed as the deals grew larger and larger. Eventually this acquisition led strategy can lead to problems, particularly if the corporate centre moves away from its real core expertise. Acquisitions of consulting companies do not provide the same potential for generating the very sizable positive cash inflows that resulted from changing the working capital structure of acquired advertising agencies. (The cash flows passing through an advertising agency represent the full value of the advertising purchased by its clients, whereas its sales revenue, i.e. its commission, is only a relatively small percentage of this advertising, and its profits only a percentage of its sales revenue.) Hence the resulting corporate centre-generated added value is significantly lower and, if other governance expertise is also less relevant, the centre can start to lose its leadership focus. This can, of course, be regained by refocusing the group back into its value-adding area, but its future growth rate may be lower.

Other similarly focused leadership roles have been particularly evident in software groups and employment agencies, where the corporate centres developed great expertise in acquiring and then controlling a large number of smaller, rapidly growing businesses. These businesses were kept as largely autonomous, decentralised business units but their management teams were significantly motivated to act in the interests of the group by their financial incentive programmes. Therefore corporate leadership is not a generic capability. The case of WPP suggests that corporate leaders must have insight into the specific portfolio of businesses in their charge.

The required leadership is highly focused but it does not need to be high profile. This leadership can be fulfilled through an indirect involvement in the businesses, without needing to create any strong group identity across the business units. They can therefore maintain their individual positions within their own markets, which may be reinforced by the strong leadership profiles of their individual business unit managers.

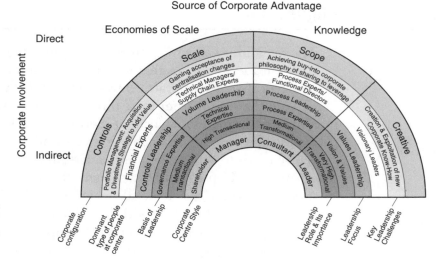

Figure 2.6
The Rainbow Diagram:
Leadership roles, focus
& challenges.

As the dominant type of people required at the corporate centre to fulfil this controls leadership focus are financial experts, they may be very happy to adopt a relatively low profile leadership role within the group. They would not, however, be happy to adopt a low control role within the group; thus the leadership profile does not equate to power.

Figure 2.6 shows this controls leadership focus, in context, for the shareholder style of corporate centre, together with the other appropriate leadership focuses for the other corporate configurations.

Creative configuration

The values leadership focus for the creative configuration should not be surprising, given the key role for this leader style of corporate centre of creating a very clear vision and set of values for the group. Consequently the basis of the centre's leadership is its contribution to the vision and values of the group, and the dominant type of people at the centre will therefore be visionary leaders, supported by communication experts who can help to get their message across clearly and consistently.

This may mean that such a corporate centre is very small as the true visionary leader may be an individual, but their leadership objective should be to be seen as the pre-eminent 'values leader' in their appropriate environment. The leadership provided by this type of corporate centre is usually high profile within the group, even if the centre is very small.

Scale configuration

The remaining corporate centre styles of manager and consultant each have a leadership focus that may not be so immediately obvious. The manager style of corporate centres create added value from economies of scale that result from their direct intervention in their businesses, normally through some form of centralisation. For these economies of scale to provide a sustainable source of added value, the corporate centre needs to achieve volume leadership in each centralised activity or process. Consequently, although the corporate centre requires supply chain expertise to decide which areas should be centralised and how these should interact with their internal business unit customers, this supply chain expertise is there to support the technical/financial managers who actually deliver the cost savings that are driving the added value. Thus the leadership focus is not to become the best supply chain experts in the world, but to achieve the highest level of added value possible from the available economies of scale. This means that the corporate centre should seek volume leadership in as many processes as possible, provided that each such process will generate real added value when the negative impacts of any required standardisation across the group are taken into account.

Scope configuration

Conversely the consultant style of corporate centre should seek to achieve process leadership status because this is the real source of the value added by the corporate centre. Any functional experts at the corporate centre are there to identify which business unit located competitive advantages have broader applicability within the group. The process expertise at the corporate centre extracts and codifies the key elements of these competitive advantages, so that this knowledge can be shared across the other business units where appropriate. Leveraging this existing knowledge is therefore made possible by the codification and systems skills of the corporate centre.

This means that, as for the shareholder style corporate centre, the consultant style does not necessarily entail high profile leadership, and this may suit the process experts who should dominate the corporate centre. Equally, despite this lower profile leadership from the centre, the business units still have to conform to the processes developed by and issued from the centre. Thus, again, the leadership profile of the corporate centre does not indicate the power and level of control exercised by the centre.

A good leader needs followers: getting business unit buy-in

No matter what leadership role and focus the corporate centre has selected, it needs to achieve some degree of buy-in to its corporate strategy from the business units within the group. If the business units are in open revolt or even are covertly hostile to the corporate strategy and the consequent corporate centre role, the result will almost certainly be the 'adding cost and destroying value' outcome that the centre is desperate to avoid.

Some types of corporate strategy require a high level of buy-in from the managers within the group if implementation is to be successful, while others can be equally successful as long as these managers are not actively against the strategy. Good examples of the need for a high level of acceptance of, and even commitment to, the corporate strategy are those involving a clear group vision and where shared values and beliefs form an integral part of creating a strong group identity.

Interestingly the other corporate strategies that require a high degree of buy-in are those where the centre takes over activities previously carried out by the business units; e.g. by centralisation. If the managers in the business units do not accept these changes, or even are really resentful of their reduced level of autonomy, they can significantly reduce the benefits achieved by the centralisation. The key difference here is that the corporate centre only needs to achieve a high level of acceptance from the relatively few business unit managers who are directly affected by the centralisation strategy.

In the case of the creative configuration the corporate centre needs to carry a large number of managers with it, as the trust and willingness to share ideas freely must permeate throughout the organisation. The scale configuration only requires a high level of buy-in from a much more limited number of managers, but this need for the high level of buy-in does indicate that this is a configuration requiring a strong leadership role at the corporate centre.

It is, of course, no coincidence that the configurations that require a high degree of managerial buy-in (i.e. the creative and scale configurations) are the ones that also show the highest leadership profiles. This leadership is essential to achieve strong commitment to the successful achievement of the corporate strategy. Equally when much less buy-in is essential, the value created by a very strong leadership role at the corporate centre is reduced.

The low degree of buy-in required for some corporate strategies can be as little as ensuring that business unit managers are not actively

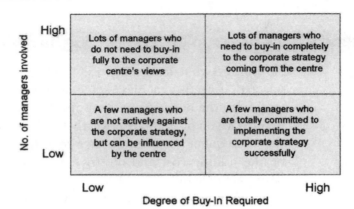

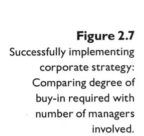

Figure 2.7
Successfully implementing
corporate strategy:
Comparing degree of
buy-in required with
number of managers
involved.

working against the corporate centre initiatives, as shown in Figure 2.7; although, of course, a less negative attitude is always preferable. However, the key distinction is that the centre does not need to win the 'hearts' of the business units, winning their minds or even playing to their own personal success criteria may be sufficient for the successful implementation of the corporate strategy. This can be used when there are relatively few significant managers involved (e.g. the general managers of the business units), as their attitudes can be influenced through the performance measures used by the corporate centre. Thus in a diverse, decentralised controls configuration, the corporate centre can achieve a relatively grudging level of buy-in from only the senior business unit managers and still be successful. It is the responsibility of these business unit top teams to run their businesses appropriately within the group structure.

It is a very different issue when there are lots of managers who need to have some degree of buy-in to the corporate strategy. This is particularly true where knowledge needs to be shared across the group, even though the corporate centre may be more directly involved in the sharing process. The knowledge may exist at lower levels in one business unit or may well need to be leveraged at lower levels elsewhere in the group. All these managers need to have some appreciation of how the group benefits from the leveraging of this existing knowledge; although the buy-in required can be reduced through very good codification and systems processes, and even through centralisation of key areas of knowledge. If centralisation is used, the degree of buy-in by the centralised managers has to be very high; as for the previous centralisation argument.

A focus on cost reduction normally requires fewer managers to be involved, but the degree of buy-in required still differs significantly, as can be seen in Figure 2.8.

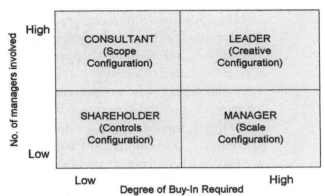

Figure 2.8
Successfully implementing corporate strategy: Alignment with corporate configurations model and style descriptors.

Note: In this diagram the four corporate configurations are not shown in their normal sequence.

Summarising the leadership challenges

These different levels of buy-in and numbers of managers involved have significant implications for the leadership required from the corporate centre within each configuration, and for the challenges they face. Drawing together the leadership issues first, it is possible to distinguish different bases of and roles for leadership and challenges to this leadership, as well as the relative rankings of importance of leadership; these were illustrated in Figure 2.6.

As discussed earlier in this chapter, the relative importance and the type of leadership differ across the four configurations. For both shareholder and consultant styles, leadership has only medium importance but, for the shareholder style, the relevant type is transactional leadership, whereas, for the consultant style, it is more appropriate for the corporate centre to exhibit transformational leadership.

Similarly, although leadership potentially has high importance for both the leader style and the manager style, the leader style should possess transformational leadership skills, while strong transactional leadership is normally required for success in the scale configuration.

The basis and focus of leadership also differs; ranging from the governance and controls expertise possessed by the shareholder configuration through the technical expertise and the process expertise of respectively the manager style and the scope configuration to the critical vision and values leadership of the creative configuration.

Controls configuration

We have also discussed the various levels of buy-in required from managers within the group and the different numbers involved in this process. Another difference across the configurations is the dominant background of the people in the corporate centre; this can affect their capability, and possibly their willingness, to undertake a leadership role. The shareholder style corporate centre is normally dominated by financial experts who are probably quite happy with their remote mode of control and their correspondingly low leadership profile. Correspondingly, their main leadership challenge is related to their management of the portfolio of businesses comprising the group. As stated in Chapter 1, the corporate centre in a shareholder configuration organisation is more likely to divest itself of any continually under-performing business unit, rather than become directly involved in trying to change the level of performance. This requires them to identify a regular supply of appropriate acquisition candidates, where their financial expertise is likely to add value. As a result, quite a lot of their efforts, including some of their leadership efforts, are focused externally to try to identify such acquisition targets.

Scale configuration

In the manager style, the corporate centre is staffed by appropriate technical managers who are actually running the centralised processes, and by supply chain experts who decide which processes should be centralised. They should have a stronger leadership role although it is mainly transactional in nature and based on their technical expertise. Consequently they should be capable of rising to their main leadership challenge which is achieving the high level of buy-in required from their key business unit colleagues to gain acceptance of their proposed centralisation changes.

Scope configuration

The corporate centre in the scope configuration also contains a mixture of expertise. There should always be process/systems experts who can codify knowledge so that it can be leveraged across the group. However, they will often be joined by functional experts who are needed to identify what knowledge is worth codifying in the first place; it is interesting that the roles of these two types of expert are reversed in the manager and consultant styles.

Quite often this consultant style of corporate centre can send out confusing messages to the business units through its own organisational structure. If a group functional director, for a key corporate process, is created within the corporate centre (e.g. group marketing director), the business units may not surprisingly see this person as being the line head of this function across the group (i.e. marketing). They would therefore expect the centre to dictate in detail what brands and products they could sell and how these were to be marketed. In reality, the corporate centre's view of the role may be to identify those excellent, leading edge brand management processes, and/or brands themselves, which have the potential for wider leverage across the group. Thus this person is much more of a technical expert than a line manager. (However, a group functional director in a heavily centralised scale configuration group, such as the group operations director, *is*, and should be regarded as, the line head of the function.)

Part of this common confusion as to the real role of the corporate centre functional experts in these organisations is caused by the assumption that the centre must have a strong leadership role within all groups. If it is accepted that there is a more limited role for leadership from the centre in this scope configuration, it is much easier to see this role as adding value through identifying best practices around the group. The real added value though is created by the process expertise that codifies the critical elements of the existing knowledge so that it has the widest possible application. Thus the corporate centre should be seeking to achieve genuine leadership in this critical area of 'process expertise'.

The main leadership challenge facing this consultant style of corporate centre is therefore achieving buy-in to the group philosophy as to how the corporate centre adds value to the group, i.e. by leveraging existing knowledge across the group. This remains true even if the corporate centre centralises certain key processes in order to accelerate the exploitation of this knowledge. The most common fault in this configuration is that the centre assumes it must adopt a high profile leadership role, possibly because of its direct style of involvement in its businesses and the high number of managers who need to be involved in understanding the role of the corporate centre.

This can lead the corporate centre to make group-wide decisions without the requisite detailed knowledge (e.g. instructing all business units in the group to sell a particular brand irrespective of their local market conditions and competitive position). These decisions are therefore not based on the real corporate advantage of this configuration. (Indeed the above example of a group-wide decision would probably be more relevant to the scale-focused manager style configuration.) Such decisions build a high profile for the corporate centre but they frequently do not lead to the creation of any added value. It is much better for the corporate centre to achieve a relatively low level of buy-in from a wide range of business managers, through it developing a reasonably low leadership profile, as long as the leadership role adopted is transformational and based on its 'process leadership'. The important role for the corporate centre in this configuration is to get the businesses to do things differently, which does not mean that all the businesses in the group should be doing the same things.

Creative configuration

It is perhaps quite surprising that the corporate configuration with the most critical leadership role is one with an indirect style of involvement. When we add in that this style requires a high level of buy-in to the corporate strategy from a large number of managers across the group, the scale of the leadership challenge becomes clear. Therefore the dominant type of people found in this values leader focused corporate centre should be visionary leaders who can create real belief in their clearly articulated vision and values for the group. The other key skill needed at the centre is a high level of communication capability so that the message does not get confused or distorted as it spreads across the group.

Even so, merely sharing the vision and values does not necessarily create a lot of added value for the group; it may add value within an individual business unit, but they could do this internally within their own division. The real value added by the corporate centre is in creating an environment of trust and group identity, through which the businesses collaborate in order to create new corporate know-how. Thus the real leadership challenge for the leader style of corporate centre is to stimulate the creation of new know-how, once it has created and communicated a clear shared vision and set of values for all the businesses within the group.

Implications for organisational culture

The leadership challenges facing each corporate configuration are therefore likely to be very different, but so are their resulting organisational cultures. We regard culture as the norms to which people in an organisation relate and which bind them together. Thus, it can be viewed as the sum of the shared values and beliefs, the shared assumptions, the common philosophies and ideologies that exist across the group. Accordingly we have developed a number of factors relating to

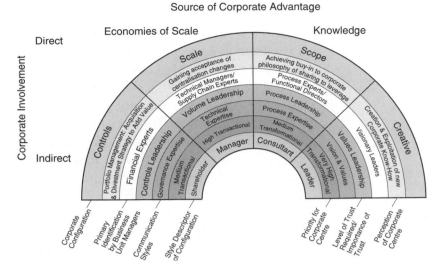

Figure 2.9
The Rainbow Diagram:
Implications for
organisational culture.

culture that can be applied to our corporate configurations model so as to further assist in distinguishing each corporate centre style.

Clearly the different styles of corporate centre have differing priorities, as shown in Figure 2.9, but they also go about achieving them in a variety of ways (e.g. in their communication styles). As a result they generate a range of levels of trust between themselves and their divisions. A relatively low level of trust is only a problem if the corporate culture requires a high level, and so we compare the resulting level of trust with the relative importance of trust for each configuration.

These factors lead to an overall relationship between the centre and its business units that is absolutely fundamental in determining the organisational culture of each group. We use two factors to describe this relationship; namely, with which level of the group do business unit managers identify themselves, and how do they really perceive the corporate centre. In Figure 2.9 we have assumed in this perception factor that the corporate centre is operating successfully in the appropriate configuration, i.e. it is adding value!

Creative configuration

If we apply all these factors to the leader style, we find that the priority for the corporate centre is, as established above, achieving an innovative culture across the group so that new corporate know-how can be created. In order to facilitate this, the centre will use a combined style of communication: it pushes out its vision and set of values (which are all but set in concrete because of its strong leadership role), but then is very willing to enter into a debate about the strategic implications of these centre given 'tablets of stone'.

It is very important that this open debate creates an environment of trust across the group (i.e. not just from each business unit with the corporate centre, but also *among* the business units) if this creative configuration is to be successful. A good test of a successful culture in such a group is that business unit managers should primarily identify themselves as being part of the group, rather than associating first with their particular division. Such a culture is often reinforced by regular managerial moves across the business units, even at very senior levels of management. These managers should also have a strongly positive view of the role of the corporate centre in this style of group, rather than a cynical tolerance of 'that lot from head office'.

Controls configuration

At the other end of the rainbow, the shareholder style of corporation demonstrates a markedly different organisational culture. The priority for the corporate centre is improving the financial performance of its business units and accordingly it employs a communication format centred on the setting of budgets and the regular monthly financially based comparison of actual performance against this target. This process can lead to a low level of trust between the centre and the divisions but, for this style of group, trust is not a critical characteristic.

This results in business unit managers who identify almost exclusively with their own business unit, so that there is no real group identity. It is by no means unusual to find employees in such business units who do not know that their division is actually part of a much larger group. These managers can regard the corporate centre as very remote and relatively disinterested, except in their financial results. In this respect, assuming that the centre is adding value as stated earlier, the corporate centre is seen as highly demanding; setting stretching but not completely unreasonable targets.

Located in between these extremes are both the manager and consultant styles of corporate centre. In both, the business unit executives primarily associate with their own division or their process or function (particularly where it has been centralised), rather than with the group. Both styles require, and normally generate, a medium (or higher) level of trust but they do this in different ways.

Scale configuration

The manager style is focused on cost reduction and tries to achieve this by using a largely command and control style of communication, in that business units are normally told which activities are to be centralised. However, the centre needs to achieve a high degree of acceptance from those managers who are directly affected by the decision. If they get this, they will normally be perceived as interfering, but cost reducing. Thus they receive a somewhat grudging acceptance of the centre's value-adding role, if not exactly a ringing endorsement of it.

Scope configuration

The priority for the consultant style is to get the knowledge based value adding processes implemented as widely as possible across the group; hence conformance with group best practice is a critical performance measure. However, in order to establish this best practice, the centre needs information on what is new and working within the business units. Thus communication needs to be first upwards to the centre, then sideways across the group to spread the knowledge, and only downwards from the centre if conformance is not being achieved.

This should engender a relatively high degree of openness and trust through the group and this is important. If all of this is achieved, the centre is often perceived as being quite value adding but only on 'those areas that they think are important'. What the corporate centre would probably regard as being a major benefit of focusing on the key corporate advantage areas is often seen by the business units as leaving them to fend for themselves in all the other areas. This can obviously be contrasted with the 'interfering' perception of the manager style of corporate centre.

Sustainability issues

Another dimension for differentiating among the four configurations is the very important issue of sustainability. If the group is to have a long-term future, it is important that the particular configuration selected is sustainable over time. Once again there are a number of factors that contribute towards an overall assessment of this sustainability dimension; these are shown in Figure 2.10.

The specific characteristics of each configuration mean that they will react differently to the same external environments. Hence it makes

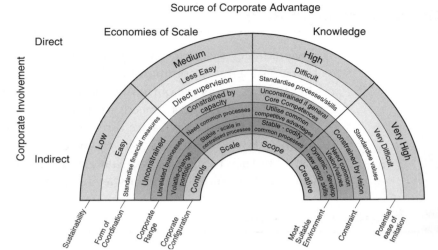

Figure 2.10
The Rainbow Diagram:
Sustainability issues.

sense for the corporate centre to identify the types of environment where its characteristics will help it to flourish. The environment facing the various business units within a group can vary in terms of their relative stability or volatility and their predictability. The idea of looking for a spread of counter-cyclically volatile environments simply so as to reduce the group's overall volatility has long ago been discarded; investors can achieve this themselves far more cost effectively than any single organisation.

However, more stable environments do allow the development and subsequent exploitation of systems and processes, such as the codification of knowledge. Also stable environments encourage the investment in specialised assets that may be necessary to achieve the maximum possible economies of scale across a group.

Dynamic and unpredictable environments favour organisations that are more flexible and capable of modifying either their behaviour or, failing that, the portfolio of businesses that they control. These factors are applied to each configuration in Figure 2.10. Another factor that affects the sustainability of any corporate configuration is the extent to which the organisation is restricted or constrained by its current configuration. This factor can be split into two related issues; the potential range or spread of the group, and any constraints on its future growth.

The breadth of the corporate range achievable by each configuration varies significantly, but all configurations can obviously support a range of businesses within the group. The controls configuration can encompass a diverse portfolio of apparently unrelated businesses, except that all the businesses must be able to benefit from the governance-focused expertise of the shareholder style of corporate centre.

The businesses within both scale configured groups and scope configurations can equally produce different products for different types of customers, but they must also benefit from the specific value-adding roles of their respective corporate centres.

In the case of the scale configuration, this requires common processes across the group so that the economies of scale from centralisation are realised. If centralisation only impacts on support activities, the corporate spread can be virtually as broad as is possible for the controls configuration. As the centralisation strategy incorporates more core processes, this potential spread of businesses is reduced by the need for these core processes to be common.

For the scope configuration, the commonality across the group is the type of competitive advantage, so that existing knowledge can be relevantly applied elsewhere by the corporate centre. This existing knowledge base can also be quite broad (e.g. knowledge about how to reduce overheads and other indirect costs) or very specific (e.g. how to sell large, long-term contracts to governments). Clearly, the corporate range is restricted by the leverage capability of this existing knowledge.

The shared factors within the creative configuration are not only the common vision and values imposed by the corporate centre, but also the ability to contribute to the creation of new know-how. This requires all business units to be innovative, and willing to share their ideas and their highly skilled people with other members of the group.

These factors can restrict the range of businesses within any such group, and they may also impose a constraint on the future growth of these creative configuration organisations. We have already mentioned, in Chapter 1, the problem of how the group actually exploits any new corporate know-how that results from such cross-divisional collaboration, without destroying the existing culture within this configuration. However, another growth constraint can be the difficulty of identifying suitable acquisition targets that can be brought into this type of group, again without severely damaging the underlying cultural fabric of the organisation.

If a creative configuration plans to grow via acquisitions, it needs to develop a suitable corporate vision and set of guiding principles that can be imposed successfully on existing businesses when they are brought into the group; i.e. enhancing rather than damaging their underlying success.

This is much less of a problem for the other corporate configurations. Indeed both the scope and controls configurations can often remove any organic growth constraints imposed by their existing mix of businesses, through an accelerated programme of acquisitions. The scope configuration needs to identify acquisitions that would enhance the potential leverage opportunities for its existing knowledge-based competitive advantages. This is much easier if these advantages are very broadly based, rather than being specific: very specific competitive advantages are individually more sustainable in themselves, but they are less easy to leverage into other business units.

A similar argument applies to the scale configuration; future growth is less constrained if only general support activities are centralised. However, organic growth in scale configurations is frequently achieved through an increasing level of centralisation; after all, this is how the corporate centre adds value. Thus a well-developed scale configuration can find it difficult to grow through acquisition, if this is only considered when organic growth rates start to decline. By this time, several core processes may be centralised, and the corporate centre is then trying to identify acquisitions that will benefit from economies of scale in these centralised core processes. This means that the corporate range of this configuration may be reduced by acquisition, rather than extended.

Controls configuration groups often become more diverse as a result of acquisition-led growth. However, as mentioned earlier in this chapter, this increased spread of businesses may reduce the leadership focus of the corporate centre. The centre applies its governance expertise to businesses where it has much less relevance and, hence, less value-adding potential.

These factors have considerable impacts on the sustainability of each configuration, but there is one really key question affecting whether the corporate centre can continue to add value to the group. How easy is it for others to imitate the value-adding role of the corporate centre, and thus reduce the existing corporate advantage to another hygiene factor that cannot add real value to the group? One way of assessing this ease of imitation is by looking at how these corporate centres tackle the problem of managing the varyingly complex set of businesses found within their corporate configurations.

All large organisations have to address two related challenges. The first concerns the issue of specialisation; how do we sub-divide the total task that we have decided to carry out – the 'who does what' question? The second follows on from the idea of breaking the organisation up, and it addresses the problem of reintegrating these sub-parts into a whole again; i.e. co-ordinating these sub-divided tasks. Clearly co-ordination can be achieved in a variety of ways.

The simplest and most straightforward method of co-ordination is that people meet face to face and sort out who is doing what, by when, etc. Unfortunately this is not practical as the sole means of co-ordination in a modern, large, multi-business group. There are five other forms of co-ordination that need to be considered: direct supervision, standardising work processes, standardising outputs, standardising skills and standardising values.

The shareholder style of corporate centre co-ordinates its business units through the setting of financial targets. Hence it is standardising the outputs required in the form of financial measures. Under the standardising outputs form of co-ordination, businesses have freedom to decide the means they use to achieve pre-set objectives or ends. This is exactly the position of business units in a controls configuration group.

Under direct supervision, the work is co-ordinated by a manager issuing instructions directly to subordinates and then checking on the results of their actions. This is precisely what is achieved through the centralisation of support activities or core processes that is the focus of the scale configuration.

Alternatively, the large task can be broken down into a sequence of simpler tasks that can then be specified as a standard procedure or routine; the standardising of work processes. Quite closely related is the co-ordination form of standardising skills, whereby a standard set of skills is trained into staff so that they can carry out all or part of the task. The scope configuration applies either of these co-ordinating forms or a combination of both of them. It seeks to capture pockets of best practice in one business unit, standardise the process or skills involved and leverage it across the group. If these processes can be described in the form of systems or processes (i.e. codified), co-ordination is achieved through the standardisation of processes. If the corporate centre trains business unit staff in the skills required, then the form of co-ordination is standardising skills.

Standardising values achieves co-ordination through employees all sharing the same values and this is clearly the form of co-ordination employed by creative configurations. Encouraging staff within different business units to collaborate and share ideas is very difficult to achieve through setting financial goals and objectives. Similarly direct supervision clearly will not work; telling people to be innovative together and to trust each other! Equally it is very difficult to identify the key elements in a collaborative creative process, in order to be able to standardise either the process or the skills involved. What is required is a corporate culture that clearly values collaboration and being a group team player, in order to facilitate the interchange of ideas among business units. As the creative configuration relies on 'mutual adjustment' (face-to-face meetings) as the primary mechanism for networking and co-ordination, this can place a constraint on group size. For example, more and/or larger meetings are required, which can demand too much of the functional experts' time. Improvements in communication technologies (e.g. video conferencing, e-enabled discussion forums) can help improve networking efficiencies of these creative groups.

All of these factors lead to an increasing level of sustainability as we progress around the rainbow diagram of Figure 2.10 from left to right. We have expressed the level of sustainability in terms of the ease of imitation by other organisations or by the market.

Controls configuration

The controls configuration is the easiest of the configurations to imitate, which explains why many of the diversified conglomerates utilising this style of corporate centre have been dismantled. To a large extent, an efficient capital market can replace the corporate centre in such a highly diversified group. Thus, where there is an undeveloped capital market, this configuration can still have a valuable role to play. However, even then the financial skills required at the corporate centre may not be in very short supply. The role required can be compared to that of an informed and demanding shareholder, unless the corporate centre achieves true leadership in its controls expertise.

Scale configuration

There are significant economic advantages to be gained from being the first to achieve the minimum efficient scale of operation. Where this is achieved by merging activities across different businesses and even industries, the advantages can be even greater. The cost advantages and the level of capital investment required to match these cost levels can act as substantial barriers to entry.

If the economies of scale are in support processes, these may be relatively easy to imitate as they may be generic across many industries. However, the more specific and specialised the activity is that generates the economy of scale, the less easy it will be to imitate. Even so, a determined competitor can eventually catch up because it is very difficult to protect over time an economy of scale advantage, other than by continually growing faster than everyone else.

Scope configuration

It can be practical to protect certain of the process advantages that are key to the scope configuration – particularly if they can be turned into proprietary systems. Even where this is not possible and there is a risk of competitors eventually acquiring each of the processes or systems, the organisation may still have a sustainable corporate advantage. This sustainable advantage is the capability to codify and leverage a continuing series of individually quite short-lived knowledge advantages across the group. In other words the ability to spread knowledge rapidly and effectively across the group can be an advantage that is difficult to imitate.

Creative configuration

Undoubtedly, however, the most difficult configuration to imitate is the creative configuration. For this to be really successful the corporate centre has to create a vision and set of values that are standardised across the group so that sharing comes naturally with innovation, creativity and new ideas as a way of life. This is not easy to achieve and hence it is not easy to copy!

The governance process

The last dimension that we consider in this chapter is the governance process that is appropriate for each configuration. This is a major issue for the practical implementation of our model and therefore each of the individual chapters on the four configurations considers the relevant planning and control process in much more detail. However, before looking at this detail, it is useful to highlight the major differences among the four configurations.

Any soundly based, strategically oriented planning and control system must be appropriately tailored to the specific needs of the business within which it is being implemented. This concept is now quite widely applied, but most of the literature on strategic management accounting, etc. focuses on the planning and control of competitive strategies, i.e. at the business unit level not at the corporate centre. The implied assumption for multi-business groups is that the corporate process merely involves consolidating the individual business unit plans; this is hardly a value-adding process.

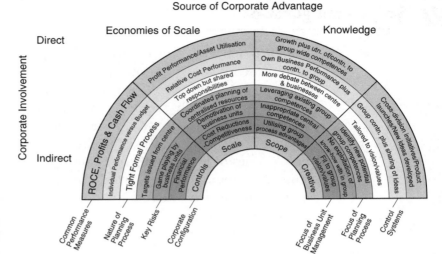

Figure 2.11
The Rainbow Diagram:
The planning & control
process.

It is clear that the corporate centre should have an equally tailored planning and control process that starts from the core elements of the corporate strategy for that organisation. As these differ across the four configurations it is likely that the resultant tailored planning and control processes will also be rather different, as is shown in Figure 2.11.

The corporate planning process should highlight the main focus of the business units in their relationship with the centre and take into account any specific role of each business unit in the total portfolio of the group. Thus, two important factors identified in Figure 2.11 are the focus of business unit management and the key risks faced by the corporate centre in implementing its particular corporate strategy.

Controls configuration

Thus, as already discussed, the business units in a controls configuration group will focus primarily on their financial performance, as they know this is considered very important by their corporate centre. The key risk created by this emphasis is that the business units will try to show good performance at all times, irrespective of what is really happening in their business. This can lead to game playing in their budgeting discussions with the centre and even in the way they present their actual performance; seeking to hide current over-performance so as to make it easier to achieve next year's targets, as well as trying to cover up current under-performance in the hope it will go away.

In this controls configuration the nature and content of the planning process, the control system, and the common performance measures used flow quite naturally from this focus and the associated key risks. The corporate centre hands out financial targets as part of a tight formal planning process; in other words, the opportunities for game playing are minimised. Strict rules are imposed on how the business units produce both their business plans and the regular financial reports that are used to track actual performance against budget; standardising outputs as discussed above. The performance measures are overwhelmingly financial; e.g. profits, cash flows and Return on Capital Employed. These actual measures are compared to the budget, last year's results and increasingly frequently other similar businesses within the group.

Scale configuration

The scale configuration has the most similar planning and control process to this, due to its corporate focus on cost reduction. However, the direct intervention of the centre and the consequent level of centralisation require some significant differences. An important focus for business unit management, in their relationship with their corporate centre, is the relative level of centralisation and its impact on their business. They do not want to see their business unit left emasculated through heavy centralisation unless they receive a very large cost advantage as a result. This highlights a key risk for the corporate centre that is the demotivation, and even potentially the departure from the group, of good quality business unit managers; this is in line with the need for a high degree of buy-in from a limited number of managers.

Resulting from this, an important element in the planning process must be co-ordinated planning for centralised resources. This not only includes capacity planning but also the service level agreements and transfer pricing levels between the centralised provider and its business unit customers. These issues can create major problems and so are discussed in Chapter 5. Consequently additional key elements in a control system for this configuration are the usages of centralised resources against planned levels and the relative cost performances of the business units across the group. As soon as the corporate centre becomes involved in creating an intra-group market it raises issues of accountability and controllability that must be carefully addressed. It is a fundamental tenet of good management that managers should only be held accountable for those things over which they can exert some degree of control; if a core process is centralised, what does the corporate centre hold business unit managers accountable for? This is also considered in Chapter 5.

Scope configuration

In the scope configuration, the corporate centre wants business units to utilise corporate knowledge wherever possible, but this raises the risk that the centre is pushing inappropriate competencies across the group. It may be that this knowledge is no longer a competitive advantage, that it is too market specific so that it has no general applicability, or that the corporate centre has misunderstood the real nature of the competitive advantage. To try to avoid this, the planning process should focus on identifying those existing competitive advantages around the group that have group-wide potential. Then the group should develop specific plans as to which business units will try to leverage which advantages.

This more strategically focused planning process leads to a looser control system because leveraging some of this new knowledge across the group requires an investment by either, or both, of the corporate centre and the business units. Also the centre needs to have a way of rewarding those business units that have developed knowledge in their own businesses that can be leveraged more widely; one common way is via a royalty fee on sales elsewhere in the group, but this can create its own quite significant problems. These issues are discussed in Chapter 6.

Creative configuration

The creative configuration faces possibly the most interesting key risk, that is that the corporate strategy appears to succeed but the group does not ever actually make any money. In other words all the business units buy-in to the group's vision and they happily work together informally in an atmosphere of trust; thus everyone is intellectually stimulated and having lots of fun. The problem is that there is never any exploitable output from all this collaborative effort.

Hence the focus of the planning process, and particularly the control system, must be on identifying new potential areas for development, which are economically attractive. As discussed in Chapter 7, this can be a major problem for this type of group; the cross-divisional project team is often very unwilling to kill their 'existing' development project, even though the economic rationale no longer exists, if it ever really did.

Summary and conclusions

This chapter has introduced a number of additional dimensions to the rainbow diagrams that we are using as a practical aid to applying the corporate configurations model.

Leadership from the centre can be either transactional (making the businesses operate more efficiently) or transformational (making the businesses operate differently, i.e. more effectively). Where the source of corporate advantage is economies of scale the leadership focus is primarily transactional, while if the source of corporate advantage is knowledge, it should be much more transformational. The consequent need to fundamentally change the type of leadership makes it much more difficult for a corporate centre to move across the configurations, to be discussed in Chapter 3. The model also highlights that the required leadership role from a corporate centre is different in each configuration, as the centre should seek to gain pre-eminence in highly tailored areas (e.g. process leadership status for the scope configuration).

Each corporate configuration also has a specific organisational culture and, as cultures can take a very long time to change, this also makes transitioning from one configuration to another more difficult.

Another dimension for differentiating among the four configurations is the very important issue of sustainability. A key factor in determining the sustainability of any value creating strategy is the relative ease or difficulty with which competitors can imitate the critical value-adding features. In this respect, the creative configuration has a significant advantage over the other configurations in that it is very, very difficult to copy. It is also one of the least constrained configurations in terms of the range of businesses that can be successfully incorporated within the group. The controls configuration is also capable of including very diverse business units. However, the creative configuration has a disadvantage in terms of its capacity for dynamic, rather than organic, growth. It is quite difficult to grow by acquisition when the acquired businesses must share the existing vision and values of the acquiring group, and also be innovative and open to sharing its new ideas with the other members of its new group. Conversely, the controls configuration can use acquisitions, and disposals, as a major source of sustained growth. This is also true to a lesser extent for the scale and scope configurations; however, their greater ease of imitation still makes the creative configuration the one with the greatest potential for sustainable value creation.

The last new dimension considered in this chapter is the governance process that is appropriate for each configuration. Yet again, it is clear that the planning and control system should be tailored to the specific requirements of the corporate centre in terms of its focus, its leadership style and the resulting organisational culture.

The next chapter develops the model still further before, in Chapters 4 to 7, we look at each of the individual configurations in detail.

Chapter 3

A proactive approach to change

Chapters 1 and 2 have already introduced a wide range of dimensions and factors that can be incorporated within the corporate configurations model. However, the model is not yet complete. We still need to refine the axes used on both sides of the rainbow and we need to consider when and how companies will move around the model. These ideas are introduced in this chapter.

When the high and low scales are properly incorporated on both axes of the model it becomes clear that there can be considerable confusion caused if certain positions within the model are occupied by the corporate centre. However, it can sometimes be less clear precisely what action such a centre should take to move itself to a sustainable value-adding situation.

It should also already be clear from the preceding chapters that any group may need, or wish, to alter its current positioning within the model. This may be in response to a change in its external business environment, its own internal organisation, or simply to improve the effectiveness of its current corporate strategy.

In this chapter, the general implications of such matters are considered. The simplest type of move is a repositioning within an existing corporate configuration; what we refer to as migrations within the model. Transitions across the model involving changing from one configuration to another are normally much more complicated, particularly if the organisation is trying to move dramatically around the model, rather than moving just across the boundary into the next-door configuration. The detailed, specific issues involved in moving just across the boundary to the next configuration in the model are dealt with, for each configuration, in Chapters 4 to 7, which deal individually with the controls, scale, scope and creative configurations. The more complex transitions around the model are then considered in Chapter 8 in Part III of the book.

Creating confusion

As already mentioned earlier in the book, for the configurations model to work to its full value-adding potential, there needs to be complete agreement between the corporate centre and the underlying businesses both on what the style of relationship between them actually is and that this style of relationship (i.e. shareholder, manager, consultant, or leader) is appropriate to the actual strategy and context of the group. Any lack of clarity in this agreement can result in dysfunctional behaviour from some or all of the business units that can destroy, rather than create, value for the group.

In order to do full justice to the new dimensions that were introduced in Chapter 2 we need to use the relative scales for both axes of the model that we developed at the end of Chapter 1, so that positions can be plotted as accurately as possible and directional strategies put in place. As was done in that chapter, it is much more helpful to place the high ends of the scales for each dimension at the outsides of the axes so that the lows are placed next to each other in the middle, as is shown in Figure 3.1.

The impact of this scaling of the vertical axis is shown in Figure 3.2, where the nature of corporate centre involvement ranges from very highly indirect to very highly direct at the extremes, with low indirect involvement and low direct intervention being placed very close together in the middle.

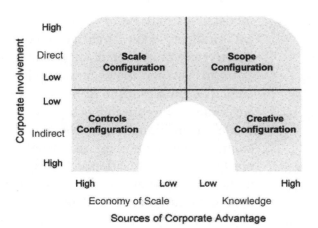

Figure 3.1
The corporate configurations model – restated.

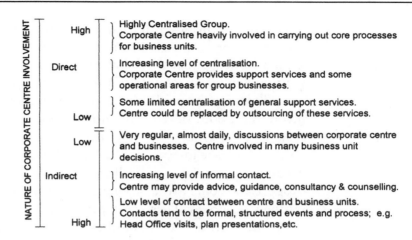

Figure 3.2
Developing the model:
The vertical axis.

Groups of companies with types of corporate centre involvement at opposite extremes look and feel very different indeed. One is highly centralised with a very large corporate centre, while the other has a very small head office that has only limited regular contact with its highly autonomous business units. These different degrees of involvement and their impacts on each corporate configuration are considered in more detail in Chapters 4 to 7, as here we are more interested in the potential problem created at the middle of the axis, where the 'two lows' meet.

At and near this intersection there is little perceptible difference between two groups with the different involvements from their corporate centres. For the manager style a low direct type of intervention can mean a centre that has only limited centralisation of some general support services or similar activities. Much of this centralisation could be replaced by outsourcing to a genuine third party supplier, and in some such groups this is in fact what the corporate centres have done themselves (i.e. they have outsourced their own centralisation).

The relationship between this type of centre and its businesses is not dramatically different to that of a shareholder style centre with a low indirect type of involvement. The highly indirect form means that there is little informal and regular contact between the businesses and the centre, but these contacts increase as the involvement becomes less highly indirect. Thus at the low end of indirect involvement, there is very regular, almost daily, discussion between the centre and the businesses, and the corporate centre is involved in many business unit decisions. (We accept that this can seem counter-intuitive at first sight due to the terms that are used to describe the indirect type of involvement, but *low* indirect involvement actually means *more* regular contact and a *greater* degree of involvement than a *high* indirect type of involvement.)

Clearly, as this level of regular contact and involvement increases, the size of the corporate centre also increases, to the point where it is similar in size to that of the low direct type of intervention. Thus there is the potential for continuous movement up and down this vertical axis. This can hopefully be made clearer by illustrating the issues involved on both sides of the model. In a cost-reducing economies of scale focused group, low *direct intervention* normally only involves the corporate centre intervening by centralising support activities (such as accounting services, payroll administration, information systems support and some areas of sourcing and supply), rather than the core business processes. These core processes are therefore left completely under the control of the business units and may differ significantly across the group.

A low level of indirect involvement also commonly involves the corporate centre taking an active interest in some of these areas but, in these cases, this is achieved through the standardisation of the required outputs from the support systems that are used throughout the group. Thus these support systems are not truly centralised, in that they may still physically be carried out within the business units, but they are very tightly specified and, therefore, controlled by the corporate centre. In many such groups, this active involvement in business decisions extends furthest in the finance areas of tax and treasury. The legal structure of these groups is often dictated by the tax planning requirements of the corporate centre finance team, even if the complexity of this structure interferes with the day-to-day operations of the individual business units. An additional requirement to remit any surplus funds, sometimes on a daily basis, to the centre removes any funding and investment discretion from the business units as major fund raising activities are also normally controlled by this type of centre. Thus tax and treasury management can be effectively centralised even in groups where the corporate centres claim to have only an indirect involvement in their autonomous business units.

On the other side of the model, where the corporate centre is focused on adding value rather than reducing cost, there can similarly be continuous movement along the vertical axis. A highly indirect, creative style of corporate centre may establish a very clear formal vision and set of values for all the businesses but this central leadership can feel somewhat remote and austere to a new employee located in one business unit. The group ethos and identity is maintained through the transfer of very senior managers (often only at divisional director level) around the group. The creation of cross-business initiatives is *simply expected* by the centre because it is built into the group culture and completely bought into by these rotating senior executives. [This can be compared to the highly indirect, shareholder style of centre, where very limited contact is maintained with the business units. The annual plan is submitted and eventually approved and the monthly management accounts review performance against this plan. It is more likely that poorly performing business units will be sold or closed down than that the corporate centre will get actively involved in trying to turn around this unacceptable level of performance.]

As the creative configuration corporate centre becomes less indirectly involved, the leaders at the centre become more accessible to the business units. This increased visibility not only provides ongoing clarification of the group's vision and values but also increases the range of mechanisms designed to facilitate the creation of new corporate know-how. The increasing number of people at the corporate centre means that the centre should have more knowledge about new interesting developments in individual business units and thus can personally facilitate the sharing of these ideas. However, this encouragement of interchange can be moved to a still more positive level by the creation of more formal but still indirect processes. Cross-divisional assignments at lower levels within the group will increase both the spread of knowledge and the idea of belonging to the group rather than to an individual division. Similarly setting up cross-divisional project teams to examine or identify new opportunities means that the centre is almost forcing the divisions to work together.

The corresponding initiatives from the equivalent low directly intervening, consultant style of corporate centre would not necessarily look dramatically different. This type of centre would codify existing knowledge gleaned from one business unit and make it generally available more widely across the group. In some groups this merely consists of establishing group best practices that are published on some internal database that *can* be accessed by interested business units. This low directly intervening corporate centre may encourage the most relevant business units to adopt this new process whereas a very highly directly intervening centre would mandate that this new process will be implemented across the group.

It is therefore quite common to find corporate centres that are not clear themselves as to the real nature of the involvement that they are implementing. In some areas they will directly intervene in their business units while, in other apparently similar matters, they will tell the businesses to get on with it and to make up their minds themselves. Other corporate centres operate differing levels of direct intervention for different business units, but without necessarily having an economically rational categorisation among their total business units. In other words, the different levels of centralisation do not appear to relate to the varying levels of economic benefits that can be generated for these various categories of business units. Sometimes these differing levels of involvement simply reflect the personal preferences of the senior executives at the corporate centre. Thus, there can even be significant differences in the ways in which different regions or business streams within a group are dealt with by 'the corporate centre'. Any such perceived differences are clearly a potential source of confusion for the business units.

To the business units within such groups there is, not surprisingly, a very limited amount of clearly perceived difference between these two 'low involvement' corporate centres. This lack of clarity can create a degree of confusion for the business units, as they can be unsure as to when and how the corporate centre will get involved in their businesses. For the corporate centre, the lack of difference at least makes it relatively easy to change the nature of involvement from the low end of one type to the low end of the other, should they eventually decide which is more appropriate.

It is possible, as shown in Figure 3.3, to describe the nature of involvement axis as a continuum, from highly indirect to highly direct. However, the middle area, where the two 'low' natures meet, has been highlighted as an area of potential confusion. There is a risk that the lack of clarity in the type of involvement could lead to the costs of the corporate centre, which can be quite considerable for both these 'low' types of involvement, exceeding the value added by the corporate centre.

Figure 3.3
Developing the model:
The vertical axis.

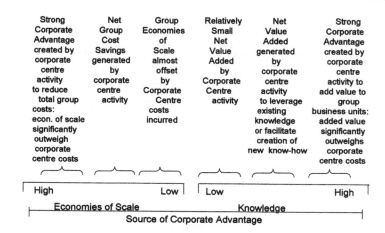

Strong Corporate Advantage created by corporate centre activity to reduce total group costs: econ. of scale significantly outweigh corporate centre costs	Net Group Cost Savings generated by corporate centre activity	Group Economies of Scale almost offset by Corporate Centre costs incurred	Relatively Small Net Value Added by Corporate Centre activity	Net Value Added generated by corporate centre activity to leverage existing knowledge or facilitate creation of new know-how	Strong Corporate Advantage created by corporate centre activity to add value to group business units: added value significantly outweighs corporate centre costs

Figure 3.4
Developing the model:
The horizontal axis.

High ⟶ Low │ Low ⟶ High

Economies of Scale ⟷ Knowledge

Source of Corporate Advantage

This is much less likely to happen when the corporate advantage being exploited by the centre is very strong; hence, the area of potential confusion is elliptically shaped, with the widest area at the low points of both types of corporate advantage. In other words, groups can tolerate more confusion in one dimension if the other dimension is stronger and hence provides the required clarity. Real problems occur when both dimensions create confusion, as is shown below.

A similar analysis can be applied, as is shown in Figure 3.4, to the scaling of the horizontal axis of the model, which considers the source of corporate advantage. Again the highest rankings for both economies of scale and knowledge advantages are placed at the extremes of the diagram, with the lowest rankings being placed next to each other in the middle.

At the extremes, the corporate centre creates a strong corporate advantage because its own costs are easily outweighed by the benefits that accrue from its activities (whether by reducing total group costs or enhancing the value of the knowledge within the group). However, as we move towards the middle of the axis from either end, there is a much closer trade-off between the corporate centre costs and its value added.

Also this horizontal axis represents a less continuous movement from one end to the other. It is not a simple matter for a corporate centre to change from trying to achieve economies of scale for the group to trying to add value by exploiting existing knowledge or facilitating the creation of new know-how. This change in focus is most difficult for corporate centres with a very indirect nature of involvement and it is easiest for those with the most direct level of intervention. Therefore the potential area of confusion for this dimension is differently shaped, as it relates to the difficulty of transitioning between the two sources of corporate advantage; as illustrated in Figure 3.5.

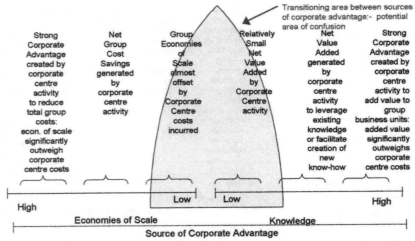

Figure 3.5
Developing the model:
The horizontal axis.

Note: This axis represents a less continuous movement from very high economies of scale to very high knowledge advantage due to a discontinuity in the middle, which can create confusion for the business units as to the true role of the corporate centre. This discontinuity is less significant in highly direct styles of involvement and much more significant in highly indirect styles.

The zone of intolerable confusion (ZOIC)

When the two axes are again combined in the full corporate configurations model, we find that the two areas of confusion overlap, as is shown in Figure 3.6. This overlapping area can create severe problems for any group because it means that the corporate centre lacks a clearly understood and agreed nature of involvement *and* is not exploiting a strong corporate advantage. This combination makes it very difficult for the centre to add value on a sustainable basis to the businesses within the

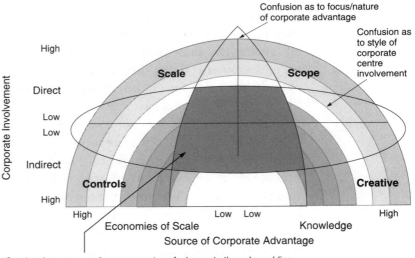

Figure 3.6
The corporate configurations model: The zone of intolerable confusion.

Overlapping area causing very great confusion as to the value adding role of corporate centre: the zone of intolerable confusion (ZOIC)

group. The options are quite stark; the centre has to find some way out of this intolerable state of confusion, as the group would be more valuable if it were split up. Hence, we have titled this overlapping area the zone of intolerable confusion (ZOIC).

This zone of intolerable confusion further restricts the sustainable value-adding positions within the model that any corporate centre can occupy. However, it also indicates some of the problems that groups can experience when they try to make dramatic transitions from one configuration to another. These are considered in detail in Chapter 8, but one has already resulted in a significant change to the diagrammatic representation of the model.

Below the ZOIC in Figure 3.6, there is deliberately a void in our corporate configurations model. As previously discussed this is to highlight that the horizontal axis is much less of a continuum than the vertical axis, and that a corporate centre cannot create added value through indirectly exploiting a weak source of corporate advantage (whether economies of scale or knowledge based). However, a further advantage of this diagrammatic presentation is that it shows the degree of the challenge facing any corporate centre that seeks to move along the horizontal axis while maintaining an indirect nature of involvement (i.e. either from the controls configuration direct to the creative configuration, or vice versa).

Moving around the model

The void shows that this move requires the centre to rapidly transform its corporate advantage from a strong economies of scale advantage to a strong knowledge advantage, or vice versa. The focuses of these two corporate configurations (i.e. controls and creative) are so fundamentally different that any attempt to reinvent the corporate centre in the alternative guise could be met with a degree of cynicism or disbelief and possibly even outright revolt by the business units in the group. It has to be remembered that a consequence of the indirect nature of involvement is that these business units are relatively autonomous and operate in a very decentralised way. This type of dramatic reorientation of the corporate advantage is a much more practical possibility when the group has a high direct nature of involvement.

An illustration may make this clearer. The organisation represented in Figure 3.7 wishes to make a dramatic change from its current position in the bottom left segment of the controls configuration to either position B or C (i.e. the top right segment of the scope configuration

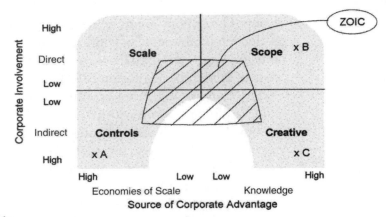

Figure 3.7

The corporate configurations model: The zone of intolerable confusion.

Note:
A represents the initial position of the organisation, i.e. strong economy of scale corporate advantage with an indirect method of involvement.
B & C represent desired new positions for this organisation.

or the bottom right portion of the creative configuration). The move from A to C would require a complete change in the nature of the corporate advantage from achieving governance focused economies of scale to facilitating the creation of new corporate know-how. Consequently the whole focus of the corporate centre would need to change, as would the skills of the managers at the centre, their leadership profile, and the entire corporate planning and control process.

It is, in fact possible to change these factors quite rapidly, as was mentioned in Chapter 2, usually by changing the top management team at the corporate centre. However, the culture of the organisation also normally needs to change dramatically. The creative configuration needs to develop a strong feeling of group identity and trust from the business units towards the corporate centre. Changing corporate cultures normally takes years rather than weeks or months and consequently such a dramatic proposed change would be incredibly risky, unless the group culture was already one that perceived the centre as value adding. The new element would be the requirement to get the business units to work much more closely together.

In 1981 Jack Welch took over as CEO of GE after 20 years working for several very highly regarded and successful group CEOs. This did not stop him radically changing the focus of the corporate centre through a series of significantly challenging initiatives. At the time of his accession GE was world famous for its centrally driven planning and control process through which the relatively small corporate centre maintained control over an increasingly diversified group, i.e. a value-adding shareholder style corporate centre. Welch set out to break through what he regarded as a centrally focused bureaucracy that was curtailing innovation and dynamism across the group. He established a new mission for the group of being 'committed to developing the sensitivity, the leanness, the simplicity, and the agility of a small company'; an interesting challenge for a group the size of GE. This meant, among other things, doing away with the group's detailed planning process and moving to what he christened 'a planful opportunism'. This entailed setting a very few clear, overarching goals for each business from the centre but then leaving the businesses free to seize any opportunities that arose to further the achievement of these goals.

The overarching goals, which included becoming No. 1 or No. 2 in any market that GE competed in, were placed in a very clear context for divisional business managers by the vision and values established for the group. GE seeks 'to improve the quality of life through technology and innovation' and believes in individual responsibility and opportunity and group-wide honesty and integrity. It also firmly believes that there is an interdependent balance between responsibility to customers, employees, society and shareholders, with no party being dominant.

This leader style of corporate centre can create what Jack Welch referred to as the conflict between numbers and values. If business units 'make the numbers' and their managers have the group's values, these managers will progress rapidly within the group. If the managers share the values but their business does not perform well, they will be given a second chance, possibly elsewhere in the group. A key element in the role of this centre is the development of general managers, and GE believes that its strong pool of talent is a major source of corporate advantage as these managers are regularly moved around the group to stimulate innovation and change. These issues are referred to later in the chapter and developed in Chapter 7.

A move from A to B is at first sight even more problematic, as it also involves a significant change in the nature of the involvement of the corporate centre from highly indirect to quite high direct intervention. In practice, this increased direct intervention by the corporate centre can make the transition more possible. The new directly intervening corporate centre can try to accelerate the rate of cultural change within the organisation, if necessary by centralising key processes and activities, even if temporarily. It is still, however, very challenging.

This overall rate of change can be further enhanced by altering the composition of the portfolio of businesses comprising the group, i.e. by the divestment of existing, but now inappropriate, businesses and the acquisition of some with the required new organisational culture, or that can benefit from the culture. This portfolio management process may use some of the already existing skills within the original controls oriented corporate centre but, as discussed in Chapter 2, dramatic acquisition and divestment activity would be less appropriate for the creative configuration.

For its final years under Lord Weinstock, GEC plc was heavily criticised for the lack of value added by its corporate strategy. Indeed some financial analysts described the albeit small corporate centre as being significant destroyers of shareholder value. Yet in the 1960s and 1970s Weinstock had restructured the UK's electronics and defence contracting industries through a series of take-overs and mergers. During the 1980s and early 1990s the rigorous financial control and incredibly tight cash management of the shareholder style corporate centre generated a vast cash mountain that none of the unsurprisingly risk averse business units was willing to access for reinvestment.

This rapidly changed with Lord Weinstock's retirement and the introduction of a new management team in the late 1990s. They very rapidly transformed the group, through very large scale disposals and acquisitions, from a well-diversified group involved in mature, relatively stable but low growth industries into a highly focused telecoms business mainly based around the USA markets (where GEC had never had any strong presence). These acquisitions were financed by cash payments, using the existing GEC cash mountain, then the proceeds from selling GEC's original core businesses, and finally from large-scale borrowings.

The renamed group (now called Marconi) subsequently suffered a dramatic crisis in the ensuing downturn in the telecoms sector. This resulted in a forced financial restructuring by the lenders that left the original shareholders with less than 1 per cent ownership of the group, as much of the outstanding debt was converted into equity. The change in role of the corporate centre from an indirect controls configuration to a more directly intervening scope configuration was therefore combined with a dramatic change in the composition of the businesses making up the group and was implemented by a new top management team at the corporate centre, none of whom actually had strong line management experience of the telecoms sector.

Clearly any such dramatic changes within organisations need to be carefully thought through before they are undertaken. The corporate centre must have a very sound justification for embarking on such a traumatic process. The possible reasons for moving around the model are thus discussed initially. The model also indicates an apparently logical 'corporate life cycle' over time but our research has highlighted that many organisations seem to want to fight against this trend, and move the other way round the model; a concept we have christened 'swimming upstream' that is considered in Chapter 8.

Migrations within one configuration

Migrating, or repositioning the organisation, *within* one configuration can be done to strengthen the added-value capability of the corporate centre, by increasing the level of the organisation's current specific corporate advantage and/or modifying the existing method of involvement. Alternatively the migration may make the group more able to move to a new configuration if that becomes necessary or desirable. Quite frequently these possible alternative migrations are inherently in conflict with each other, and these conflicts are highlighted in the corporate configurations model.

Figure 3.8 shows the position for the corporate centre of an organisation within the scale configuration; the initial position of the corporate centre has been plotted at point A. One way for this corporate centre to enhance its added value would be to increase its direct intervention in its business units and to enhance the existing economies of scale based corporate advantage. This could involve an increased level of centralisation by the corporate centre, such as bringing into the centre certain core processes rather than restricting centralisation to support activities. A highly successful migration could result in the corporate centre being repositioned at point B in Figure 3.8, a position where the centre should be able to add sustainable value to the group.

However, this migration also moves this corporate centre as far as possible away from the borders with the neighbouring controls and

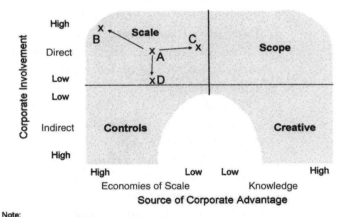

Figure 3.8
The corporate configurations model: Migrations within a configuration.

Note:
A shows the existing position of a corporate centre.
Positions B, C & D show 3 possible migrations within the Scale configuration.

scope configurations. Consequently, if a sudden transition to either of these configurations became necessary, this corporate centre would find it much more difficult to change following its move to position B. Indeed, if the centre felt that such a transition was likely to be required, it might prefer to migrate to either position C or D, depending on the predicted direction of the required transition. Such an early migration would greatly facilitate any subsequent transition across the boundary to the desired future configuration. This is despite both these migrations appearing less attractive than the move to B, and no more attractive than staying at point A.

It is therefore clearly very important that organisations fully understand the reasons for needing to change their corporate configurations and that they can predict, quite well in advance, when circumstances will require such a change.

Reasons for moving

The first and most obvious reason for wanting to move to a different corporate configuration was mentioned at the beginning of Chapter 2. After carrying out the initial analysis of where they currently are and where the group really should be, many groups find that either they are not currently in any of the four value-adding configurations or they are definitely in the wrong one. Even if the corporate centre is currently in the correct configuration, the analysis should be forward looking to try to predict whether this situation is likely to change, and how these changes could affect the future role of the corporate centre. A major cause of transitions is a change in the external environment that affects the major business units of the group. For multi-business groups this is obviously a less common occurrence than for individual business units within the group, but there are significant changes that could force the corporate centre to review, and possibly to change, its current configuration and style.

Major changes in the competitive environment may be caused by technology (such as are happening with the internet and the whole digital revolution). These may create significant new opportunities to leverage knowledge across the group or to centralise more activities in order to reduce total group costs, or they may present significant threats to the businesses currently within the group. Any of these impacts could require the corporate centre to change from its current configuration.

Equally customer expectations change over time so that today's competitive advantage becomes tomorrow's hygiene factor. Unfortunately this can also happen very suddenly, so that the basis of competition in one or more of the major business units within the group moves from perceived use value to selling price, and hence relative costs become much more important. As already discussed the corporate centre has to decide whether it needs to change its role and/or the composition of the group.

Similarly supplier initiatives can force the group to reassess its corporate strategy. Suppliers may dramatically reorganise their level of the value chain so that even centralised activities can no longer compete on cost. Alternatively they can move vertically down the supply chain of the industry so that they now compete directly with the business units within the group.

Of course, the most common examples relate to activities of competitors, either in reaction to the group's existing success or as a separate competitive initiative. Competitors may match or even exceed the group's current offering in the marketplace (as mentioned in Chapter 1 these group-wide competitors may be competing for shareholders' attention rather than for product customers), or indeed they may completely change the rules of the game.

The rules of the game can also be dramatically altered through legal or regulatory changes. The regulatory changes in an industry (e.g. financial services, telecoms, information technology, transport) can force corporate centres fundamentally to rethink their overall corporate strategy. Similar changes can occur through the privatisation of other players in an industry that is very important to the group.

However, there are also changes in corporate configuration that are caused by factors internal to the group. The relationship between the corporate centre and its business units may well change over time. The business units can develop or acquire the skills previously provided by the centre; this is particularly likely, as they grow, for those skills that rely on critical mass. It is also quite likely if the group becomes increasingly diversified, through acquisition led growth for example, because the corporate centre may become ever more distant and the business units have to provide the necessary skilled inputs themselves. These locally held skills may be more relevant to the marketplace of the specific business than those provided across the whole group by the corporate centre. Thus the centre needs to review how it can continue to add value to the group.

Conversely the competitive environment facing some of the business units may intensify and the business unit's skills may no longer be adequate for its marketplace. It now needs a different type of input from its corporate centre. This type of change may require the centre to become more directly involved in the affairs of the business unit.

Another set of changes can be caused by internal management changes within the group. Clearly this includes the normal successions at the corporate centre and at the top of the divisions, but it can also be caused by sudden unexpected management alterations. These sudden changes can be due to the unexpected departure of key personnel, which alters either the skills at the centre or the relationship with the business units, or by internally stimulated departures (i.e. the removal of part, or all, of the top team). As discussed elsewhere, this internal stimulus can be a way of creating the required change in the corporate configuration.

The remaining main causes of transitions across the model are changes in the expectations of other key stakeholders (e.g. shareholders, lenders, etc.) that impact on the group's ability to continue with its current corporate strategy. This may occur through a change in the ownership structure of the group, rather than a direct change in the competitive environment in which the group operates. Initial Public Offerings onto Public Capital Markets can significantly change the major shareholders in the group. These new shareholders may have different expectations and return requirements from the previous owners. The reverse movement, which is becoming increasingly common, involving taking an existing publicly quoted group private, can have similar implications requiring a review of the corporate strategy. 'Going private' can be achieved through some form of leveraged buy-out, which quite often makes the top group executives into significant shareholders in the group and this may change their own stakeholder perspective.

Perhaps the most extreme form of change is when a previously mutually owned or government owned group is rapidly transformed into a fully fledged publicly quoted company. This happened to the majority of the originally mutually structured building societies in the UK that have now been converted into publicly quoted banks or even more diverse financial institutions. It has also changed the role of the corporate centre for demutualised life assurance businesses but the scale of such a change is magnified significantly when the flotation is made, or includes a listing, on an international capital market that is not the home base of the transformed group. Suddenly the corporate strategy and the corporate centre's value-adding role is subjected to a dramatically more rigorous review. A very good example of this is the recent rapid transformation of Old Mutual plc.

For over 150 years Old Mutual had been a very successful South African based mutual life assurance organisation. Over this period it had developed a dominant position in the life assurance and savings industries of South Africa and some neighbouring African countries. The effective direct ownership of the business by the policyholders and the tight focus of the business units comprising the group enabled the corporate centre to have a very directly intervening method of involvement that sought to leverage knowledge across the group. In 1999 Old Mutual demutualised and gained listings on the London, Johannesburg and other African Stock Exchanges, immediately becoming part of the FTSE 100 Index. It relocated its Head Office base to London and the initial sale of new shares gave it access to capital that enabled acquisitions outside South Africa to be undertaken. This was part of a publicly stated objective to reduce the group's dependence upon the volatile South African Rand for its future stream of profit. Several significant acquisitions were rapidly made, both in the UK and the USA, and these included large investment and fund management companies as well as some relatively small insurance businesses. This resulted in the establishment of a much more formal divisional and regional organisational structure for the dramatically changed group.

Of course, the strict reporting requirements from the new professional international shareholders meant that the external focus of the corporate centre increased significantly, at the same time as did the spread of businesses comprising the group. This required a significant shift in the role of the corporate centre if it was to continue as a value-adding contributor to the future success of the enlarged group. The challenge that faces all groups during any such periods of rapid and dramatic change is to make a conscious choice as to which new configuration to move to. For Old Mutual, a logical move is for its corporate centre to become less directly involved in the underlying business units; but should the resulting indirect involvement style be that of a shareholder or a more creative leader?

The more simple transition may be to retain the value-adding knowledge source of corporate advantage but to apply this less directly in future. However, much of the previously relevant knowledge that could be leveraged across the group was specifically to do with the South African market where, for example, the Old Mutual brand is tremendously strong. This has much less relevance to the new collection of businesses and it may be more appropriate for the centre to focus on the role of effectively controlling these businesses. In order to do this the corporate centre needs to develop a group-wide planning and control process and to design tailored short-term and long-term

incentive schemes that will appropriately motivate the more autonomous heads of its new, far-flung business divisions. For the group to
achieve this, it may need to develop or bring in a different set of skills
to those that currently exist at the corporate centre. However, there is
also a strong argument that even a move from the scope configuration
to the creative configuration would require significantly different
skills from the centre. Establishing a clear vision and set of values that
is relevant to the geographically much wider and more disparate set
of businesses in the new external environment of much more demanding shareholders and professional analysts could be difficult for a top
team that was used to a very different managerial style and a different
type of environment. As has been said about Old Mutual, 'it's no longer
old and no longer mutual!'.

A similarly dramatic review of corporate strategy, and the corresponding role of the corporate centre, can be needed in the face of a
crisis of confidence. This may be related to the overall sector in which
the group is placed by the capital markets (e.g. 'old' economy versus
'new' economy) or it may be geographically focused (e.g. the Far East,
Eastern Europe crises). The group may feel it is only marginally
affected, but the perception of capital market investors can have a
dramatic impact on its ability to raise new capital, or even to sustain
existing levels of financing. This may lead to a much changed corporate
strategy, with a consequent need for a very different style of corporate
centre.

There were several examples of this type of change being attempted
by large relatively mature groups during the dot.com boom of the very
late 1990s. Many well-established, cash generating companies saw their
share prices slashed as investors dumped these boring 'old economy'
shares in order to buy shares in completely new, highly cash negative
start-ups. In response, some of these groups tried to package themselves
as 'quasi dot.coms' with highly creative, know-how creating focused top
management teams, whereas they had been, for many years, firmly
entrenched in much more appropriate but very different corporate
configurations. Fortunately the dot.com bubble burst before these
corporate centres could do too much damage by reconfiguring their
underlying businesses to fit their newly stated corporate emphasis.

However, there is also a strong argument that it is inevitable that
organisations will need to review the role of their corporate centres
from time to time. The successful exploitation of one 'style' leads eventually to the need to change to a different corporate centre style.
In other words the group may go through some form of corporate
lifecycle, as is shown in Figure 3.9.

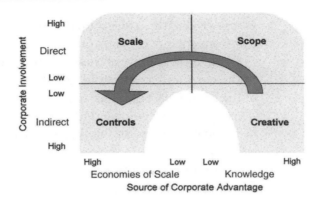

Figure 3.9

The corporate configurations model: A corporate lifecycle?

Transitions over time – a corporate lifecycle?

[It is important to note, up-front, that the configurations are by no means limited to the types of group considered in this following discussion.] The creative configuration can incorporate many very new innovative groups, where the culture and shared vision and values are seen as very important to the success of the group. Thus this can be argued to be the start of a corporate lifecycle, particularly since many of these groups currently contain no, or very few, profit making and cash generating businesses; their current value is therefore totally based on their future prospects.

If this type of group is successful at developing a major new innovation through its cross-business division initiatives, it then faces the dilemma of how best to exploit this exciting potential corporate advantage. The possibilities are several, and are considered in detail in Chapter 7, but our research indicates that there are two common solutions. One is where the group decides to create a new business unit to focus exclusively on leveraging this new innovative business opportunity. The second is to centralise this new area so that the corporate head office can get directly involved in maximising the value created from this corporate centre sponsored initiative.

These corporate centre stimulated changes are normally intended to accelerate the exploitation of the newly created corporate know-how; this problem of 'know-how exploitation' was raised in Chapter 2 as a key challenge facing corporate centres in this creative configuration. It is, therefore, not surprising that some corporate centres seek more direct involvement in the scale-up phase of know-how exploitation.

One way of accelerating the process is to try to codify the new know-how into transferable knowledge, so that it can be more readily shared across the group. Codified knowledge is, of course, not only more easily transferred within the group but also is more easily imitated by competitors outside the organisation.

Quite clearly some of these solutions immediately transform the role of the corporate centre and, to a large extent, the fundamental nature of the group. Part of it has, in reality, moved to the scope configuration. This should be recognised by the corporate centre so that the nature of its involvement and the skill sets of managers located in the centre can adapt accordingly.

The scope configuration can function very successfully when the group is involved in quite rapidly growing businesses, where competition is not primarily based on price. Thus specific competitive advantages built around brand management expertise, technological development, product innovation, customer service enhancements, new channels of distribution can often be leveraged group-wide by scope configuration corporate centres. These centres may have very high costs, as may the business units, but these may be considered irrelevant as long as the leveraged knowledge based advantages generate even higher profits as they spread across the business units.

However, once it has been fully applied across the group, the particular knowledge based core competence is fully exploited and the corporate centre is no longer adding value. Yet it may still have high costs. Acquisition of new businesses to which this core competence has relevance can prolong this value-adding stage but, eventually, any individual competitive advantage becomes a hygiene factor that is required to survive rather than flourish. Customers' requirements change over time or competitors catch up, so that the corporate centre needs to keep identifying new sources of advantage to which it can add value by leveraging them across the rest of the group. An obvious potential problem is that the new knowledge based advantage may not be relevant to all of the businesses within the group.

Also, as industries mature, the basis of competition often tends to become focused on selling price. This means that the corporate centre now becomes more cost conscious, both of its own costs and those of its business units. A seemingly logical extension of the corporate centre's existing direct intervention in its business units is frequently seen as centralisation of certain activities in order to reduce the total costs of the group. There are obvious and substantive resulting problems in that this represents a fundamental change in the source of overall corporate advantage, in response to a possible change in, or removal of, a competitive advantage for certain businesses within the group. Also the corporate centre does not currently possess the supply chain management skills necessary to achieve these economies of scale effectively and efficiently.

Further, as discussed in Chapter 2, the type of leadership that is required from the corporate centre differs in these two configurations. In the scope configuration, the focus is on transformational leadership as the centre seeks to change what the underlying businesses are doing. With the move across to the cost reducing scale configuration, the emphasis changes to a transactional leadership role by which the centre makes the businesses do the same things more efficiently; changing 'the how' rather than 'the what'.

Notwithstanding these issues, the group may now find itself with a set of maturing businesses, where cost is likely to be a fundamental competitive issue. Consequently the corporate centre continues to centralise in order to reduce total group costs still further. Indeed, other similar businesses may be added to the group so that extra economies of scale and, potentially, overall volume leadership in this centralised process can be achieved.

Ultimately, in many such industries, competition will respond to this corporate centre led activity. This response can take several forms: outsourcing or strategic alliances could be used to equal or better the corporation's cost levels; the competitors within any industry may consolidate by merger or take-over, or rationalise the industry capacity, so that they remove the volume leadership advantage. Alternatively, the group may grow so large that the centralised processes reach a diseconomy of scale level. This seems to be rare but, more commonly, the economy of scale benefits flatten out at a volume of activity that renders centralisation for the whole group irrelevant; this is quite often caused by the introduction of new technologies, e.g. information processing technology.

Thus the centralising, economies of scale focused corporate centre may find itself under pressure. One apparently attractive response is to reduce the level of direct intervention in the businesses and become an indirect, shareholder style of corporate centre. The focus is still on cost reduction and profit improvement, but the centralised processes are either given back to the businesses, treated as stand-alone profit generating business units within the group, or sold off to the independent outside third party suppliers that have normally now established themselves.

Our research has revealed several examples of this type of lifecycle development, which unfortunately has the corporate centre in the role of reacting to changes in the competitive environment of its businesses rather than focusing on the source of its corporate advantage and its continued relevance to the businesses in the group.

Application to single business groups

As mentioned in Chapter 1, the research was originally aimed at multi-business groups but it soon became clear that it was equally applicable to any groups that had a separate corporate centre; therefore, it also encompasses 'single' business groups. Although all these businesses, by definition, sell very similar products to similar types of customer, it is quite likely that the individual business units face significant differences in their specific competitive environments.

Thus the similar products could be sold in different markets that are at very different stages of development, as is the case for multinational groups such as McDonald's, Coca-Cola, Microsoft and Intel. Alternatively similar products may be sold in specific segments of the same market where the bases of competition are different. This is done by several automotive manufacturers where major components are shared across different car brands, such as Audi, VW and Skoda. Another variant of this occurs where the similar products are sold in different markets against totally different competitors or to significantly different customer profiles; major multinational consumer goods companies can find themselves up against very locally focused competitors in specific markets where market segmentations are completely different.

This can lead to a conflict in terms of the appropriate value-adding role for the corporate centre and hence for its appropriate style. This is illustrated in Figure 3.10 where the same product can be sold in a new, rapidly growing market where competition is based on brand imagery, and also in a mature or even declining market where the product is regarded as much more of a price sensitive commodity. At first sight these different competitive environments would seem to require different roles from the corporate centre.

Figure 3.10
Single business groups:
Similar products in
different markets.

Some types of changes and developments in these geographical markets or internal market segmentations should be much more manageable by these large single business groups, because they will have been seen several times before. Indeed a group should be able to predict the next stage of development in the later developing markets. However, many such groups have organisation structures that do not assist in this 'learning from experience' process (i.e. leveraging the knowledge that already exists within the group). The scope configuration can still be relevant even to the mature cost-based markets as long as the knowledge that is then shared is 'how to reduce costs'. The consultant style corporate centre can also apply its process skills to leverage the knowledge that had been gained when these now mature markets were themselves growing rapidly across the later developing markets where such information is both relevant and very valuable.

Alternatively, the corporate centre may decide to focus its attention on the particular needs of one type of competitive environment and the correspondingly required role for the centre. This can lead to the group moving away from its single product focus as the skills at the corporate centre can prove more relevant to other products that now face the same type of competitive environment. These issues for single business groups are discussed in Part II.

Applications of model in different contexts

The corporate configurations model can be applied to all large organisations but there are some slight differences in its application in specific contexts. In the non-corporate sector, the model can be used to analyse the relationship between the organisation, with its particular style, and its sponsoring parent body which may have a different style and will certainly have its own stakeholder expectations and objectives. If these criteria change at the parent level, the style and configuration of the subsidiary organisation may also need to change. This need could be highlighted through a two tiered centre/business analysis to assess any conflicts within the styles now being used.

A two or even three stage analysis may also be needed in some very large groups, where individual business units are formed into sub-groups and these sub-groups are themselves further consolidated together to establish the final reporting relationships to the ultimate group centre. This can mean that the sub-group centres are operating in different configurations from those that they are being subjected to at the overall group level. If these different centre styles are particularly appropriate for the specific needs of the business units in each sub-group, this tailored approach to the roles of the various levels of 'centres' can be value-adding to the group. However, it can also create significant confusion within the group and hence become value destroying.

Another slightly different context is the application of the model at the main board level of a publicly quoted group. The model highlights significant differences among the potential value-adding roles of corporate centres, particularly with reference to leadership, culture and control mechanisms. It would therefore be beneficial to the group if non-executive directors were appointed who understood the relevant issues arising from the corporate centre's current style. This can be particularly value- adding where a change in this style may be planned or needed in the future, or where a complex, hybrid, multi-level centre is being operated.

Having it all

At the beginning of Chapter 2 we stated that many top managers could see the corporate centres in their groups being in all four configurations at the same time. We have already agreed that it is almost inevitable that some centre activities can be described as being in each segment of the rainbow, but the real value-adding reason for the existence of the corporate centre should be concentrated in only one configuration. We can illustrate the all too common phenomenon of trying to 'have it all' at once by a classic example of a large multinational single product group.

The Chief Executive of the group is very clear about the critical role of the corporate centre that he heads up (unfortunately, but not atypically, all of the group directors that we refer to in this illustration are male). This is to provide a clear vision and set of values for the large number of operating businesses within the group. The centre has established an overall objective for the group, which is to become the No. 1 international player in its industry but, in recent years, its internally generated organic growth rate has been lower than the existing industry leader. Thus the CEO's emphasis is on stimulating innovation and building a winning culture across the group; he believes that the group is currently very good but that it is not yet a 'great company'. Beyond this focused role for the centre, the group should be based on a decentralised philosophy but where the primary identity and loyalty should be to the overall group rather than to the individual business units: an apparently clear example of a leadership style from a creative configuration corporate centre.

The Chief Financial Officer of the group, whose office is not surprisingly down the corridor from the Chief Executive, agrees wholeheartedly with the idea of decentralisation and the resulting freedom and responsibility concept that is central to the group's guiding principles. To him, responsibility is the same as accountability. Thus his focus is on setting specific annual profit targets for each business unit that should be regarded as firm commitments to the centre from the business managers. After all, he effectively has to give a commitment to the stock markets to achieve the expected earnings per share growth for the overall group. Further, partly because of the lack of organic growth but also because he strongly believes that there are still excessive levels of cost within the group, the annual profit targets include an element of cost reductions for virtually all business units. Tax and Treasury management are largely centralised in this group and in the past few years these areas have contributed significantly to the overall earnings per share (eps) growth of the group. This is also a clear example from our configurations model, but this time it is of a controls configuration.

The Group Operations Director also feels that it is quite practical to reduce the cost levels within the group. He is seeking to achieve this by centralising significant parts of the supply chain. This started by looking at the plethora of third party suppliers that were used by the group. A major cause of this was the amazingly wide range of component specifications that were in use for what were supposed to be the same product produced and sold in different markets. The next stage was to rationalise the number of manufacturing plants, thus moving away from each end market being relatively self-sufficient. As several smaller factories were closed, the supply of product became a more centrally driven activity. Indeed, this centralisation was being extended into other aspects of the supply chain, including raw material sourcing and logistics. Thus many end market business units are now dependent upon this centralised supply chain process for the timely and cost efficient supply of their finished products; their line management responsibilities now being focused on the sales and marketing of these products. Indeed, in one geographic region this whole supply chain, including the remaining larger factories, is now managed by a separate centrally reporting operations management team: a good example of a manager style corporate centre operating within the scale configuration.

The Group Marketing Director has a different view from his colleagues, which comes as no surprise to any of them. He believes that as a consumer products company the future success of the business is dependent upon the group's brand portfolio and its trade marketing effectiveness. In fact, as the group starts with the significant corporate disadvantage of not having the dominant global brand in this category (not surprisingly this is owned by the industry leader and accounts for half of their global sales volumes), a particularly key marketing issue is how well the company understands its consumers. As a result, the centre has identified some leading edge marketing segmentation techniques that enable consumers to be grouped together by relevant lifestyles and behaviours, so that specific brands can be appropriately targeted. The central marketing team has also identified some best practices from around the group (e.g. to do with evaluating new brand launches, and creating trial through different channels of distribution) and are looking to leverage this knowledge as widely as possible. In addition they have identified a limited number of key brands that they believe have almost global potential. These 'drive brands' are being pushed very strongly to the business units and each is supported by a centrally reporting brand management team. However, it is also well accepted that the successful development of any of these brands in a highly competitive marketplace requires a consistent and significant level of marketing investment over several years before any positive financial returns are likely to be achieved. Once more, a clear style of corporate centre; a consultant style in the scope configuration.

Each of these corporate centre roles is clearly aimed at adding value to the group and, of themselves, may well make financial sense. However, the result within a single group is a massive level of centre stimulated initiatives and demands for information that creates confusion, resentment and perceived unnecessary workloads within the supposedly decentralised and autonomous business units. The centre directly intervenes in some aspects of the business, but this may be either to reduce costs or to spread knowledge. Not surprisingly there is a strong view across the business units that any centralised activity ends up costing them more than if they had done it themselves. Many of the business unit managers do not believe that these centrally sponsored brands are relevant to their end markets and pay, at best, lip service to their development by investing the minimum that they can get away with each year.

Also, as the achievement of this year's profit target is the most important driver of their managerial bonus scheme, even this level of expenditure may come under threat if their business unit's performance falls below that included in the annual plan. In other words the complete freedom of the business units to implement their specifically tailored long-term strategies that are all aimed towards the group's vision may be somewhat constrained by the conflicting messages that emanate from this multi-faceted corporate centre. It is difficult to see how the high level of trust and respect between the centre and the business units that is essential for the success of the creative configuration can be achieved in such a complex and confusing relationship. Not surprisingly, the conflicting requirements have demoralised many of the senior business unit managers and increased their level of cynicism. This is clearly not helping the group to achieve its already challenging growth and long-term value-creation targets. Of course, we would willingly admit that if this group's corporate centre actually does create significant value while operating so blatantly in all four configurations it would be a 'world class' achievement.

Review of corporate configurations model

We can now apply the overall model, utilising the additional factors discussed in this chapter, in order to build up a fairly detailed profile of the characteristics of organisations that fit into each configuration.

To recap, the basis of the model is the combination of the nature of the involvement of the Corporate Centre and the source of the Corporate Advantage. The involvement of the centre can be either direct or indirect. By direct intervention we mean that the strategy of the business unit is directly affected by actions at the centre. This can come about in two ways: either processes or activities critical to the divisions are performed at the centre, or critical elements of the business units' strategies are determined by the centre (so that both means and ends are strongly directed from the centre).

There are also two forms of indirect involvement: either targets and control processes are set centrally with the business units having discretion to decide how to achieve their targets; or the centre sets the vision for the group and facilitates its achievement, but does not dictate detailed strategies to the business units. In both cases, the ends are specified by the centre, with some constraints on how these are to be achieved, but the detail of the means is left to the division.

Thus, from the perspective of business unit managers, the centre activities may be directly interconnected with their activities through the sharing of critical resources and processes. Alternatively, the corporate centre's indirect influence may not necessarily impinge on the day-to-day activities of the division. As discussed in this chapter, this range of involvement is a continuum and the two extremes provide clear illustrations of the substantial differences between their respective organisations.

At the extreme indirect end, the business unit managers are left to determine virtually all the elements of their specific competitive strategy. The only influence exerted from the centre is to provide some critical parameters within which this strategy must be developed. In one case, this is done by establishing financial performance measures that the businesses must achieve; while, in the other, the centre establishes a clear group vision and set of guiding principles for the businesses to adhere to.

At the other extreme, the highly directly intervening corporate centre performs large areas of activity for the business units. Thus the divisions can focus on a smaller sub-set of the total business process. The difference here is that in one configuration the centre centralises in order to reduce total group costs, while in the other configuration the economic rationale is to ensure that existing group knowledge is optimally leveraged across the group.

We have highlighted a wide range of dimensions and factors that indicate how the four possible corporate configurations differ from each other. It is clearly not realistic to expect any specific group and its corporate centre to comply exactly with each and every dimension and factor. However, the ways in which these various elements fit together in many large groups are illustrated, for each corporate configuration of the model, in Chapters 4 to 7; these deal individually, in turn, with the controls, scale, scope and creative configurations.

PART II

The individual configurations

The individual configurations

Chapter 4

The controls configuration

As its name clearly implies, the focus of the corporate centre in the controls configuration is on establishing excellent control processes that add value to the businesses within the group. This means that the dominant skills at the relatively small, indirectly involved centre will be financial management so that stretching, but not completely unrealistic, targets can be set and appropriately tailored, but primarily financial, performance measures established. The best examples of this shareholder style of corporate centre develop world leading expertise in this area of governance so that the costs incurred at the centre are easily outweighed by the improved performance of the underlying businesses. These issues are re-shown in Figure 4.1.

A classic characterisation of the controls configuration is therefore a small, financially focused corporate centre controlling a portfolio of relatively independent business units. The centre exercises tight financial control despite its indirect involvement in these autonomous units and is normally only concerned with the end results (both promised and achieved) rather than with the detailed competitive strategies implemented by each business. The only common benefit holding this type of group together is that all the individual business units can improve their financial performance by applying the disciplines, processes and controls that have been identified or developed by the corporate centre. This means that highly successful groups in this configuration can contain a very diverse range of businesses.

Consequently an additional key role for the corporate centre can be to alter the composition of the group through both acquisitions and divestment. Divestments can be an essential component of the

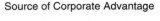

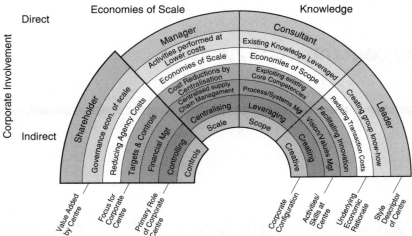

Figure 4.1
Coporate configurations:
The Rainbow Diagram.

development of these groups as is clarified below and developed later in this chapter. Quite often, the majority of the potential value added by group membership is generated very rapidly after the business becomes part of the group and the corporate centre imposes its financial disciplines through its planning and control system. This involves tight financial controls over expenditures and stretching performance targets, which are closely aligned to the incentive schemes of senior business unit managers. The business unit's managers rapidly become very focused on delivering what their new corporate centre wants, or they leave the group.

This may cause the new business unit to modify its existing competitive strategy and this can include divesting itself of, or closing down, any under-performing elements of its own portfolio. As the focus of the shareholder style corporate centre often tends to be on the short-term financial performance of its businesses, this can lead to new business units refocusing away from any major investments in longer-term growth where the expected financial return will be deferred and the risk profile is relatively high.

Thus there can be a significant step change improvement in the financial performance, often in terms of both profits and cash flow generation, quite soon after acquisition. This is particularly the case if the corporate centre had identified perceived flaws in the existing competitive strategy of the target prior to the acquisition. Of course, many of these corporate centres are therefore actively searching for businesses where they believe that they can add value through their governance expertise.

However, this creates a subsequent challenge for the corporate centre once this 'one-off' improvement has been achieved. The controls configuration corporate centre can find it difficult to continue to add value to this particular business unit through its focused indirect method of involvement. One quite practical option is to divest these new high performance businesses, particularly if the short-term performance improvement can be reflected in a significantly higher selling price. Thus the controls configuration group effectively captures the majority of the value from the future enhanced profits stream of the business unit. This may be especially attractive where part, if not all, of this short-term performance improvement has been achieved at the expense of the long-term strategy of the business.

If divestments are likely, there is an even greater need for new acquisitions to be brought into the group if it is to maintain its current size, let alone grow. This increases the external focus of the corporate centre away from its existing established businesses. The centre is interested in finding new attractive take-over targets and identifying potential buyers for existing business units that are considered fully developed. Its internal focus tends to be concentrated in the first few years of membership of the group as it seeks to ensure that the new business unit conforms to its planning and control processes. Thus, controls configuration groups often comprise quite dynamic portfolios of businesses, where there is no 'core business' that is considered sacrosanct.

Not surprisingly this has a significant impact on the culture prevailing within such a group. Employees in each business unit identify almost exclusively with their own business unit, so that there is no perceptible common group culture, other than possibly a common resentment of the remote and demanding 'owners'. This means that the corporate centre need not adopt a high profile leadership role within the individual businesses, as it needs to achieve only limited buy-in to its role from a few very senior managers within each division. Indeed it is not unusual to find that the corporate centre has a higher leadership profile outside the group than it does inside. It may not only be very active in the acquisitions and divestments area, but it also needs to justify, to the outside world, how its corporate centre can add value to what can appear to be an almost random assortment of businesses.

In some cases, the shareholder style corporate centre is unwilling to sell off businesses, even when they are fully implementing the group's governance processes. In an attempt to continue its value-adding role, these centres may try to change the way in which they interact with such business units. Having initially refocused their performance by setting clear targets, the centre moves to more of an advisory, counselling role in an attempt to continue this performance improvement. The role is still indirect but the movement up the vertical axis of the model means there is much more regular ongoing, less formal contact between the centre and the business units. This clearly requires a very different set of technical and managerial skills at the corporate centre; but it also requires much more knowledge at the centre about the competitive environments and strategies of each business unit.

Ultimately this increased contact and involvement can lead to the direct intervention by the corporate centre in the operations of the business units. This obviously represents a transition to the scale configuration. Alternatively the centre may seek to maintain its indirect type of involvement but change its source of corporate advantage and jump across to the creative configuration; a very difficult but just about possible leap, as was discussed in Part I.

The classic examples

An excellent early exponent of this idea of decentralised responsibility within a framework of tough financial controls and appropriate managerial performance incentives was the Hanson group (known as Hanson Industries in the USA). The group primarily focused on businesses at the maturity stage of a relatively low technology, and hence long, industry lifecycle. Through a succession of increasingly large acquisitions Hanson built up a wide-ranging portfolio of mainly UK and USA based businesses. Many of its best acquisitions were of groups that had themselves tried to diversify into growth areas, using the cash generation of the original, but now mature, business to fund such diversification. Many of these moves were proving unsuccessful as the corporate centres involved did not possess the skills necessary for adding value to the new growth industries that their groups were entering. Neither did Hanson, but the lack of performance of these acquisition targets enabled it to buy these groups at what it deemed a 'good price'. The genuine growth parts of the acquired groups were then normally rapidly sold on (or floated off as independent companies), often recouping for Hanson the bulk of its original total purchase cost. This was possible as stock markets can find it very difficult to value complex diversified groups that comprise high growth elements as well as mature and declining businesses. Not only is it complicated to assess the overall price earnings (P/E) multiple that should be applied to the earnings of such a group, but also the most appropriate financial strategy, in terms of the dividend pay-out ratio and the debt to equity ratio, can be unclear.

Hanson avoided any such ambiguity by ensuring that all its retained businesses were relatively mature operations that would benefit from the financial disciplines that would be imposed by its corporate centre. This meant that the key skills of acquisitions and subsequent financial control were critical to the success of Hanson and these were the focus of the top management team. The group was built up by a small corporate centre headed by Lord Hanson and Lord White. Lord White looked after the new acquisitions, while Lord Hanson oversaw the management of the current portfolio.

The ideal target businesses would operate in comprehensible technologies (like Warren Buffett, Lords Hanson and White did not believe in buying into industries that they did not understand) and be based in markets where the published financial statements, legal frameworks and capital markets made the pursuit of hostile take-overs an economic practicality; hence the USA and UK focus of the group. Further, they preferred businesses that were not facing very tough competition and hence had not already had to become lean and mean to survive, let alone flourish. This meant that the group did a vast amount of financial analysis on potential acquisition targets and could track companies for a number of years before, if ever, it decided to attempt an acquisition. Indeed these deals were tremendously driven by the existing financial numbers and what Hanson considered that the business could achieve when under its guidance. One of Lord White's famous quotes was that he had never physically visited any business that Hanson was acquiring.

As part of its pre-acquisition screening, Hanson would have already decided on which, if any, divisions of a target company would be rapidly sold off after completion, so that it could then focus on improving the performance of the remaining business units. This performance improvement was first generated by the rapid imposition of tight financial controls over expenditure (if it is not essential, then do not spend it, being the basic maxim). This was followed by the imposition of a strong results oriented focus, reinforced by very high levels of incentivisation for the senior managers at each business unit. There were also severe sanctions for non-performance!

The emphasis was on short-term improvements in key financial ratios so that year on year profitability ratio increases were key; improving the bottom (profit) line was considered much more important than growing the top (sales revenue) line. This highlights why the orientation towards mature, long-life businesses can be so important to this type of strategy. High growth strategies in mature or slowly declining markets can destabilise the whole industry by reducing the total profit pool available to all the companies in the industry. One player's volume growth must come at the expense of another competitor and this may well force an aggressive competitive reaction; the most common being the start of a price war that can destroy value for everyone in the industry.

Also in mature industries the short-term focus of annual profit improvements should have a smaller negative impact on the long-term profit potential of the business, compared to a high growth industry where the impact can be disastrous. Indeed, in many such industries, the sustainable cash generation capability is actually greater than the profit level due to the non-reinvestment of all the depreciation expense and potential reductions in the working capital tied up in the business. Hanson not only completely understood these issues but the corporate centre could provide the expertise to show the new business units how to achieve considerable savings in net assets employed as well as operating costs.

This targeting process was not exclusively top-down as there does need to be buy-in from the senior divisional managers that, although stretching, the key performance measures that they are being given are possible. Thus a sense of realism has to pervade the planning process, otherwise the business unit management teams can become totally demotivated very early in the financial year, as significant potential bonuses move increasingly out of reach no matter how much effort they put in. However, the planning process can concentrate on agreeing these stretching targets without having to get involved in the detail of the competitive strategy that is needed to produce this required level of performance. This is left to the management team in each individual business and the group may therefore be implementing a number of specifically tailored competitive strategies. After all, Hanson was involved in a wide range of industries (cigarettes, bricks, energy, electrical consumer products, zips and fasteners, etc.) that all had their own distinct competitive environments and bases of competition. The small corporate centre could not, and did not need to, be experts in the specifics of each of these industries.

The major problem with this very successful corporate strategy is the relatively short period during which the specific skills of the centre add significant value to the business units. This can be sustained through the dynamic acquisitions and disposals strategy that was an integral part of Hanson. However, as the group increased in size, the corporate centre had to identify ever larger acquisitions in order to have the same proportionate impact on the overall group's profit and cash flows. Further, the presence of such aggressive players in the market forced a number of potential targets to review their own corporate strategies, before it was done to them by Hanson or someone like it.

Several large groups were created on the same principles and, indeed, some had probably learned the concepts while at Hanson. Thus Greg Hutchings, who with Ian Duncan built Tomkins into a similarly widely diversified group (from cakes to guns), had been an acquisitions manager with Hanson. Most of these groups have now themselves been split up which indicates the problem of long-term sustainability that we return to at the end of the chapter. In Hanson's own case, this was in fact done by Lord Hanson after the death of Lord White. It is testimony to the lack of excessive cost at the corporate centre that this eventual self-imposed demerger of the group into four separate companies created no real shareholder value, even though no large acquisitions had been done in the preceding few years.

The planning and control process

The discussion of the Hanson group's success has highlighted that the planning and control process designed and implemented by a share-holder style of corporate centre is critical to its value-adding role. Although such a centre only has an indirect involvement in the under-lying businesses, an appropriately developed planning and control process across the group can still give the centre a very effective level of control over these businesses.

This level of control is achieved through a focus on measuring the individual achievements of each business, with the result that there is normally virtually no cross-fertilisation of new ideas or current practices among the business units within a controls configuration group. (This can be contrasted with the creative configuration where a key objective of the other indirectly involved style of corporate centre is to stimulate such activities across the group.) The perceived importance of these measurements is normally increased by tightly linking the overall remuneration of the senior business unit managers to their relative levels of performance. Thus a large proportion of their total potential income consists of incentives, but these incentives are based almost exclusively on their own business unit's performance. Whereas in many large groups, a significant proportion of such incentivisation schemes for top business unit managers would be based

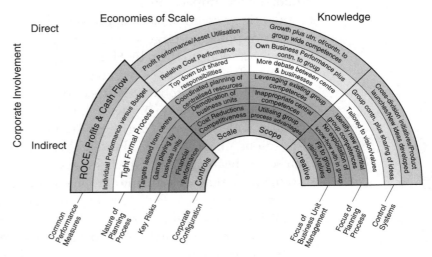

Figure 4.2
The Rainbow Diagram:
The planning & control
process.

on the performance of the total group; such as by granting stock options over shares in the ultimate parent company.

Consequently the corporate centre needs to identify appropriate measurable outputs that can be objectively assessed at the divisional level, but that also motivate the business unit managers to act in accordance with the aims of the overall corporate strategy. Not surprisingly, these shareholder style corporate centres utilise almost exclusively financial performance measures, as shown in Figure 4.2, and then normally establish group-wide accounting procedures so as to ensure that all business units are playing by the same rules.

The use of such financial performance measures is, however, only the first element in the required planning and control process. The performance of each business unit has to be placed into its appropriate context and this is achieved through the targets that are issued by the centre to each business unit. It is now well accepted that managerial performance measures should only include areas over which the specific managers can exercise some degree of control. Thus, as more constraints are placed on managerial discretion by higher levels of management, the relevant performance measures that should be used become more and more limited. If a shareholder style corporate centre wants to hold its business unit managers fully accountable for the actual profits and cash flows generated by their businesses, it needs to give them a high level of freedom in how they actually manage these businesses. This is, of course, exactly what this indirectly involved corporate centre wants to do, but this can, in some groups, be subject to a number of caveats. It is very common in controls configuration groups for the corporate centre to allow only a very low level of business unit discretion in terms of capital expenditure. This means that the business units have to request permission from the corporate centre before they are able to commit to any sizeable investment expenditure. In some cases, as was mentioned for Hanson, this is done quite deliberately when the business unit is new to the group in order to create a frugal, cost conscious culture within the business unit itself, that will rigorously challenge the justification of all expenditures. This is normally fine as the final decision is in reality left to the business unit managers but, in other cases, it can impose an unnecessary restriction on the ability of the business unit to achieve the targets that are set for it.

An alternative is to introduce a set of investment approval procedures across the group that allow business unit managers a much higher authorisation level as long as the return from the proposed expenditure is expected to beat the group's financial requirements. After all, the key measures that are used to assess the performance of the business unit management team are the profits, cash flows and Return on Investment of the business unit. If these managers believe that making additional investments in their business is likely to enable them to achieve their targets then, as long as these targets take into account the additional return required on the new investment, the corporate centre should be willing to let them have the funds to make the investment. In most controls configuration groups, any substantial shortfall against expected performance has a dramatic effect on a managerial career! This downside can have a significant impact on the risk taking appetite of business unit managers.

The emphasis on the achievement of objectively measurable outputs as the basis for the high managerial incentive payments means that the centre-established targets are usually focused on short-term performance; normally one to three years ahead, with the greatest focus on the first year. This has resulted in the widespread use, within controls configuration groups, of the pay-back technique (whether discounted pay-back or simple pay-back), rather than the more sophisticated full discounted cash flow computations. Investment proposals that immediately start to generate high levels of return are very highly rated by the pay-back technique while slower starting, but ultimately more value adding, projects would be more highly ranked by a full discounted cash flow appraisal. The unsurprising consequence of this short-term focus in most controls configuration groups is that the underlying business units are unwilling to undertake long-term strategic investment projects that do not generate high short-term returns, such as developing new technologies, new brand building expenditures, entering new markets or some very new segments, and launching completely new products. Business units within controls configuration groups tend to concentrate on doing better what they already do quite well, rather than trying to do something different. As discussed later, this is also normally in line with the transactional leadership style of the corporate centre; the centre is focused on trying to make these underlying businesses more efficient at what they already do. If new businesses are needed to generate growth for the group, these businesses can be acquired by the corporate centre.

Although the short-term financial targets are issued by the corporate centre, as stated in Figure 4.2, they should not simply be arbitrarily imposed on the business units. There needs to be a level of agreement with or, at least, acceptance of the targets by the top managers of the business unit as being 'just about achievable'. If these targets are seen as completely unrealistic by these managers then their incentive plans, which are based on achieving these targets, will cease to offer any incentive at all. Different controls configuration groups obviously have their own ways of actually implementing their incentive plans depending upon how stretching their targets are. Thus bonus payments can start to be paid even though the business unit performance only reaches 90 per cent, or even 80 per cent, of the very stretching target. In another group with more realistic targets, the incentive plan may only start when the target is reached, but increasing payments may be earned for out-performance, but often up to a maximum level.

The details of these incentive plans and their inter-relationship with the target setting process can have a major impact on the behaviour of business unit managers. The corporate centre is normally showing an exclusively financial interest in these business units, particularly where it is well known that it is willing to sell them to any sufficiently high bidder. Not surprisingly, this tends to be reflected in the relationship that business unit managers have with the corporate centre. They are motivated almost totally by their remuneration package and this is largely controlled by the high incentive plans and their targets.

This can lead to very sophisticated 'game playing' by the business units both in the target setting process and in their financial reporting of actual results against this target. During the planning process, the business unit will try to get its target for next year set at the lowest possible level as this will obviously make it easier to achieve. This tends to make planning an iterative round of negotiations between the centre and the business units before a final target is agreed, but this means that the corporate centre needs both good negotiating skills and the knowledge of what is actually achievable by the business unit. As many targets with controls configuration groups are set by reference to the actual current performance, e.g. year-on-year profit improvement or cost decreases, etc., the business unit has an incentive to be ultra conservative on its current performance until the target for next year has been agreed.

Also the business unit may not want to outperform in total this year if this will lead to a tougher target for next year or the year after. This is particularly the case where the incentive scheme has no increased payments for out-performance. Once the current target is reached the business unit managers may seek to hide away (in the form of conservative accrued expenses and provisions) any excess profits, so that these provisions and accruals can be released in the following year when they can help to achieve that year's bonus. Clearly if this game playing becomes excessive it can significantly reduce the value added by the corporate centre. Either the centre has to incur additional governance costs to check the business units' plans or the actual performance of the business units, after incentive payments, is less than it should be.

The performance of the overall group is assessed from the consolidated results of all the business units minus the costs incurred by the corporate centre. One of the strengths of many controls configuration groups is that the diversified nature of their business units makes them relatively unaffected by industrial downturns and even quite substantial economic cycles. If one, or more, of their businesses is suffering an adverse economic environment, the corporate centre can increase the required target slightly from the other business units so that the overall financial performance of the group is still in line with its shareholders' expectations. This ability to maintain short-term overall financial performance in terms of profits and dividend payments is a major attraction to investors in this type of group. Of course, this is much easier to achieve if the performance problem is identified during the planning process, i.e. before the targets for the other businesses are agreed. In order to emphasise this need for early warnings of potential problems, control configuration groups often implement a very strong 'no surprises' or even 'no changes' culture across the group, whereby the delivery of the planned profit level is regarded as a firm commitment by the business unit to the centre. Some shareholder style corporate centres in larger groups even allow for the under-performance of some business units by ensuring that the sum of the expected profits from the businesses exceeds the total group profit requirement. In other words, they build a central contingency into the planning process.

Developing a portfolio of businesses to which the shareholder style of corporate centre can apply its tight formal planning and control process is very important to the controls configuration. This centrally controlled targeting and monitoring process, through which the centre standardises the financial measures used by the businesses within the group, removes the need for each of these businesses to develop its own process. Thus these businesses hopefully gain access to an excellent process and the group generates a governance based economy of scale by applying its process across a large number of businesses. It is important to remember that the key value-adding element is the focus on relevant measurable outputs in order to improve financial performance. It is not necessary, and can be very counter-productive, for the corporate centre in a highly diversified group to force all the business units to go through exactly the same *detailed* planning process. The centre imposes the targets on the business units and dictates the way in which the actual performance against those targets will be reported. It should not get involved in the details of the competitive strategy that will be implemented to deliver the required performance, and the detailed planning process in each business unit should be tailored to this competitive strategy.

Common misfits

Theoretically there is no reason for a controls configuration group to restrict itself to only one type of business unit (e.g. the mature businesses of Hanson and Tomkins). As long as the corporate centre can develop appropriately tailored performance measures for all of the different businesses in the group, the indirect involvement can still create value. However, as already discussed, the indirect type of involvement and the emphasis on improving performance makes the use of objective measures very important. It can be very difficult to continue to motivate business unit managers through the commonly used high incentive payments based on performance, if the assessment of that performance is felt to be extremely subjective and judgemental, particularly if that judgement is being exercised by a corporate centre that is perceived to be quite remote from, and uninformed about, the underlying businesses.

Hence there is the already discussed strong tendency for shareholder style corporate centres to emphasise financial performance measures and to specify throughout the group how this financial performance is to be calculated. This has often resulted in the use of standardised financial measures (such as profit, cash flow, return on capital employed) across *all* the businesses in the group, sometimes with very detrimental results.

GEC, during Lord Weinstock's period as Chief Executive was a good example of a controls configuration group, as already mentioned in Part I. Its business units were set annual profit improvement and cash generation targets that helped the group to generate a £2 billion cash mountain that was held at the corporate centre. Unfortunately not all of the businesses in the group were completely mature and could probably have benefited from greater levels of reinvestment. The corporate centre would argue that investment funds were always available provided a good financial case was put forward. However if, as a divisional manager, you are going to be expected to generate a higher rate of return on the capital employed in your business next year than you achieved this year, you may think twice before you put in a request for substantial new investments.

Thus the shareholder style of corporate centre can be a constraint on the organic rate of growth that is generated within a given set of businesses. However, a bigger negative impact can be generated from running a mixed portfolio, particularly when the whole portfolio is built around one large, mature, cash generating business. BAT Industries, like several other tobacco based groups, was a good example of this. For most of its 100 year history in tobacco, the tobacco business was run from the corporate centre as four completely separate groups that actually competed against each other in certain parts of the world. These groups were each set profit, return on assets and cash generation targets, and the free cash flow was basically remitted to the centre. Using this very strong cash flow, BAT's corporate centre acquired a sizeable portfolio of diversified businesses (financial services, retailing, and paper businesses in both the UK and the USA). All of these acquired businesses reported into the corporate centre separately and were initially run as stand-alone businesses by the shareholder style centre.

It was during this period of rapid diversification with the consequent pressure on them to generate increased profits and dividends, that the combined tobacco businesses lost their overall leadership of the international cigarette market to Philip Morris. During this period the profitability of this international cigarette market increased substantially. The much changed BAT plc is still, nearly 20 years later, trying to regain this leadership, as is discussed elsewhere in the book.

Not too surprisingly, the stock market was not wildly impressed by BAT's diversification strategy with the result that the share price was based on a very low earnings multiple of the group's current profits. At the end of the 1980s BAT was attacked by a special purpose vehicle called Hoylake, with a view to splitting up the group and closing down what was perceived as a value-destroying corporate centre. It is interesting that one of Hanson's most successful acquisitions was of Imperial Group, following which the more highly rated businesses such as Courage Breweries, Golden Wonder and KP Nuts were sold off, recovering over £1.5 billion of the £2.1 billion total acquisition cost, and the mature, cash producing Imperial Tobacco was retained. Also RJR Nabisco in the USA was subjected to a very famous leveraged buy-out by KKR at the same time. Philip Morris did not suffer the same fate due to the different role of its corporate centre, as is discussed in Chapter 6 when the scope configuration is considered in detail.

BAT Industries rapidly implemented a change in its corporate strategy. The paper businesses were merged together and floated off onto the stock market, as was the UK retailing business. The USA based retailing business was sold and the group's substantial cash mountain was used to finance a share repurchase programme in the stock market. There was also an announcement that the future dividend pay-out ratio would increase from below 25 per cent to around 50 per cent of normalised post-tax earnings. This left two types of businesses, tobacco and financial services; a cynic might regard cigarettes and life insurance as an interesting form of diversification. What is interesting from our perspective is that this response to the external threat is totally in keeping with the controls configuration. The corporate centre changes the portfolio of businesses that it owns rather than becoming more involved in managing them through direct intervention. The main changes that such a centre does implement are externally focused; the share buy-back and change in dividend policy were reinforced by the adoption of a more aggressive debt based funding strategy. This strategy change became more fundamental following the retirement of Sir Patrick Sheehy. The new group board, led by Martin Broughton, brought together the four tobacco companies into one global group and then exited from financial services by merging all its interests with the Zurich group. This left a totally focused tobacco group and this group has since then made a number of significant acquisitions and new market entries. The corporate centre has now established a clear vision and set of guiding principles for the group which, although exclusively focused on tobacco, is currently still regionally structured. Although it is not yet possible to conclude that the corporate centre has made a clear transition from the controls configuration to the creative configuration, it does illustrate that creative configuration groups do not have to be in high growth, high technology industries as is made clear in Chapter 7.

A more sustainable role model?

Neither is the controls configuration only relevant to mature, cash generating businesses. The shareholder style of corporate centre can add value wherever excellent governance processes can improve the financial performance of the group's businesses. This has been demonstrated in many service industries but, as already mentioned, the best example comes from the advertising industry through the development of both Saatchi & Saatchi and WPP.

The traditional structure of the advertising services industry was based around a small creative team, who set up their own agency on the back of a limited number of client accounts. If this initial start-up was successful, a constraint on the ultimate size of the business seemed to be the tendency for a few of this now expanded team to leave and set up *their* own advertising agency. This created an impression to any outside potential investors (such as public stock markets) that clients were primarily loyal to the account team handling their advertising and promotions, rather than to the advertising agency employing this creative team. It was also largely true that the main strategic thrust of these businesses was based on delivering a high quality service to the customer; thus there was a low emphasis, within most of these small agencies, on financial management and control. During this period of development, a relatively small number of large, international agencies did develop, but even these tended to be built around either a limited number of very large international clients or a leading industry creative figure. Thus there were independent USA based names such as J Walter Thompson (JWT), Ogilvy & Mather (O & M) and Ted Bates, but all this was to change!

In August 1970, Charles and Maurice Saatchi launched their own advertising agency. Charles Saatchi, at 26, had already established a reputation as a brilliantly creative advertising copywriter, but the innovative element in this equation was Maurice. Aged 23, Maurice Saatchi had been working in the publishing industry and his expertise was much more on the finance and administration side of the business than in developing creative advertising. Their new business was quickly successful and growth was rapid. The brothers were able to attract other small agencies to join them and so the initial growth was both organic and dynamic. In 1975 they made their first major take-over of the larger and publicly quoted agency Garland-Compton (this brought them the prestigious Procter and Gamble account). It was also the stimulus for the company to become publicly quoted itself in 1976. This led to the recruitment of Martin Sorrell as financial director to help Maurice in controlling the embryonic empire.

The pace of acquisitions was intense and the acquisition strategy had two main themes. First, acquired businesses were relatively left alone from a creative stand-point but the original principals behind these agencies were motivated to maximise their medium-term growth in profits by making the final acquisition price dependent upon the profits achieved over an earn-out period. These earn-out periods were normally three to five years, but could be as long as seven years. Second, Saatchi & Saatchi developed a very strong central financial control system that concentrated on tight cash management, so as to maximise the benefit of potential cash flow timings from the client through the agency and on to the media supplier. Thus, if successfully implemented, these acquisitions could almost guarantee to generate growth in profit yet not to use excessive amounts of cash in funding this growth in the early years after purchase.

This shareholder style corporate centre also had an external focus as Maurice Saatchi put considerable effort into demonstrating to financial analysts and investment institutions that there was actually a low rate of change by clients in the advertising agencies that they used; thus improving the perceived value of current profit streams and raising the earnings multiples that were applied by the stock market to the advertising industry.

The resulting twenty-fold growth in earnings per share over its first 10 years as a publicly quoted group gained Saatchi's a premium stock market rating over its re-rated sector, and a share price that out-performed the FT All Shares index by around 2000 per cent. The acquisition of Ted Bates in 1986 made Saatchi & Saatchi the world's largest advertising agency group, with over half the world's top 500 corporations as clients.

However, in 1985 Martin Sorrell had left to set up his own marketing services business, using an existing small quoted company called Wire and Plastic Products plc which he and an original partner bought into. The originally stated strategy was not to compete directly with Saatchi's, but to focus on promotional activities (referred to as 'below the line', while media advertising is termed 'above the line' activity, although nobody really seems to know where this 'line' should be drawn nowadays) and other value-adding marketing services (such as marketing research, design and public relations). Rapid growth through acquisitions followed, mainly using the earn-out formula, and these businesses were then also subjected to a much more rigorous financial planning and control process that was driven from the small corporate centre. WPP Group plc (as it had been renamed) also delivered spectacular shareholder value with its share price growing from below 40p in 1985 to over £10 by May 1987, which gave the group a market capitalisation of £125 million.

In its first quarter results for 1987 JWT surprised the stock market when it reported a loss and there were clearly senior management conflicts as some key personnel had left the organisation; the share price fell to around half its level at the end of 1986. WPP launched a $560 million (£375 million, i.e. three times its own market capitalisation) bid for JWT, financed by a very large (2 for 1) rights issue together with a substantial level of new borrowing. The excellent governance skills of WPP's corporate centre rapidly restored JWT's previous operating margins *and* released around $150 million of cash by implementing a much tighter working capital management process. As a result WPP announced a 71 per cent increase in its earnings per share for 1988 over 1987.

Despite the stock market crash in October 1987, both Saatchi & Saatchi and WPP were actively looking for acquisitions but, as with Hanson, these were getting more difficult to find. Saatchi was starting to talk about 'globalisation' and 'cross-fertilisation' between its communications businesses as being key to its future. This took the public form of abortive approaches to both Midland Bank and Hill Samuel, the merchant bank. It then made a shock 'profits warning' announcement, which resulted in a dramatic fall in its share price.

This did not stop WPP from launching, early the following year, an originally hostile bid for Ogilvy & Mather that, if successful, would make it the largest advertising group in the world. Eventually, after a very public and highly volatile series of negotiations, WPP announced an agreed bid of $864 million (around £550 million) for O & M. This bid value was over twice the market capitalisation of WPP at the time, but the reputation of WPP's top management made it possible to raise the required financing. However, O & M was a very different acquisition from the JWT turnaround deal, as it was already achieving industry average profit margins and did not demonstrate the same level of potential for freeing up excess working capital. Despite this apparent lack of dramatic growth potential, the enlarged group achieved earnings per share growth of 34 per cent and 77 per cent in the two years following the deal.

Then WPP announced its own profits warning since when both groups have required fundamental changes to their capital structures. These have included significant modifications to their shareholders, as much of the financing originally raised as redeemable debt had to be converted into permanent equity capital. The Saatchi brothers left their group to restart on their own, but Martin Sorrell is still at the helm of WPP. WPP is now the second largest advertising and marketing services group by market capitalisation despite its subsequent take-overs of Young & Rubicam, Tempus and Cordiant Communications (which is the renamed Saatchi & Saatchi group, although their original business had been sold to Publicis).

Clearly there are alternative corporate configurations that can be applied in the marketing services industry, but these have to be appropriate to the corporate strategy of the group. One major element of the total advertising process that can show significant economies of scale is media buying, due to the volume buying power of the large-scale specialist. This volume buying service also needs specialist research facilities, including sophisticated computer based research tools. Given the vast size of the global media space buying market (estimated at over $200 billion), this has resulted in the development of focused media buying groups that do not necessarily need to have in-house all the other aspects of a full-service advertising agency, i.e. they can operate successfully in the scale configuration.

The controls configuration corporate centre has been applied by groups in other people-based, fast growing, owner-managed industries such as employment bureaux, consultancies, software companies, and even contract catering. Obviously the specific issues of each industry make the detailed implementation slightly different but, in each case, the corporate centre can add value through its ability to change the group's portfolio of businesses significantly through acquisition and, where necessary, subsequent divestment. This element of added value comes in two parts. The first part is generated if the centre has very high acquisition skills, so that it can buy businesses at good prices (i.e. below their full economic value). It can, however, add much more value through the second part by improving the financial performance of the acquired business once it has been incorporated within the group. As a result we now need to consider the nature of this shareholder style corporate centre in more detail.

Leadership and organisational culture

The implications of a shareholder style of corporate centre for the organisational culture of a group are quite clear; there is no cohesive group culture across the whole group. As shown in Figure 4.3, the business unit managers identify primarily with their own businesses, rather than 'the group'. Below this senior level, employees may not even be aware that their business is part of a greater whole. This retention of the discrete business unit identity is actually very helpful if an active acquisition and divestment strategy is being implemented by the corporate centre. The focus on, and consequent reporting of, the stand-alone financial performance of each business unit also minimises the disruption that is caused by a change in ownership, if and when the business unit is sold off by its corporate centre.

This arm's-length, financially dominated relationship between the business unit and the corporate centre is unlikely to generate a high level of trust between these parts of the group; business unit managers may feel concerned that too high an increase in profitability could actually make them a candidate for disposal. However, even a resulting low level of trust is not a problem for this configuration, as long as the corporate centre can properly motivate its business unit managers through its performance related incentive schemes. This means that a shareholder style corporate centre can create value even though it

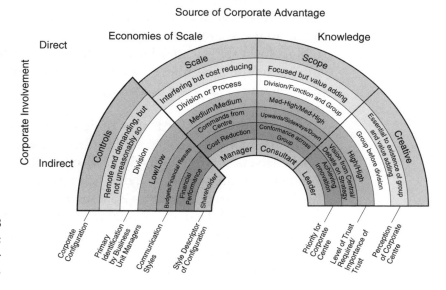

Figure 4.3
The Rainbow Diagram: Implications for organisational culture.

only gains quite limited acceptance of its corporate strategy from a very few people within the group. These senior business unit managers do not have to 'like' their corporate centre, but they must at least feel that it is in their own interests to try to achieve the targets that are set for them by this centre. It is then their responsibility to get buy-in from their employees to the specific strategy implemented within the business unit.

The good news for these business unit managers is that they are likely to be left alone to run their 'own' businesses, as long as these financial targets are met. There is unlikely to be much interchange with other divisions in the group; indeed, in many cases, the corporate centres in controls configuration groups seem to actively discourage any such communication and collaboration. Thus the business units operate as self-contained entities but with a very interested, financially focused shareholder. As discussed at the end of this chapter, this is particularly true for the newer types of controls configuration groups that are being developed by private equity investors.

The focus of the shareholder style corporate centre dictates the type of executives that it will require. The vast majority of the people in these corporate centres will have financial expertise; both corporate finance skills for analysing and structuring acquisitions and management accounting skills for controlling the current portfolio are relevant. In an excellent controls configuration group, the centre will have developed pre-eminence in its planning and control processes, including the design of appropriate incentivisation schemes. The skills and background required for this relatively technical leadership role do not automatically go with highly extrovert and charismatic personalities. Thus many shareholder style corporate centres deliberately adopt quite a low profile leadership role within the group, but they will definitely exercise a high level of authority, particularly when things are going wrong. Profile, in this configuration, must not be confused with power!

As already mentioned, it is quite common to find the corporate centre adopting a higher profile role outside the group, as the only public face of a large diversified collection of apparently independent businesses, than within the individual businesses, where the perceived leaders are clearly the business unit managers. This relatively low profile internal leadership role is completely compatible with the needs of the group as the corporate centre's emphasis is on improving transactional efficiency, not achieving transformational revolution, as is shown in Figure 4.4.

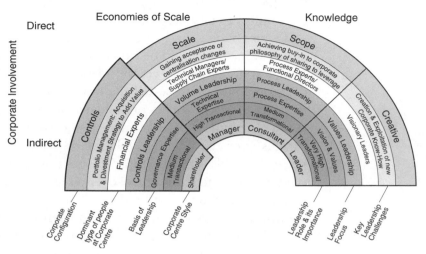

Figure 4.4
The Rainbow Diagram:
Leadership roles &
challenges.

Possible positions within the controls configuration

In Chapter 3 we developed both axes of the corporate configurations model so that we can now consider different degrees of indirect involvement and also a range of levels for the economies of scale corporate advantage. The shareholder descriptor for the controls configuration was selected because of the idea of this corporate centre acting as a very well informed controlling shareholder in its underlying businesses. This implies a predominantly financial attachment to any of these businesses and hence a willingness to sever the attachment if it ceases to be value adding.

Hanson provides our best example of this as expressed in Lord Hanson's quote, 'Everything is potentially for sale, it is just a matter of price'. In other words, if Hanson received an offer for any of its businesses that was above its internal assessment of the business' ongoing value to the group, it was willing to sell that business. It did not therefore have anything that it regarded as a core business. Such a sale would be most likely to occur once Hanson had increased the level of financial performance of this business so that the future growth potential was expected to be much less dynamic; say, after three or four years in the group.

This can be contrasted with WPP's acquisition and long-term retention of JWT. Within two or three years, the governance skills of WPP's corporate centre had restored JWT's profit margins and dramatically improved its working capital management. [Incidentally, after the acquisition, it also found that JWT *owned* the office block that it occupied in Tokyo; the rapid sale of which provided a further significant cash inflow to offset another large part of WPP's initial purchase cost.]

These changes had in a short time created most of the potential added value that could be expected to be generated from WPP's shareholder style corporate centre. Hence the most focused and objective decision could be to re-sell the now more valuable business, whether in parts to trade buyers or refloated as a single entity. One possible counter-argument is that such a sale would not have realised any surplus over the ongoing value if retained or the original purchase price, but this would simply mean that the group had originally paid too much to gain control over a business that was self-evidently in trouble. This should not be the case for any corporate centre that has acquisitions as one of its core competences. However, WPP did pay a significant premium over the sharply discounted JWT share price in order to guarantee that it would succeed with its pre-emptive bid.

A further argument for a subsequent sale is that any move, let alone such a large move, into advertising agency ownership was not part of the group's original corporate strategy; it had intended to focus on 'below the line' marketing services businesses. However, having bought one large advertising agency, the subsequent opportunity to overtake Saatchi & Saatchi (which, by then, were in trouble) as the world's largest advertising group through the acquisition of Ogilvy & Mather may have been too good for WPP's corporate management team to turn down. Unfortunately there is normally a distinctly negative correlation between satisfying an ego and creating shareholder value.

Our detailed examples of successful controls configuration groups have been built through a large number of acquisitions using the shareholder style of corporate centre. Also they have each consciously focused on developing very strong governance skills at the centre of the group, i.e. very good acquiring skills and a well-honed financial control process. This means that they would seek to be positioned on the left-hand side of the controls configuration segment of the overall model, as is shown by position A in Figure 4.5.

These corporate centres can create significant added value through their well-developed, highly tailored competencies. However, for the acquisition created groups, achieving a rapid change in the financial performance of a new addition to the group normally requires a greater level of corporate centre involvement for the first year or so. This initial stage of ownership by this 'interested, focused shareholder' often results in a step change in the financial performance, as many non-essential and non-value adding cost items are cut. Once the business unit

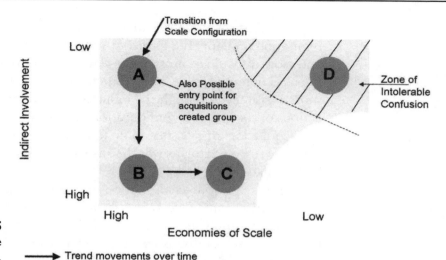

Figure 4.5
Positioning within the
controls configuration.

Transition from
Scale Configuration

Low

Indirect Involvement

Also Possible
entry point for
acquisitions
created group

Zone of
Intolerable
Confusion

High

High   Low
Economies of Scale

⟶ Trend movements over time

understands the rigorous cost conscious culture of the centre and has
been through the whole planning and control cycle at least once, the
level of corporate centre involvement can be reduced to the highly
indirect position B of Figure 4.5. At this point, the financial performance of the new business unit is still improving significantly as the
benefits of the corporate centre's governance processes feed through
into increased financial returns. The reduced involvement of the corporate centre (and hence attributable cost levels incurred by the centre) in
this business unit can mean that the 'net' value added to the group
during this second stage of ownership is still very high.

Even for these world-class examples of the controls configuration,
there is a relatively short period of high value generation from any
specific business, unless the corporate centre can continually improve
its targeting and control processes. Thus, for any fixed set of businesses,
there will be an automatic tendency to move to the right, as shown by
position C in Figure 4.5, as the value created by the centre's indirect
involvement declines. As long as the group actively manages this portfolio of businesses, this natural movement can be resisted by a regular
influx of new challenges for the corporate centre to work on.

The divestment of more established business units in order to realise
the bulk of the value created is not essential, as long as the corporate
centre can maintain this now improved level of performance with
only a very minimal level of involvement. This avoids the need for the
centre to grow significantly in size as the portfolio of businesses grows;
indeed, the corporate centre should be realising its own economies of
scale as the total group expands. The challenge for such groups is to
continue to identify suitable acquisitions and to complete the purchase

at prices that subsequently allow them to create added value. As their reputation and appetite for acquisitions spread, this can become more and more difficult, as prospective vendors seek to gain a greater share of the total potential value of the targeted business. In other words, prices start to rise, even though the value is created by the post acquisition actions of the controls configuration group. Alternatively these potential acquisition targets start to 'do it to themselves before it gets done to them' by the predator, as was the case of BAT Industries when attacked by Hoylake.

There are, of course, also groups that do not start out in the controls configuration but move there as the external environment changes. They may simply have moved to the next stage of the corporate lifecycle that was discussed in Chapter 3 and thus have progressed down the model from the scale configuration. As already discussed in Chapter 3, it is not possible for a corporate centre to add sustainable value if it falls into our 'zone of intolerable confusion', where it has a confusing type of involvement and is exploiting a weak corporate advantage. This is shown as the shaded area of Figure 4.5 and means that position D is not viable for a value-adding shareholder style corporate centre.

For groups transitioning into the controls configuration from the scale configuration, the challenges are reversed from those faced by the acquisitions led group. A good acquisitions led group has already developed its governance skills but has no detailed direct knowledge about the new business unit to which its processes are now to be applied. The ex-scale configuration group has a lot of knowledge about its businesses and probably quite a large corporate centre; it was, after all, previously operating certain centralised activities on behalf of these business units. However, it does not have the required governance expertise that will create significantly improved performance from these underlying business units. Either it has to acquire or develop these skills rapidly so that it can occupy position A, or it has to move very quickly to a highly indirect type of involvement that would place it in position C. This would normally involve some significant cost reductions at the corporate centre, as this would have had the capability to directly intervene in certain operations of the business units in the past. Hence, it is not unusual to find controls configuration groups positioned at point D of Figure 4.5; they have neither developed value adding governance expertise nor have they reduced their corporate centre costs sufficiently. This tendency is exacerbated when centre executives find it difficult to withdraw from intervening in business unit strategies and activities.

Transitions out of the controls configuration

Fairly obviously the most common destination for any shareholder style corporate centre to move to within the model is up to the scale configuration, as this does not require a change in the focus of the centre. It is still seeking to reduce the total costs of the group but is doing it in a more directly interventionist way. As discussed in Chapter 8 this is an example of 'swimming upstream' against a normal lifecycle trend over time in large groups.

The interesting logic is that it is much easier to achieve this transition successfully if it is attempted while the corporate centre has a low indirect involvement in its business units (i.e. ideally from position A of Figure 4.5 but even from position D). If the corporate centre already has regular, more informal contacts with the business units, there is a closer relationship and business unit managers are more used to consulting with and being advised by the centre. When the centre is remote with only very limited, formal points of contact with the businesses, there is likely to be much more resentment of, and negative reaction to, the more dramatic move to any direct intervention in the management of the previously very autonomous business units.

This highlights a challenge for the shareholder style centre that considers a move to the manager style of the scale configuration. The transition is easier if the decision is made when the controls configuration centre has a low indirect involvement. Yet our previous discussion demonstrated that the normal trend over time within the controls configuration is to become more highly indirectly involved in the businesses, i.e. to move further away from the scale configuration rather than closer to it, thus making the potential transition more difficult. This is why, in Chapter 3, we considered migrating within any particular configuration not only in terms of improving the current value-creating capability but also in terms of positioning the corporate centre for any future potential transitions to other configurations.

There are potentially more dramatic transitions out of the controls configuration to either the creative configuration (where the involvement of the centre remains indirect but its focus shifts to stimulating the creation of new corporate know-how) or the scope configuration (where both the nature of the involvement and the focus of the corporate centre change). These are covered in Chapter 8 in Part III of the book, when all of these more dramatic transitions around the model are considered together.

Conclusion – the sustainability of the controls configuration

It should by now be clear that it is quite difficult for a shareholder style corporate centre to sustain a high value-adding role over time if it maintains a stable portfolio of businesses in the group. Any initially high level of performance improvements is likely to decline over time as each business unit fully adopts the best governance practices from the corporate centre. Thus, to continue to add substantial value the centre must either develop its own skills to another level or change some of the businesses to which its skills are applied. This does not mean that it is inevitable that a static controls configuration group will become value destroying over time. If the corporate centre adopts a highly indirect level of involvement in its business units, it can keep its own costs very low. As we explained, the centre has to be more involved in the acquired businesses immediately post-acquisition. Over time the centre can withdraw as the disciplines of financial control become embedded within the business unit. In this sense the business unit managers may develop self-control, reducing the requirement for the centre's involvement. Also it can maintain the pressure on performance through its planning and control process, so that the existing high levels of financial return do improve, albeit more slowly than in the earlier years.

However, the controls configuration is the least sustainable of the four configurations in terms of creating high added value from a constant mix of businesses. The counterbalance is that it is the best in terms of the ease with which this configuration can be significantly changed, as is shown in Figure 4.6. In a volatile external business

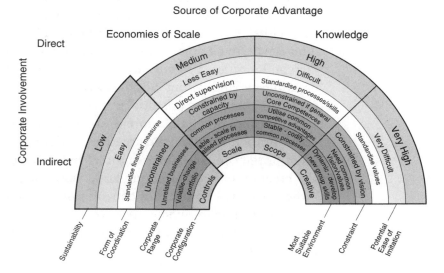

Figure 4.6
The Rainbow Diagram:
Sustainability issues.

environment, its governance expertise can suddenly become highly relevant to a new range of businesses and, if it also has acquisition expertise at the corporate centre, the controls configuration group may be very willing and able to apply its skills in these new areas.

Thus, although several of the original acquisition led highly diversified controls configuration groups have themselves been unbundled, they are being replaced by a whole new set of shareholder style corporate centres. These are the private equity businesses, many of which are investing on behalf of major financial institutions that are now building up very sizeable and increasingly diversified groups. These groups are being developed by acquisition, often of already mature, cash generating businesses, and the corporate centres are run by experts in deal structuring and execution. It will be very interesting to see, over the next few years, whether these corporate centres possess, or can develop, the planning and control expertise that is so essential to continue to add value to their acquisitions.

Chapter 5

The scale configuration

Introduction and overview

Organisations within the scale configuration have corporate centres that directly intervene in the operations of their underlying businesses. This direct intervention is aimed at reducing the total costs of the group by exploiting economies of scale that would not be available to the individual business units within the group. This manager style of corporate centre will therefore have identified some common support activities, core processes or even complete functions where significant savings across the group can be generated by centralisation.

Any such centralisation inevitably results in some loss of independence by the individual business units as they become more integrated within the group. However, the level of this integration varies considerably across this configuration depending on the nature of the centralisation. At one extreme, the low level of direct intervention is restricted to a few common support activities, like legal services and public relations. This means that the group can still comprise a relatively diverse range of business units and these business units should maintain a high level of autonomy. Such scale configuration groups do not look dramatically different to the low indirect involvement controls configuration groups where the shareholder centres have regular interaction with the business units, as was discussed in Chapter 4. Equally the sustainable value added by these corporate centres may not be sufficient to ensure the long-term viability of the group, and the group could even fall into the problem 'zone of intolerable confusion'.

As the level of centralisation by the corporate centre increases to include some core processes of the divisions, there is a much greater need for cohesiveness across the group's portfolio of businesses.

Centralisation clearly only reduces costs if the centralised activities have common features that generate economies of scale. This can increase the value created by the corporate centre's interventions but it may also act as a constraint on the future growth potential of the group. The centre ideally needs to find (either through organic growth or acquisition) other businesses that can add to the total cost savings from centralisation of these common core processes.

The corporate centre in the scale configuration creates value by reducing costs for the group as a whole, but this does not mean that this has to be the basis for the competitive strategies of all, or any of, the business units within the group. Indeed they can pursue their own independent and potentially very differing competitive strategies that may include core competences in branding, customer service, technology, innovation, research and development, etc. The only economic rationale required for their continued group membership is that they can contribute to and benefit from the lower cost levels that are achieved in the group's centralised activities.

This centralisation frequently leads to the standardisation of the common activities in order to maximise the cost savings. Any adverse impacts of this standardisation on the business units must be taken into account so that the 'net' value added by the interventions of the corporate centre can be assessed. In the extreme cases, some business units may 'opt out' of the centralisation due to the perceived adverse impact of the required standardisation on their individual competitive strategies, despite the negative effect that this can have on the group's cost levels. Another important potential impact on the divisions can be caused by the decrease in independence and loss of control that results from an increasing level of centralisation.

The impact can be positive if it enables business unit managers to focus on the key elements of their individual competitive strategies. Thus the business units can effectively delegate to the corporate centre the provision of many essential, but non-value adding activities, but they should be provided with these activities at a lower cost than they could achieve by doing it themselves. This is often the argument used when non-core support activities are centralised. A more negative impact can arise if business unit managers become demotivated through a perceived loss of control over '*their*' business. This happens most frequently when centralisation incorporates any of the perceived critical, value-adding core processes of the business unit. The corporate centre needs to ensure a high level of buy-in to the centralisation by the key business unit managers who are most affected by this centralisation. It should also take great care in designing the service level agreements and transfer pricing arrangements between the centralised provider and its internal customers, i.e. the business units. These customers need to trust the corporate centre to provide the centralised goods and services at lower prices than they could achieve themselves. In many large groups, there is a strong feeling within the business units that *any* centralised activity is much more expensive than it would be if they provided it for themselves. Also the business units should be able to rely on the fact that these corporate centre provided goods and services will properly meet their requirements. This will enable them to concentrate on their remaining controllable areas of activity. To achieve this, the manager style corporate centre not only requires a high level of operational management expertise in each of the centralised processes but also needs excellent supply chain management skills whatever processes are centralised, as is shown in Figure 5.1. This supply chain expertise is needed to identify those activities and processes where economies of scale can be achieved through corporate centre intervention. It will also allow the centre to avoid any damaging demotivational consequences from centralisation through the implementation of appropriate service level agreements and transfer pricing mechanisms.

The scale configuration corporate centre has an increasingly important leadership role within the group as more core processes are centralised. As discussed at the end of Chapter 1, if all the key value adding activities are centralised the corporate centre's role dominates to the extent that the group has really reverted to a single business. However, below that level of centralisation, the corporate centre should be focusing on its transactional leadership role. It is not trying to change how

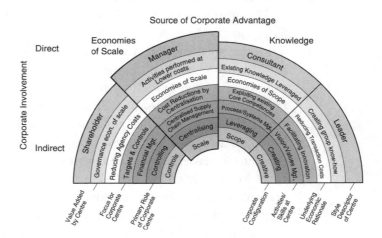

Figure 5.1
Corporate configurations:

the business units interact with their own customers, it is simply trying to reduce the total costs that are incurred in doing what the group is already doing. Thus the corporate centre ideally wants to achieve overall volume leadership in the centralised processes so that it becomes the lowest cost supplier possible to all its business units.

Comparison to the scope configuration

As both the scale and the scope configurations have directly intervening corporate centres that can effectively centralise certain activities and processes within their groups, it may be useful to highlight the key differences early in this chapter. The key difference is not *what* has been centralised but *why* it has been centralised. In the scale configuration, the corporate centre's intervention is aimed at reducing the total costs incurred by the group while, in the scope configuration, any centralisation is aimed at spreading knowledge across the group so that all relevant business units can take advantage of it. Not surprisingly, the greatest confusion can occur when the knowledge that is being shared across a scope configuration group is to do with how to reduce costs within the business units. This knowledge sharing should ultimately result in the business units that apply it reducing their own costs themselves, but this *cost reduction* does not directly result from the intervention of the corporate centre. Normally, in the scope configuration, the intervention of the corporate centre in spreading knowledge actually *increases* the total costs incurred by the group. The value added is generated from the application of this knowledge within the business units whereas, in the scale configuration, the value added can be directly seen in the reduced costs of the centralised activities.

Another important difference was discussed in Chapter 2 in that the scope configuration's corporate centre normally wants to change in some way what the business units do, i.e. it has a transformational role. As already mentioned, the manager style corporate centre has a primarily transactional leadership role that seeks to make the group more efficient at what it already does. This means that the direct intervention of the manager style corporate centre need have no visible impact on any external customers of the group unless, of course, some of the business units decide to utilise part of their cost savings by reducing their selling prices to their external customers. Thus the manager style corporate centre enables the group to capture a greater share of the existing total industry value chain. This is achieved either by generating input price reductions from suppliers through gaining greater negotiating power from the combined group volumes or by using less input resources per unit of output (i.e. a normal volume related efficiency improvement). The consultant style of corporate centre in the scope configuration can actually create more total value from the total industry supply chain, as the knowledge that is more widely leveraged across the group can transform the way that individual business units conduct their own businesses.

An alternative business unit view

The value-adding role of the corporate centre in the scale configuration is therefore one of reducing total costs through achieving economies of scale by centralising certain common group-wide activities or processes. However, one of the very interesting paradoxes to come out of our research is that it is quite common to find business units preferring centralisation, or some other form of outsourcing, even though it does not save them money. As stated in the introduction to this chapter, the ability to 'get rid of' essential but non-value adding activities enables the business unit managers to focus on the limited number of key value-adding processes that really matter. Of course, many companies try to achieve this by setting priorities within each function of the business, but this cannot create the same very high level of focus within the business unit.

A real-life example may make this more clear. A country general manager of a fast moving consumer goods company had recently launched a premium brand into his highly competitive marketplace. He faced a dominant, but declining, domestic competitor and a few, quite well established international players that were also currently importing products into this market. His company had been trying to gain a viable foothold in this market for over ten years without any significant success and the local business unit was still loss-making. The government had recently announced phased changes in tariff levels that necessitated an early decision on whether to build a factory on-shore or leave the market. Clearly this decision would be primarily based on the projected sustainable market share that could be gained, initially with the new premium brand. This made the strategic focus of the business unit gaining distribution, trial and consumer acceptance for this repeat purchase branded product. The new general manager wanted everyone in the company to be exclusively focused on the success of this brand as, if it failed, the business did not have a viable position in this market. In order to accentuate this focus, he would have paid a premium cost if it enabled him to outsource, whether to the corporate centre or to an external third party, as much of the general administration activity of the business unit as possible.

This creation of focus within this business unit should enable its management team to develop a highly tailored competitive strategy that will increase its chances of success. However, this marketing led strategy is likely to require a great deal of flexibility and very rapid responses to any changes in the competitive environment. Sales volumes will hopefully grow very quickly but this makes them very difficult to forecast accurately. As new distribution channels are opened, the business unit will need to expand its sales and distribution resources immediately and the timings of these events cannot be predicted exactly. Rapid flexibility and high levels of volatility are a complete anathema to a normal centralising cost reduction strategy, which really thrives on stability with good periods of notice of required changes. Thus the business unit wants to delegate non-essential activities but not if that robs it of the essential capability to respond to the demands of the marketplace. It is perfectly willing to pay for the required level of flexibility and responsiveness. Further, it is launching a premium priced brand into a very quality conscious marketplace and therefore requires a correspondingly high quality imported product. The challenge for the corporate centre is that, if this product is successful, the high ongoing volumes will need to be produced in a new on-shore manufacturing facility as the new tariff structures are implemented.

In this example, as with many others, the specific requirements of the competitive strategy of the business unit are almost diametrically opposed to the standardisation principles that can lead to the greatest economies of scale. This particular issue is developed in more detail later in the chapter but, clearly, where there is likely to be disagreement between the objectives of the corporate centre and the needs of a business unit, it will be difficult to achieve the required high level of buy-in from the senior business unit managers.

Degree of centralisation

The manager style corporate centre has to decide on the level of direct intervention that it is appropriate for it to have in the operations of its business units. It can add *some* value by centralising only certain support activities but this is unlikely to produce a very high level of sustainable corporate advantage as is shown by position 1 in Figure 5.2. In most

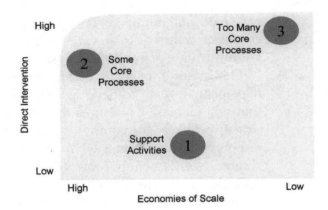

Figure 5.2
Degree of centralisation.

cases the level of cost reduction achieved by this sort of centralisation can be matched by competitors implementing the same or similar strategies. Thus, if accounting services (such as accounts payable, payroll or even general ledger processing) are centralised in order to reduce costs through economies of scale, smaller more focused competitors may be forced to try to reduce their own costs by outsourcing these same services to a large third party supplier (such as one of the big accounting firms) that can achieve at least similar levels of economies of scale. A cost reduction may have been achieved but the competitive advantage can be rapidly removed as these lower cost levels may have to be totally passed on to external customers.

In order to develop a sustainable corporate advantage, the corporate centre needs to identify a centralisation strategy that cannot easily be matched by competitors. This could be attempted by the group investing in its centralised support activities in order to produce significantly lower cost support services than can be achieved by anyone else, but this would represent a very high risk investment on behalf of the group without any guarantee of a sustainable level of return. Also this does not build on any existing strength of the corporate centre unless it has previously achieved such breakthroughs in its centralised activities. It is possible for some corporate centres to exploit the unique competitive position of the group to gain an advantage but most examples of this only result in relatively short-lived gains until competitors find ways to respond.

In the insurance industry, a number of UK based groups centralised their policy administration and claims processing functions in order to gain significant economies of scale. The cost savings generated were increased by locating these centralised functions physically away from both their London based head offices and the externally focused business units that retained total responsibility for winning new business.

For any such group possessing international business units that were based in lower cost economies a significant further cost saving could be achieved by locating the centralised group back-office operations in this lower cost country. If the country was South Africa, the logistics problems of serving UK and continental European customers remotely were also minimised by the small time differences involved. Of course it may be difficult for competitors to rapidly develop a large-scale back office business from scratch in South Africa, but they do not need to. They can look for an even cheaper international location such as India and they may find a third party that can run these operations for them at lower costs still.

For many industries therefore it is now fair to argue that a move to an in-house shared service centre or to a third party operated call-centre based in India cannot of itself be regarded as a *sustainable* competitive advantage. Competitive reaction will often rapidly make the new cost levels a hygiene factor that is needed to survive in the industry. As mentioned already and developed in more detail later in this chapter, the aim of the scale configuration is to achieve volume leadership in each centralised area as that should enable a sustainable cost advantage to be realised. It is however difficult to achieve such volume leadership in most support activities, particularly where these activities can be provided for a wide range of companies by specialist third party suppliers.

This means that many groups have moved to centralising more fundamental core processes in an attempt to move to the more value-adding position 2 of Figure 5.2. The first impact of centralising core business unit processes is that it imposes a greater degree of context across the group. If fairly generic support activities are centralised the group can contain a very wide range of different business units; after all, most businesses need to pay bills, collect outstanding money from customers, pay their employees, etc. Once the corporate centre decides to intervene by taking over the provision of more key activities, these centralised processes must be relevant to all the business units within the group.

As with the vertical axis for the controls configuration that was discussed in Chapter 4, there is also a continuum of levels of direct intervention by the corporate centre in the scale configuration. Also what are generic support activities in one group may be key value-added processes in another; but, in the scale configuration, the central-isation strategy is the glue that binds the group together and therefore determines the potential spread of the businesses that the corporate centre can logically add value to. For example, if a corporate centre decides that it will centralise the logistics process across its group, this will have significant implications for the types of business units that are now appropriate for this group. First, logistics costs should be relatively significant to each such business unit so that any cost advantage achieved should be material. Second, the actual details of the logistics processes involved in all the business units must have sufficiently common elements that their centralisation will achieve economies of scale. This would not necessarily be the case if one business unit made all its sales of its standard products in very large bulk quantities that were centrally delivered to each of their few customers on a monthly cycle, while another delivered its individually tailored products to its thousands of customers according to each customer's specific requirements.

This means that, for most groups, there is an optimum level of centralisation that will produce the highest level of corporate advantage. If more processes are centralised the group will move to the right of the scale configuration segment of the model, as is shown by position 3 of Figure 5.2. The corporate centre is now too highly involved in the operations of its business units, so that the negative impact of the required standardisation in these centralised processes is more than offsetting the economies of scale generated by the centralisation. The corporate centre can either reduce the level of its direct intervention so that it moves back to position 2 or it can try to change the composition of the group by divesting itself of those business units for which the high level of centralisation is inappropriate, and acquiring more suitable businesses.

From Model T to today

These issues could be illustrated by using a number of detailed industry examples but we have chosen the car industry as it is an industry that was really originally built on the concept of economies of scale from standardisation of core processes.

In 1907 Henry Ford announced that his company would 'democratise the automobile' by producing a car 'that everyone will be able to afford' so that 'everyone will have one'. At this time Ford Motor Company, which had been founded in 1903 as one of over five hundred new car manufacturers started in the USA, was by no means the market leader. It had already launched five models (A, B, C, F and K) into the market before the Model T in 1908, but the Model T was the first to utilise the full concept of a mass-production line manufacturing process.

Effectively Ford Motor Company reverse engineered the Model T Ford because the end selling price had to be affordable by the average American family. This meant that every car produced was exactly the same, e.g. it was only available in black, in order to gain the maximum economies of scale in the total production process. The new model was such a wonderful success that Ford was able to reduce the selling price by 58 per cent from its launch in 1908 to 1916 during which period 15 million cars were sold. Demand outstripped even this level of supply, so that Ford could in fact have raised prices rather than reducing them; the company was very strongly challenged by some shareholders and much of the business press for not taking advantage of this pricing opportunity. Henry Ford replied that he much preferred to sell large volumes of cars at a reasonable profit as that made more customers happy and enabled the company to employ more workers at reasonable wages.

It also, of course, made Ford Motor Company the USA market leader and gave it a sustainable cost advantage that could potentially be transferred to later models in order to maintain this market leadership. General Motors had been formed in 1908 to acquire and reorganise several small car manufacturers; by 1910, it owned Buick Motors, Cadillac, Pontiac and Oldsmobile, with Chevrolet being added in 1918. The new group suffered severely as the Model T gained market dominance and it very nearly went bust. Then in 1921 Alfred Sloan took over GM and the group deliberately gave the now car-owning public a choice of replacement models at different pricing levels. General Motors rapidly overtook Ford to become and stay the largest auto manufacturer, as Ford was very reluctant, and hence very slow, to give up its total focus on reducing its cost base through economies of scale.

This very early but classic example highlights one of the major constraints on the scale configuration; maximising economies of scale requires great standardisation in business processes. Such levels of standardisation can have opportunity costs that significantly outweigh the benefits of the cost reductions generated by the economies of scale. Of course, the global car companies are now much more sophisticated in their use of centralised processes and activities but there can still be real dangers involved. In these global companies, centralisation obviously does not necessarily mean establishing a single physical facility for the world-wide group, but it does entail removing these centralised facilities from the direct control of the end market focused business units. Thus Ford Motor Company does not have manufacturing facilities in every country in which it sells vehicles and, even where this is the case, the manufacturing plant is unlikely to produce solely for its local market. Thus the centralised sourcing strategy seeks to achieve economies of scale by allowing individual plants to concentrate on a limited range of outputs (e.g. assembling Fiesta cars or manufacturing diesel engines), even though this results in a very high level of components and finished vehicles being shipped around the world. Ford was one of the earliest exponents of this more global approach to the industry and set up, for example, its central Ford of Europe organisation a long time before most other similar international groups.

Nowadays many of the large automotive groups seek to reduce their total costs by sharing major components across their 'differentiated' range of products. Thus one car group can have similar sized cars that are sold as different brands at very different pricing levels. If these cars were all completely different, this would increase the group's manufacturing complexity enormously and hence reduce its economies of scale equally significantly. However, if the group was able to utilise major elements across all this range, it could be possible to obtain major economies of scale while still positioning the cars in different segments of the market. A good example of this is the VW Group that owns the very distinct brands Audi, Volkswagen, Seat and Skoda. Each of these car brands is positioned in a different market segment but the group seeks to achieve economies of scale in design and manufacturing by sharing some major components across the range, including even some basic body platforms and engines. These economies of scale are gained at the risk that consumers may downtrade from a 'top of the range' Audi Quattro to a 'top of its range' Skoda if they realise that under the surface the cars share several features. Thus these car groups are normally very careful to ensure that the marketing and distribution of the individual car brands are kept distinct and separate, even though this reduces any opportunities for generating economies of scale at this level in the group.

This tendency to centralise the production or operations process but to leave the ultimate externally focused sales and marketing processes under the total control of individual business units can also be seen in many other industries. In the car industry it has also led to a number of significant acquisitions, including some by Ford Motor Company. Although its greatest global rival, General Motors, has consistently used a number of different car brands (particularly in the USA market) that are not instantly directly associated by the consumer with the ultimate parent company, Ford has basically used its group name on every vehicle that it has sold. This can be argued to have limited the premium brand positions that its offerings can occupy as Ford is known world-wide as a volume automobile manufacturer. The counter argument, not surprisingly, is that Ford achieves a significant economy of scale in its marketing expenditure as every communication reinforces the 'Ford' brand. This is true but it may reinforce it as a 'value for money' brand rather than as a premium brand such as BMW or Mercedes Benz. Indeed consumer research indicated that if Ford Motor Company could put a different 'premium' badge on its largest, 'top of the range' offering it could sell *more* of these cars at a significantly *higher* price. In other words, these cars were viewed as being very well engineered with excellent manufacturing quality, but their generic branding and lack of imagery meant that consumers would not pay a premium price to acquire them.

However, at this time, Jaguar faced the reverse problem. It had a wonderful brand image, particularly in the USA, but a terrible reputation for product quality. Ford's acquisition of Jaguar therefore gave the combined entity the opportunity to apply Ford's expertise in cost efficient manufacturing and engineering design to Jaguar's styling and brand imagery expertise. A critical element in the success of this acquisition is that the corporate centre of Ford Motor Company knows exactly where it should directly intervene in its new Jaguar subsidiary and where it should leave well alone. Following its other related acquisitions it has now formed a luxury products sub-group where the businesses definitely do not brand their vehicles as Fords (i.e. Jaguar, Volvo, Land Rover, Aston Martin probably have more brand appeal to consumers than if they were all called Ford Whatever!). Bringing together these business units under one central management team may enable the group to generate some further economies of scale through centralisation of additional processes, but trying to achieve cost savings through standardising brand marketing is not likely to be a value enhancing strategic initiative.

The group has generated significant economies of scale in other areas through direct intervention of the corporate centre but the implementation of any global standardisation has to be done very carefully in order to ensure that it does not impact on critical business areas that need to be specifically tailored to the needs of different markets, etc. In other marketing areas it can be quite logical for the corporate centre in a scale configuration group to centralise media buying and to negotiate a global deal with one advertising agency, as long as the different product groups and end markets are still able to design and deliver appropriately tailored advertising. Global contracting of this type can not only reduce the group's total costs but also it frees up local management's time to concentrate on their competitive strategies (instead of having to negotiate local deals with a range of suppliers) and it enables the group's internal audit function to validate, in a cost effective way, that the group is only paying for what it should under the terms of the global agreement.

Another common area for corporate centre intervention in such global groups is Research and Development as centralisation can avoid the wasteful duplication that often arises when several business units each investigate the same areas. However, there are some very common problems that are quite well illustrated by Ford Motor Company. Ford has large R & D functions in North America and in Europe; their European facilities are based in England and Germany but they operate as a centralised entity. Apart from more fundamental research projects, these facilities are responsible for the vitally important development of the group's new automobile models, but the centralisation of this process adds significant complexities that have to be considered. Starting at the European level, the development of a new model has to take into account the often conflicting requirements of the different end markets in which the new model will be sold and the centralised manufacturing group that will produce it. Manufacturing clearly wants to minimise the various combinations and permutations of options, fittings, etc. that can drastically reduce any possible economies of scale that will significantly reduce total production costs. (Some years ago, one of the authors calculated that there were three million possible versions of a single Ford model if all the potential derivatives and options were combined. It can be difficult to achieve large economies of scale if you are only producing two million units in total of this model each year.) However, the individual markets need to offer relevant product attributes and a viable range of choice to their target consumers. Unfortunately some of these 'relevant' product attributes are not 'as relevant' in other markets. Heated seats and heated wing mirrors and windscreens are highly appropriate in northern European markets, but are less necessary in the warmer southern European countries where air-conditioning and soft-top cabriolet versions are considered more important issues.

The design process has to decide on which elements are to be incorporated into the core product, which are to be available as options, and which are to be excluded completely. These decisions can make dramatic differences to the complexity of the manufacturing process and the actual costs involved. To take one specific example; it is much simpler and cheaper to incorporate an opening sunshine roof into every vehicle that goes down an assembly line than it is to try to install the same roof opening into only some cars as they actually go down the line. Clearly if all cars are to have one fitted, the basic body shell will be pressed appropriately while, if it is an optional extra, a hole will have to be cut into the originally solid roof. However, incorporating this feature in all cars will mean an on-cost for everyone, albeit a small one, compared to charging an increased price to only those taking up the option. This extra cost may, of course, have a negative effect on those customers to whom this added feature is completely irrelevant (e.g. those who are having electronic climate control fitted to their car).

This requires that the centralised processes consider very carefully where total standardisation can be applied and where the centralised operation must allow for much greater flexibility. In simplified terms for the car industry, corporate centres seek to standardise as far as possible on major components (such as body platforms, major body panels, engines, gearboxes, wheels, etc.) but allow a great level of flexibility in the final assembly operations. Thus, allowing the end consumers to specify in amazing detail what their car will actually look like does not cause excessive disruption to the very flexible paint shops and assembly lines that now exist. However, most of these 'very different' vehicles have a common set of key major components and changing any of these does increase the total cost dramatically.

There is a higher level of commonality that could be applied by Ford's R & D function, i.e. developing a world-wide model that would be common to North America, Europe, the Far East and the Rest of the World. Such a project has, to date, proved to be a step too far for the North American based car manufacturers but has, of course, been the basis of the highly successful strategies of both Japanese and European producers, which do not have completely different models for the different regions of the world. Some of the issues involved are considered later in the chapter.

Using scale to manage risk

Centralising R & D can have other benefits as well as avoiding unnecessary duplication. The corporate centre should have the ability to assess the total potential for a new product or technology across the whole group, whereas any individual business unit will tend to consider only the potential from its own more restricted sphere of influence. Thus, if the R & D is centralised, the initial project can take account of the different requirements of all of the potential markets where a successful outcome can be exploited. Building these issues in at the beginning will normally be much cheaper and more successful than trying to subsequently modify a highly market specific development.

For several industries, the lack of any significant differences across almost the total global market makes the prospective benefits from a successful research breakthrough incredibly attractive. However, the likelihood of developing a globally successful product is also very low, and the research expenditure required will normally need to be substantial with only these small chances of success. There are therefore considerable benefits in scale as sheer size and financial muscle can enable the corporate centre to contemplate taking on this level of expenditure and risk without putting the total business at risk. Of course, the group must have the capability to exploit the full potential of any outputs from this significant resource commitment and for this type of activity, this will require global reach.

This has proved a major issue for many high technology industries including the pharmaceutical industry. There have been several examples of large-scale mergers and acquisitions in order to achieve critical mass in R & D in major therapeutic areas or to gain access to all the main markets for pharmaceuticals, which not too surprisingly are North America, Japan and Europe. The immense size of these global groups enables them to devote very large resources to research into many areas at the same time, but this multi-pronged investment in the future requires the active intervention of the corporate centre. The key driver for the share price performance of publicly quoted ethical pharmaceutical companies is the new product pipeline and this is intensely scrutinised by investment analysts. Thus the corporate centre needs to ensure that the group's R & D portfolio is relatively balanced in terms of the time scales and probabilities of bringing any new molecular entities to the market. In the pharmaceutical industry, as with other primarily patent protected technology industries, outside financial analysts can quite accurately assess the very high profit streams that will be generated from existing patented drugs. Even more importantly they can precisely identify when these profits will all but disappear; the *sales revenues* of such products tend to fall by over 90 per cent in the year following patent expiry. If the centrally driven R & D activity cannot deliver an adequate replacement stream of profits, the share price is likely to decline dramatically.

Such pressure on new major breakthroughs has led some corporate centres to change their R & D strategies. This can involve focusing its total expenditure on fewer therapeutic areas in an attempt to increase each project's chances of success through greater economies of scale. It can also include effectively outsourcing the new areas of research to a number of smaller, more focused companies (such as biotechnology businesses). If one of these proves successful, the larger group that has financed the research obviously has the exclusive rights to exploit the new technology for a period of time, but normally the smaller company is simply taken over by the mainstream pharmaceutical company.

This is an interesting development of the quite common strategy of a corporate centre outsourcing its own centralisation of a support activity but now it is being more widely applied to the centralisation of core business processes.

Potential problems of centralisation

There are clearly some very significant implications of the corporate centre directly intervening so dramatically in such a key value adding process for the group. Particularly if the justification for the intervention, and the consequent focus of the centre, is cost reduction while the emphasis of the business units may be on 'speed to market' or 'effectiveness of the new product' rather than cost. This requires the corporate centre to be very clear as to its reasons for centralising any core process or support activity; is it really still in the scale configuration or should it now be positioned in the scope configuration as its focus is on leveraging knowledge rather than reducing cost? An example of such a transition is given at the end of this chapter. The centralisation of the process may generate substantial economies of scale in the level of expenditures that are incurred but it is now the corporate centre that is deciding which areas to spend the funds on. There can be a danger that the centralised research function becomes too removed from the real opportunities in the marketplace and is excessively internally focused. Many groups have large centralised research facilities that are regarded as remote ivory towers by the business unit managers who are supposed to use the new developments from this centralised process.

It is therefore very important that the corporate centre succeeds in getting the high level of buy-in from the relatively few key business unit managers who are most affected by any particular centralisation, as was discussed in Chapter 2. Although the centre has the power potentially to force the centralisation of any activity or process, such centralisation will not prove effective if these key business unit managers are actively opposed to the resulting level of direct intervention. Trust between the centre and its businesses is more important in the scale configuration than for the controls configuration, as is shown in

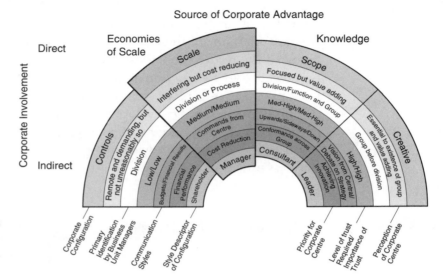

Figure 5.3
The Rainbow Diagram:
Implications for organisa-
tional culture.

Figure 5.3, and the level of trust required increases as the centralisation incorporates increasingly core business processes. Thus the general managers of major business units may not be too bothered if some peripheral support activities are centralised by 'diktat' from the centre, but they will want to be much more involved in any decision affecting what they perceive as a key value adding process for their businesses.

This is not an insuperable problem as the corporate centre can give the business units their desired involvement and still achieve its own objectives. The dominant general skill at the corporate centre in the scale configuration is supply chain expertise so that the centre can identify those areas where its direct intervention can generate significant savings. These tend to come from the removal of duplication and the standardisation of practices across the group as well as the increased bulk buying power of the total group. Of course the lowest level of direct intervention is only to centralise the actual 'buying' process but to leave the business units complete freedom as to what to buy. The next level restricts the choice of suppliers to those that are approved by the centralised buying function. Then the centre takes more direct managerial control of what is being bought, and then what is done with it when it is bought! Thus the corporate centre also needs appropriate skills in managing each area that has been centralised.

However, this managerial skill will be focused on improving the operational efficiency of each centralised activity or process and this need not include the ability to set the longer-term objectives and strategic focus for this area. The corporate centre can get this more externally, market focused input from its business unit managers if they are likely to have much more relevant insights. Thus the business units could still set the priorities for any centralised key business process (which may be R & D, information systems development, logistics, manufacturing or even sales and marketing) and the corporate centre would then deliver these agreed priorities but at a lower cost than could be achieved by any individual business unit.

Indeed in some cases the corporate centre may delegate the actual delivery to one business unit if that business unit already possesses most of the specifically relevant skills. This happens quite frequently in the case of R & D projects and major information systems activities, where one business unit takes on the prime development role and therefore works for the corporate centre. An example may make this clearer.

The European Human Foods Division (the division's title sounds strange but the group is also the world's largest petfoods producer) of Mars Inc. had identified a very exciting new product development idea that could potentially have a global market. Arising out of its research and development activities for its new UK based processed meat products business (mainly convenience canned products sold through retail, catering and industrial channels), the division has started preliminary work on an artificial meat product made out of soya protein. This basic concept was not revolutionary as soya based textured vegetable protein products had already been introduced to a relatively poor consumer response. Masterfoods used a completely different approach based on spinning technology (similar to that involved in producing artificial fibres such as nylon) to create a much finer spun vegetable protein. Each individual fibre could be coated with an appropriate meat or other flavouring and the fibres then woven together to form a meat textured end product. This product did not require specialised storage and could have a dramatically longer shelf life than 'the real thing'. Of course there was a massive amount of work to do to bring such a completely new idea to an actual product launch and the division was not sure that its profit potential justified the scale of investment that would be required.

The group's corporate centre agreed that the project looked interesting and had potential outside the European division's area of control. Accordingly the centre directly funded the project so that this expenditure did not affect the short-term performance of the division. If the project were successful, the division would get what it had wanted anyway in terms of being able to sell the resulting products, but it did not have to bear the entire project risk itself. The centre would obviously have the ability either to make any resulting products available to other divisions around the world, without them paying

Masterfoods a royalty or licence fee, or it could itself licence the product to external third parties. Also the corporate centre could ensure that there was no duplicated effort taking place elsewhere in the group by centralising all the appropriate resources in the one division and it could effectively directly manage the project through the funds allocation process.

This type of 'delegated centralisation' tries to avoid the corporate centre becoming too distant and remote from the real competitive environment of the underlying businesses. However, there is another potential remoteness issue that can be caused by a strongly centralising corporate centre that is totally focused on reducing costs. This can be illustrated by comparing, in general terms, the differing approaches of the automotive industries of the USA and Japan. This was explicitly highlighted by the well-documented experiences of NUMMI, which was a joint venture operation set up in the USA between GM and Toyota.

The USA based car companies were primarily following a cost reduction focused strategy in their operations processes. This meant that all new in-house generated component designs were sent out by a centralised sourcing team to a number of potential suppliers for competitive tendering. Some of these 'suppliers' could be other parts of the same group. These companies maintained flexibility through only granting short-term contracts to any successful bidders. The role of the suppliers was therefore seen to be to deliver exactly what had been ordered and any departures from the tightly defined group procedures would normally result in severe sanctions on the defaulting supplier.

The usual Japanese approach was to work much more closely with a limited number of suppliers. These suppliers were supposed to contribute to the development of new products and this capability for innovation by the supplier was a key issue in developing a close and long-term relationship with the major auto manufacturer. Once selected for such a long-term relationship, the supplier went through a quality certification process that meant the customer could do away with goods inwards inspections. Also the car company worked with its suppliers to develop joint designs and developments and was willing to give these suppliers long-term contracts to supply these parts. This enabled the suppliers to commit to investments in highly specific assets that could ultimately result in lower costs to its customers. The selling price to these customers also reflected the lower required rate of return that resulted from the reduced risk perception generated by the long-term contract and high volumes. Thus the higher level of trust that is generated from this closer working relationship means that it does not necessarily lead to higher costs. In many cases, the adversarial approach can cause a substantial increase in the total governance costs needed to manage such a relationship. This is still true even if the adversarial relationship is completely within the group, so that the corporate centre must be clear as to the type of relationship that it wants to see following any centralisation decision.

Service level agreements

The most common way to regulate these relationships between any centralised activity or process and its internal customers (i.e. the business units that are required to take the output from the centralised function) is by establishing a Service Level Agreement (SLA). The SLA should set out very clearly the agreed responsibilities of each party to the agreement. This enables full accountability to be associated with each party's responsibility that is, as stated earlier in the book, critically important to establishing appropriate managerial performance measures. Where all the specific responsibilities are clearly identified it is much easier to gain the required high level of buy-in from the business unit managers who are most affected by the centralisation.

Thus, if the production processes of a manufactured goods group are being centralised, the SLAs between the sales and marketing focused business units and this centralised production process must clarify how the relationship will work. This means that the frequency of ordering, the order to delivery lead times, the delivery schedules, the quality specifications, the responsibility for defective products, as well as pricing levels, must be explicitly stated to the satisfaction of both parties. If the relationship was being set up with an outside third party it would be automatic that such a contractual agreement was reached prior to commencing working together. Yet, in many large groups, there are a multitude of informal, unspecified commercial relationships that can lead to significant problems as soon as things start to go wrong. It is very common to find a culture of 'blame apportionment' between the business units and the centre in scale configuration groups, and this is often exacerbated by the absence of the clearly defined responsibilities that can be created by the design of appropriate SLAs.

Designing these SLAs obviously requires some skill as they should not become excessively bureaucratic and over-detailed but, as the manager style corporate centre should contain supply chain expertise, it should be able to develop practical, value enhancing agreements for the group. One major issue that the SLA should cover is the internal

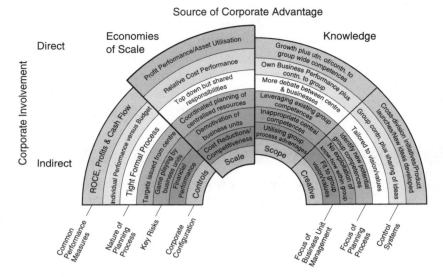

Figure 5.4
The Rainbow Diagram:
The planning & control
process.

pricing mechanism that will be used for each centralised activity or process. It is important that this is seen by both parties as a 'pricing' arrangement and not a method by which the centralised area simply apportions its total costs across the business units. As shown in Figure 5.4, a key risk in the scale configuration is the demotivation of business unit managers and this is easily achieved if they are held accountable for things over which they can exercise no control. The business units are still primarily focused on their own divisional financial performance and the level of costs that are transferred to them from centralised parts of the group can have a material impact on the profit performance of these business units.

The corporate centre in the scale configuration, of course, has a more complex control role in that it has to control not only the business units and the centralised activities and processes, but also the relationship between these discrete areas. The primary control system for all the centralised resources will be their relative cost performance, as this should be demonstrably lower than could be achieved by the individual business units. However, the actual cost savings generated by such centralised facilities will obviously depend upon the utilisation levels achieved through the demand that comes from the group's business units.

Therefore the group planning process needs to consider the appropriate scale of the centralised resources and this requires that the internal business unit customers are involved so that a properly integrated and co-ordinated plan is produced. Thus the planning process for the scale configuration can be described as driven from the corporate centre (as they are looking for cost reduction opportunities) but with shared responsibilities for the actual usage levels of centralised resources. There are many examples of corporate centre driven initiatives to create very large centralised facilities that remain extremely under-utilised by the group's businesses. This is clearly disastrous for a scale configuration group as the economic justification for this type of centralisation is to reduce the total costs of the group. The centre should only therefore be centralising activities and processes that are essential to the business units and for which it has obtained their commitment. This required commitment by the business units to use these 'essential' centralised resources can be reflected in the transfer pricing system that is used within the group. If business units are prepared to guarantee to take a specified level of output from a centralised activity, the transfer price should be appropriately reduced to reflect the greater certainty that this provides for this centralised resource.

This means that transfer prices should be structured to reflect the real business decisions that the group faces in deciding whether to centralise any particular activity; exactly as would be done if the group were negotiating an outsourcing contract with an independent third party supplier. Unfortunately, in most large multinational groups, the only factor that is taken into consideration in designing a group-wide transfer pricing system seems to be gaining approval from the tax authorities around the world. Hence the most common transfer pricing system is 'cost plus 10 per cent' (or some similar add-on to the basic cost). In any group where the focus of the corporate centre is on cost reduction, it is bizarre that the 'return' generated by an internal centralised activity should increase if its costs actually go up!

A strong leadership role

This type of externally focused tax driven transfer pricing system would seem more appropriate for the much less involved shareholder style corporate centre of the controls configuration. The manager style centre has a significantly greater leadership role within the group, although it may adopt a lower external profile in some cases. The focus of this leadership is on achieving the greatest economies of scale possible for the group. This can result in acquisition led growth strategies if the existing portfolio of businesses does not generate a sufficiently large critical mass for certain activities and processes. It can be perceived that 'the tail is wagging the dog' if new businesses are acquired solely so that the corporate centre can increase the level of

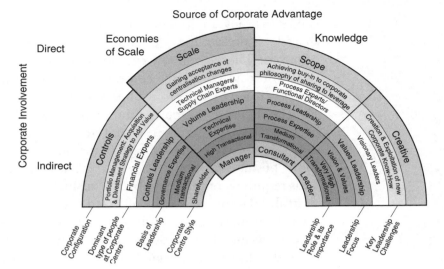

Figure 5.5
The Rainbow Diagram:
Leadership roles &
changes.

economies of scale. However these increased economies of scale should also reduce the costs of all the existing business units, as well as benefiting the newly acquired business. Also the main economic justification for the group remaining as a group is this economies of scale driven value-adding role of the corporate centre.

Indeed the objective of the scale configuration corporate centre is to achieve volume leadership in at least one core business process that has relevance across the entire group, as is shown in Figure 5.5. As already discussed it is important that the corporate centre selects both the core processes that are to be centralised and the business units that will be involved very carefully. The negative impacts on the business units of any required standardisation in these processes can more than offset the economies of scale achieved by the centralisation. Alternatively this can lead to those business units that have more specialised requirements opting out of the centralisation process and destroying the potential economies of scale savings.

This gives the corporate centre a critical challenge of gaining acceptance of its planned centralisation changes from those managers most highly affected, e.g. those with the specialised requirements. These most important managers must give high commitment to the centralisation strategy rather than merely reluctantly complying with a change that is mandated by the centre. They need to be involved in developing the SLAs that will be implemented and should also have input to the proposed transfer pricing system. A relatively simple ploy to increase the level of buy-in is to guarantee that their costs will fall after centralisation. The level of guaranteed cost reduction that is needed will be related to the amount of change that the business unit will need to make because of any standardisation in the centralised process. If this cost reduction cannot be guaranteed, given the technical management expertise and supply chain skills in the group, the corporate centre probably should reconsider its plans to centralise this core process.

Sustainability

As with the controls configuration, scale configuration groups normally have a limited period in which the corporate centre can continue to keep adding significant value to a fixed set of business units. During this period the total value added by the centralisation of some core processes and many support activities can be very significant. However, once these have all been centralised and the associated economies of scale cost savings realised, the corporate centre will find it difficult to reduce the group's costs still further. [As already mentioned, there is a danger of over-centralising so that the adverse effects on the business units more than offset any additional economies of scale.]

This does not necessarily mean the group is no longer economically viable. If the corporate centre has attained volume leadership in its centralised processes it should have established a continuing cost advantage for its business units. Such a cost advantage will persist, even though it will not increase, until competitors are able to respond and either achieve similar economies of scale or find an alternative competitive strategy. As discussed earlier in the chapter, this is much easier for competitors to achieve if the centralisation only affects support activities. Thus the more sustainable corporate strategy is to centralise some core business processes but, as might be expected, this has some downsides.

The group becomes much more constrained in terms of the businesses that it can logically contain, as shown in Figure 5.6; they must be able to benefit from the economies of scale that are being produced from the centralisation. Also the large-scale investments made by the corporate centre to create the required capacity start to become increasingly specific. This increases the risk associated with the centralisation strategy due to the lack of alternative uses and this may make the group seek more stable external environments in which its business units can exploit these lower cost but centralised core processes. This more stable external environment can sometimes be created by the group itself if it develops a protectable core process (such as a patented technology or product that comes out of the centralised R & D process). In such a case, the group's external environment may be

Source of Corporate Advantage

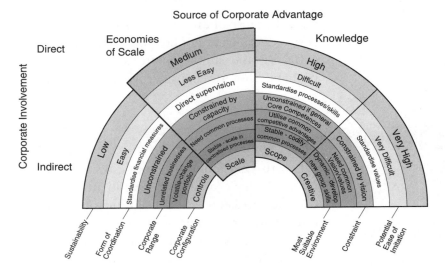

Figure 5.6
The Rainbow Diagram:
Sustainability issues.

sufficiently stable that it can take the risk of investing in large-scale production volumes before competitors can enter the market. The resulting economies of scale can then give it a significant cost advantage that can sustain its market dominance even when competitors are able to enter the market.

As the value-adding centralised core processes become more and more specific it becomes increasingly difficult for the corporate centre to identify new business units that will benefit from this very focused centralisation strategy. It may decide to stay as it is and simply try to maintain its existing cost advantage for as long as possible. This strategy is often extended to include centralising other processes and activities of the existing business units, usually with much less successful results. Alternatively the corporate centre can look for other types of core process that it believes it can add value to; i.e. it tries to broaden out its technical management expertise and leverage on its supply chain knowledge. In reality it is seeking to move to the scope configuration by seeking to leverage existing knowledge, while still staying in the scale configuration with its original businesses. A more logical strategy may be a total transition to a neighbouring configuration.

Transitions to neighbouring configurations

There are obviously two possible transitions out of the scale configuration to neighbouring configurations, but these moves will have very different impacts on the corporate centre of any group. A move down the model to the controls configuration does not require the corporate

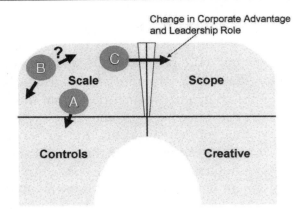

Figure 5.7
Transitions to neighbour-
ing configurations.

centre to change its focus on cost reduction, but its involvement in its business units becomes more indirect. This is most easily achieved when the current direct intervention encompasses mainly support activities, as shown by position A in Figure 5.7. With this low level of direct intervention, the underlying businesses will already be relatively autonomous and a greater degree of freedom should not cause too many problems.

As discussed in Chapter 3, this type of transition can be regarded as the next stage in a corporate lifecycle. The centralised support activities can either be set up as a separate 'independent' business unit within the group, or these activities can be outsourced to a truly independent third party. The loss of this 'management' role for the corporate centre should enable it to make the change to the indirect involvement role required of the cost conscious shareholder style centre of the controls configuration.

The much more interesting transition is the move across to the right to try to go to the scope configuration. Such a transition requires a change both in the source of corporate advantage and in the leadership role of the corporate centre. Instead of being focused on cost reductions through economies of scale, the corporate centre has to identify areas of knowledge that can be leveraged more widely across the group. Also the scope configuration requires that the corporate centre adopts a more transformational leadership role as it tries to make the business units do different things. In the scale configuration the centre will have had a primarily transactional leadership role. Thus this transition is very challenging as was discussed in Chapter 3 and shown by the barriers between the two configurations in Figure 5.7. However, it has been achieved very successfully.

From Figure 5.7 it can be seen that a logical start point for this transition is position C; i.e. the top right-hand part of the scale configuration. This means that the corporate centre has a very high level of direct intervention in its business units and has centralised many core processes as well as a lot of support activities. At this stage the level of corporate advantage may be reducing due to the imposition of completely standardised procedures across the group in order to maximise the economies of scale. However, it is quite possible that some of these centralised processes may have generated information that can be utilised by the group to add value rather than reduce costs still further. If so, the corporate centre may be able to generate significant new added value if it moves across to the consultant style role of the scope configuration. An example may make this clearer.

Supermarkets in the UK, and in most other major markets, started their rapid growth phase by operating very clearly in the scale configuration. The corporate centres intervened very directly in the operation of the stores by centralising most core business processes and almost all support activities. The focus of this intervention was to reduce costs through maximising the level of economies of scale generated by the group. A critical area was obviously the centralised buying department that enabled the supermarket to negotiate not only significant volume discounts but also generous settlement terms from suppliers. These suppliers became increasingly subservient to the buying power of these dominant supermarket chains as they grew their market share by opening more and larger stores. Thus the initial maxim of the supermarkets can be described as 'pile it high, sell it cheap and pay for it tomorrow'. Indeed a financial analysis of the published financial statements of a leading discount supermarket chain, such as Kwik-Save, during these early rapid growth years would highlight that the group actually only broke even on its retailing activities and made its total net profit margin by investing the substantial cash mountain generated from its negative working capital.

The next stage in this scale configuration strategy was to strengthen its negotiating power still further by putting its own name on an increasing proportion of the products that it sold. These 'own labels', as they were originally known, turned their suppliers into more commodity manufacturers than the branded goods companies that they had previously been. Indeed several new manufacturing groups grew up that specialised in producing only retailer branded goods, but many of the previously high margin branded manufacturers saw their profits dramatically squeezed by this increasing retailer power.

At the same time, the centralised support activities were finding new ways to reduce costs in the stores. Point-of-sale automation removed the need for individual product price marking in the store and for check-out operators to key-in price data. However, this computerised database system had several even more important benefits. It obviously provided real-time information on what was being purchased by customers. This could be used to make inventory management and even store layouts more dynamic but, much more important, it could give detailed information on who was buying what and how frequently they did it! Of course in order to capture this potential information the supermarkets needed customer details and these could be obtained from some form of loyalty card, store card or in-house credit card.

As a result, the supermarkets developed very detailed information about their customers in terms of shopping frequency, purchasing habits, product combination, etc. This information could then be added to through direct communication with their 'loyal' customers so that tailored special offers could be designed in order to increase this 'level of loyalty'. This increased level of 'knowledge' about who their customers were and what they really wanted further tilted the industry playing field towards the supermarket and away from the manufacturers. Originally the fast moving consumer goods (fmcg) manufacturers were the experts on consumers as they did all the research on potential consumer demand, etc. However, now the retailers were able to collect real factual information from every transaction that took place; this has forced the fmcg companies to upgrade their consumer research to consider more fundamental reasons for buying (e.g. psychographic segmentations) as is considered in Chapter 6.

The generation of this in-depth customer information and increased focus on customer loyalty is inconsistent with the cost reduction focus of the scale configuration. The corporate centre is now seeking to add value to the group by leveraging its knowledge about consumers and their shopping habits and preferences. This has been consciously reinforced by the leading supermarket groups through repositioning their retailer brands. These are now seen as perfectly acceptable quality products in their own right and, in some cases, they are even themselves being segmented into different positionings; such as 'value', 'simple', 'finest', 'organic', etc. Such new propositions have also enabled the supermarkets to broaden their product ranges dramatically and to move away from their previous dependence on their store outlets.

The competitive advantages that the supermarkets initially brought to many of the services that they now sell (e.g. insurance, banking and utilities) was their trusted branding and their customer insights, rather than their buying power. This knowledge could be leveraged by the corporate centre through entering into partnerships with established companies in each of these new product areas. Undoubtedly this new trend has *transformed* the way in which these groups will develop in the future. Of course the retail stores will remain important but increasingly they will be only one part of the group as directly sold services (e.g. banking and insurance) and goods (e.g. internet based retailing) grow much more rapidly in the future. It is therefore helpful that we now move on to consider the implications of operating in the scope configuration in Chapter 6.

Chapter 6

The scope configuration

Introduction and overview

As with the scale configuration that was considered in the previous chapter, the consultant style corporate centre of the scope configuration directly intervenes in the operations of the business units within the group. However, the objective of this intervention is not to reduce directly the total costs of the group. Rather the consultant style corporate centre seeks to leverage existing value-adding knowledge as widely as possible across the group.

It is important to emphasise immediately that the corporate centre does not necessarily have to develop this knowledge itself. The centre can add substantial value to knowledge that already exists in one part of the group by making it available to all those other parts of the group where it has relevance. By doing this, the corporate centre enables the group to generate economies of scope, as is shown in Figure 6.1. In order to maximise the relevance of any particular knowledge-based competitive advantage, the corporate centre may need to codify, refine, or generalise the specific knowledge that is being applied by one business unit. It may well be that it is actually the business process or functional way of working that is transferable rather than the resulting local business unit competitive advantage. It is quite possible that these business unit managers may not know exactly why they are so successful. The critical value-adding role of the consultant style corporate centre is then to identify the key elements and codify them into a potential group-wide resource. In other words, the centre can turn tacit know-how of the business unit into leveragable knowledge for the group.

Of course this role has significant implications for both the costs incurred and the variety of skills that are required by the corporate

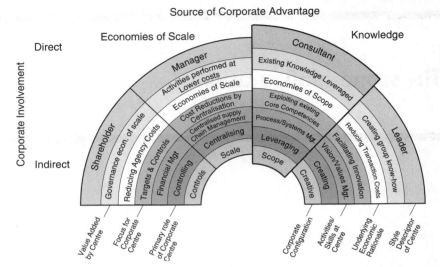

Figure 6.1
Corporate configurations:
The Rainbow Diagram.

centre. It needs functional skills to identify existing value-adding knowledge that may have more general relevance across the group. The centre also must have sufficient knowledge about its business units and their particular competitive situations to recognise exactly where and when this knowledge should be applied. However, the most important component is the process and systems expertise that ensures that the existing knowledge can be successfully applied by the other business units. It is in this area of process and systems expertise that the consultant style corporate centre should seek to establish its own pre-eminence so that it is recognised as a leader in this field.

The existing knowledge that it seeks to leverage may be to do with the core processes of the underlying business units or it could be associated with more generic support activities. Thus scope configurations can encompass a very wide-ranging spread of businesses, or can appear as quite integrated, high context groups (including single business groups). The glue that binds together any scope configuration group is the exploitation of similar sources of competitive advantage. This similarity makes the more general exploitation of existing knowledge across the group so relevant and value adding.

However, it also indicates a very significant challenge to the sustainability of the value-adding role of a consultant style corporate centre. Any specific knowledge-based competitive advantage has a tightly defined economic lifecycle for the corporate centre. Once it has been codified and leveraged across all the relevant business units, the consultant style corporate centre has added all of its potential value to this knowledge. The business units may continue to exploit this knowledge-based competitive advantage for many years but they no longer need the corporate centre, with its attendant costs, to achieve this. An important characteristic of the scope configuration is that, although the corporate centre is directly intervening, the benefits are realised in the business units that receive the knowledge while the costs of acquiring or codifying this knowledge are incurred at the corporate centre or in the originating business unit. This has implications for the planning and control systems and these are discussed later in the chapter.

This is why the systems and process expertise is so important in the scope configuration. A sustainable consultant style corporate centre needs to be able to leverage a succession of different competitive advantages across a possibly changing portfolio of businesses. Thus the centre could try to find new businesses in which it can leverage its existing knowledge-based competitive advantages or which may provide new knowledge that it can leverage across the rest of the group. A steady flow of knowledge that can be leveraged by the consultant style corporate centre is more easily achieved if the business units are themselves innovative and face severe competitive pressures in their own competitive environments. It is also important to remember that the leveragable knowledge can relate to how to reduce cost levels. In this type of group, external competitive pressures can force all the business units to come up with their own innovative cost reducing solutions that may have relevance more widely across the group. The consultant style corporate centre may have quite high costs itself, but it can still help the business units to reduce their own costs by making specific cost reducing strategies more generally applicable within the group.

The culture within a scope configuration group needs to be open and trusting so that the business units are willing to share their advances in knowledge with the corporate centre. This means that the initial communication flow should be up the organisation from the business units to the centre, so that the centre is made aware of new value-adding opportunities. The centre should, once they have been appropriately packaged, spread this knowledge across the organisation but, ideally it should not need to *force* other business units to adopt the new best practice. Once the centre gains a reputation for only spreading useful and usable knowledge, the business units should not only readily adopt each new centre driven initiative but also should willingly share their breakthroughs with the centre. This can make the process self-sustaining if the business units keep getting more value back from the centre than they provide to it, so that they

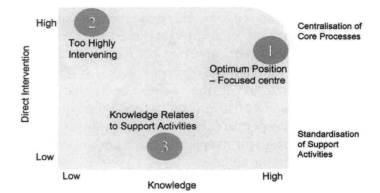

Figure 6.2
Alternative positions
within scope
configuration.

have an incentive to keep the corporate centre in its value-adding role.

It is quite possible for the consultant style centre to get into an unsustainable position within the scope configuration as is shown in Figure 6.2. Position 1 shows the optimum position for the group where the corporate centre has identified a few critical, core business processes to which it can continue to add a lot of value by leveraging existing knowledge across the group. Thus it focuses its attention on these limited processes, which may be new product development, brand management, customer service, etc.

In Position 2, the corporate centre has become too interventionist in the business units and this is constraining their ability to compete in their specific competitive environment. This type of corporate centre may actually have directly centralised several core processes rather than leaving the enhanced and standardised processes under the management of the business units. The consultant style corporate centre should have a transformational leadership role within the group in that it acts to change how the business units operate. However, in the top left-hand segment of the configuration, as discussed in Chapter 3, the centre's role can become much too transactional as the centre gets too involved in the detailed daily operations of the business units. This can have a highly negative impact on the performance of the business units, as well as increasing the cost base of the corporate centre significantly.

Position 3 shows a corporate centre that is focused only on support activities so that its value adding potential is limited. This type of group may contain a wide range of business units as it is not constrained by any commonality of core processes. Not surprisingly our first case study example looks at a group that has maintained a highly value adding position for its corporate centre for over 50 years.

Leveraging brand building expertise

Philip Morris Inc., recently renamed as Altria, has a publicly stated mission of being 'the most successful consumer packaged goods company in the world'. Its main strategy to achieve this is through 'building and protecting' very strong consumer brands that are product based, with the first and still leading example being Marlboro.

Unlike Coca-Cola, which is discussed at the end of this chapter, Marlboro has not always dominated its market in the USA. Philip Morris only entered the USA cigarette market in 1934 when volumes were already over 100 billion units per year. Marlboro itself was launched in 1937 and peaked at sales volumes of 2.3 billion cigarettes in 1945. By 1953 Marlboro had a negligible share of the market and was targeted specifically at female smokers. It was relaunched in 1955 as a filter-tipped cigarette aimed primarily at male smokers. Then, in the late 1950s an advertising campaign featuring a cowboy and wide-open spaces was introduced! At this time the leading USA brands, which were Lucky Strike, Camel and Chesterfield, were all non-filtered, plain cigarettes. These brands did not launch filtered versions until the 1960s, by which time Marlboro was well established.

Marlboro's growth was steady rather than spectacular and was fuelled by very high marketing support (i.e. brand development investment) so that in 1975 Marlboro became the largest cigarette brand in the USA market. In 1983 Philip Morris became the largest USA-based cigarette company, selling 205 billion cigarettes out of 597.5 billion, of which 120 billion were Marlboro. This was interesting because the USA market volume peaked in 1981 at 638 billion cigarettes, and then went into a slow but continual decline. This meant that PM had followed the well-established shareholder value enhancing strategy of gaining market share while the market was itself growing.

Once it had the leading position in the now mature market, its strategy changed and it looked to increase both its own profitability and that of the total market. Accordingly, as the price leader with the dominant brand, PM took retail selling prices up significantly faster than inflation: through the 1980s, price rises averaged 7 per cent per annum in real terms. Consequently, although total industry volumes were declining at 3 per cent per annum, the total profit pool was still increasing. This meant that the profits of all the other cigarette companies could increase, even though PM was taking an increasing share of this profit pool.

Moving international

The initial success of Marlboro in the USA led the group to make a major corporate strategy move. In the 1960s the group CEO, Joe Cullman, identified international cigarette markets as the best opportunity for long-term growth. Thus, well before Marlboro had actually achieved leadership of the USA industry, he reassigned George Weissman, who had been running the USA domestic business (then 99 per cent of total group sales volumes) and put him in charge of the embryonic international operations. He refocused the business on Europe and Australasia and based the long-term strategy around Marlboro. This meant that Marlboro also became the best selling cigarette brand outside the USA, mainly by taking large market shares in similarly mature markets. This is important because PM's group-wide marketing competences are most suited to particular types of competitive environment.

Marlboro has been able to build very high brand recognition globally through consistent marketing investment, such as through sponsorship of Formula One motor racing. The actual product has been modified where necessary to meet either specific market requirements (such as using Virginia tobacco rather than the normal US blends) or changing consumer requirements. Thus as the age profile of full flavour Marlboro 'Red' cigarettes increased, the company introduced Marlboro Lights to appeal to a younger age group. However, the brand imagery has always been maintained and other cigarette brands sold by PM are carefully positioned to be compatible with Marlboro. For example, in many markets PM has brands called Philip Morris and L & M, with L & M often being referred to as Little Marlboro.

The very high brand awareness generated by PM for Marlboro should make it easier for the group to gain distribution through wholesalers and retailers in any market. However, PM is most successful in markets where the distribution channels are well organised so that it can negotiate national or regional deals with distributors, wholesalers or multi-outlet retailers. Marlboro has only very small market shares in several less developed countries where many cigarettes are still sold to smokers as individual 'sticks' by street vendors.

Also Marlboro is a premium priced cigarette in most markets around the world. This means that the issue of affordability is critical to gaining a dominant market share and explains why well-off countries such as Germany, France, UK and Italy have been such successful competitive environments for Marlboro. In fact the group has also learnt how to identify when Marlboro becomes very attractive in a specific market, so that it can launch its aggressive marketing campaign at the most opportune time. This can be illustrated by looking at its development in Argentina.

An appropriately tailored strategy

The Argentine economy had been ravaged by hyperinflation and the 1980's debt crisis. Early in the 20th century, Argentina had been in the world's top ten countries in terms of trading and GDP per head. However, following the election of Juan Peron as President in 1946 the country went into a long period of economic decline. This resulted in a series of military coups until democracy was restored in 1983 following the Malvinas/Falklands war with Great Britain. Democracy was restored but the economy was not, as rampant inflation took over. Annual inflation for 1989 was 4,923 per cent and for 1990 over 2,000 per cent; it actually peaked during 1990 at an annualised rate of 20,266 per cent.

In 1989 Carlos Menem was elected President as leader of the Peronist Party. However Menem, with Domingo Cavallo as his finance minister, used free market policies to try to turn the economy around. The government ran a fiscal surplus by increasing the tax base and reducing expenditure, and privatisation of inefficient state-owned industries was rapidly introduced. The previously tariff protected economy was opened up through the development of Mercosur as well as establishing closer trading links with the USA and the rest of Latin America.

In 1991, the government launched the Convertibility Plan which fixed the local currency against the US dollar. However, the critical point of the Plan was that the internal monetary base of the country had to be backed by foreign currency reserves. Thus if foreign currency reserves fell, the government had to reduce the domestic money supply. Government deficits could no longer be financed by printing money. No more printing money should, in theory, lead to no more inflation; or at least only the same low rate of inflation as the USA to which the currency was tied. Also the government did not have to increase the domestic money supply if foreign currency reserves increased.

Inflation fell dramatically to 4.1 per cent in 1994 and 1.9 per cent in 1995 (below the rate in the USA) but GDP growth in this period was substantial (1991, 8.9 per cent; 1992, 8.7 per cent; 1993, 6.0 per cent; 1994, 6.5 per cent). This phenomenal run was obviously too good to continue and the economy moved into recession towards the end of

1995 and Argentina faced another currency and political crisis at the end of the century.

Before the hyperinflation period, Philip Morris already had, through a local company, a presence in Argentina with Marlboro. However, its market share was very small and the market was dominated by local brands. The leading cigarette company was the BAT Industries local subsidiary that had the largest local brand, Jockey Club, with around 30 per cent market share. Although Marlboro's actual market share was very low, the company was aware through its consumer research that it had a much higher penetration of adult smokers, with around 25 per cent smoking Marlboro at some time. This indicated the minimum potential market share for the brand if smokers could afford to buy it on a regular basis.

During the previous economic plan, PM had launched a very low price brand into the market that, not surprisingly, had started to gain market share. This prompted a rapid response by the leading competitor that launched its own equally low price brand. This brand not only recaptured the share that had been lost but took a sizable proportion of the total market. By 1990 its share was over 20 per cent but most of this volume had been gained at the expense of its own higher priced Jockey Club brand. While its total market share had been protected, the profitability of BAT's Argentine company had been decimated.

As inflation started to fall and GDP per head to grow, PM supported Marlboro much more aggressively with much higher levels of marketing expenditure. The company's market support for Marlboro had, for some years, been excessive by reference to its current low market share. As consumers' purchasing power increased, the industry looked to recover some of its former profitability by increasing selling prices in real terms; particularly of the marginally profitable, but dominant, very low priced products. This gave Marlboro a significant competitive opportunity as it had always been established in the higher priced category and its pricing had not been discounted in the earlier price wars.

PM was able to close the *relative* price gap between the very low price brands and Marlboro by maintaining the *absolute* price differential through 1991 to 1995. This made Marlboro much more affordable in the eyes of the target consumers and its market share grew very rapidly to over 35 per cent by the end of 1995. This gave PM's Argentine company a total market share of over 50 per cent, which it has maintained since.

Not surprisingly the group has sought to implement very similar competitive strategies in other countries that face equivalent economic challenges. Argentina's much larger neighbour, Brazil, with its five times larger population and comparable government driven economic plans was an obvious target. To date, BAT's local subsidiary has retained its market leadership but PM has been more successful with a very similar strategy in several Central and East European markets.

Moving away from cigarettes

The very strong cash generation of its highly successful Marlboro-led cigarettes business enabled PM to acquire other branded product companies. At the same time, all the other major cigarette companies were also diversifying out of tobacco as a defensive measure against the increasing threats to their existing earnings streams. However, PM has had by far the most successful acquisition-led growth strategy as it deliberately set out to leverage the key existing knowledge held by the group. PM had already demonstrated its ability to build a domestic market-leading brand that could then be translated into equally leading positions in many international markets.

Its acquisitions of non-cigarette businesses were of brands in 'not-so-healthy' consumer products where the group felt that its marketing expertise could add value. All of these had quite good positions in their domestic markets but had not established similarly strong brand values internationally. Thus these acquisitions were in brewing (Miller), soft drinks (Seven-Up), coffee (Maxwell House from the purchase of General Foods), processed cheese (Kraft), and chocolate (Jacob Suchard). Not all of these were successful but PM did try to ensure that it learnt from its mistakes. The best example of this was its purchase of Seven-Up in 1978 that never worked out and ended when it was sold in 1986 at a loss. In several subsequent publications senior executives have openly discussed the thousands of hours of management time that were spent in trying both to make the acquisition successful and then to learn why it did not work as part of the group. Miller brewing would be classified as a successful beer company by most of its competitors. However it could not achieve the relative brand strength, compared to its global rival Budweiser, that PM expects of its leading brands. As a result PM recently merged Miller into SAB (South African Breweries) to give it a significant minority stake in the greatly enlarged SAB Miller business.

PM's main USA based competitor, RJ Reynolds, from which PM took leadership of the USA cigarette industry, also made a large number of acquisitions. Some of these were of fast moving consumer goods (fmcg) businesses (Nabisco) but Reynolds also bought a large shipping container company (Sea-Land) and an oil company (Aminoil). These true diversification moves actually destroyed a lot of shareholder value; e.g. Sea-Land was sold five years later at a significant loss. Even the more related food acquisition did not create value as the group had no really relevant knowledge that could be leveraged across these acquisitions. At the time of its acquisition Nabisco had brands that still had leadership in their domestic market; spreading the knowledge of how to lose this leadership is not value-adding! Subsequent to RJR Nabisco's highly leveraged buy-out by KKR in 1989 and the disposal of its international tobacco business to Japan Tobacco in 1998, RJ Reynolds sold its Nabisco food businesses to Altria. This left Reynolds as a focused USA based cigarette company and in 2004 it merged with BAT's USA based subsidiary, Brown & Williamson.

BAT Industries' own value-destroying diversification strategy was discussed earlier in the book but BAT plc is now totally focused on the global tobacco industry. However, as it does not possess the leading global brand, it cannot apply exactly the same knowledge leverage as PM. Indeed the challenge facing BAT is that its success in the many markets around the world where it is the leading cigarette company (e.g. Canada, Brazil, South Africa and Malaysia) seems to be based on significantly different factors. Identifying any key knowledge that can be leveraged across the group is not therefore as straightforward for BAT as it is for PM, should BAT decide that it wants to be in the scope configuration.

This need not of itself be a bad thing as long as the corporate centre focuses its attention on identifying this key knowledge. PM has really been applying a 'one-size fits all' branding strategy that works very successfully as long as the marketplace is not highly segmented. If different groups of consumers really want different things, it should be possible for a competitor to develop an appropriately tailored brand portfolio where each brand is targeted at a different segment of the total market. Such a segmentation strategy may restrict the total market share of any single brand as it cannot be the *most* relevant brand to several different groups of consumers. Indeed its previous broad-based general appeal may mean that it is not the most relevant to *any* single segment!

In this kind of focused marketing led strategy, the critical knowledge to the businesses becomes how to understand the specific requirements of individual consumers and how to group these consumers together into meaningful market segmentations. Thus, although the brands used in individual markets where BAT is market leader may be different and even the consumer segments may be unique to that market, the marketing research *processes* that were used to understand the particular needs of these markets may be very relevant to many other markets. This means that the role of the corporate centre would be to identify and codify these key marketing processes through which each separate market will develop its own specifically tailored brand portfolio.

A company like PM can be much more prescriptive and almost formulaic in the knowledge that it spreads across the group. Its direct competitor may need to be less directly interventionist but could still add a lot of value by identifying the real value-adding knowledge that has general application across the group.

Cultural implications and leadership challenges

Clearly these differences impact not only on how far up the vertical axis of the configurations model any scope configuration group should be, but also on the organisational culture within the group. Where the competitive strategies being implemented by the individual business units within a group are very similar, the corporate centre may be able to identify a number of highly significant developments in the external competitive environment that should enable the business unit to implement the next stage of the strategy. For example, it is now well established that the demand for various categories of consumer products increases dramatically when GDP per head passes through certain critical levels (such as consumer durables at $1000 GDP per head). This group knowledge can clearly be leveraged to optimise the timing of marketing expenditure in markets approaching such critical points. If this knowledge has already been validated in many markets, the resulting high level of confidence means that its implementation may be absolutely mandated by the corporate centre. The upwards communication that is needed from the business unit is the prediction of when the triggering event will occur; e.g. when will Marlboro become generally affordable in a particular market?

Of course the knowledge that is to be leveraged may be less precise and require much more interpretation or modification before being applied successfully in other parts of the group. In these cases it may be sensible for the corporate centre to be less prescriptive in the way it spreads the knowledge across the group. The knowledge may be expressed as best practice or described as a 'successful case study' of

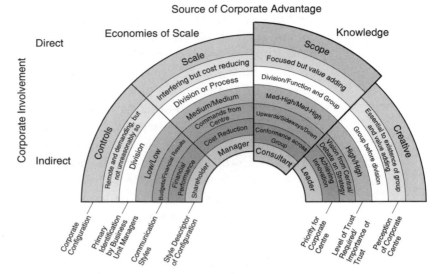

Figure 6.3
The Rainbow Diagram:
Implications for
organisational culture.

what was done by a specific business unit. The danger of this approach is, of course, that there will be much less take-up by other business units with a correspondingly lower level of conformance achieved across the group. Achieving conformance across the group in the application of leveragable knowledge is important to the success of the consultant style corporate centre, as is shown in Figure 6.3.

A very interesting result of our research is the identification of a common difference on this dimension between USA led groups and European based ones. Altria and BAT have already been mentioned but the same differences can be highlighted between Procter & Gamble and Unilever, or by comparing Shell to its USA based competitors such as Exxon-Mobil.

Procter & Gamble (P & G) was founded in 1837 by two brothers-in-law who found that their businesses used the same raw materials. William Procter was a candle-maker while James Gamble manufactured soap. Although the early business grew quite slowly from its base in Cincinnati, the founders established the very strong culture that still pervades the group today. There is a P & G 'way of doing things' that new entrants to the group learn by a process that has been described as indoctrination. Successful employees have to be totally comfortable with this 'tightness of fit' which is applied in all the countries where the group operates. The P & G culture is therefore seen as coming before the specific national culture of the employees. This is strongly reinforced by a promotion from within policy, so that senior managers will all have developed within this cultural environment.

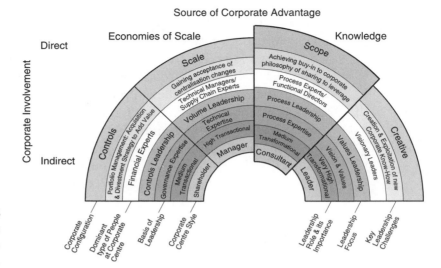

Figure 6.4
The Rainbow Diagram:
Leadership roles &
challenges.

However, the group avoids becoming outdated through its internal processes and fundamental beliefs in product excellence and continuous improvement. Sales and marketing are absolutely core business processes of P & G and it was the first major group to introduce the idea of self-competing brands in 1931. Also, even further back in 1919, it revolutionised the industry's distribution system in the USA by going straight to retailers rather than selling through wholesalers. Since then it has continually leveraged its brand building expertise and sales management knowledge across the group. Attaining the essential buy-in to this philosophy of sharing in order to achieve economies of scope by leveraging existing knowledge is quite easy in a group that has such a strong culture and a willing acceptance of a P & G way to do things.

It also enables the corporate centre to take a quite strong leadership role within the group without creating resentment at the business unit level that the centre is interfering too much. This is much more difficult in a less centralised group such as Unilever. Unilever was formed in 1930 by the merger of two already well-established businesses, Margarine Unie and Lever Bros. The group developed into four global business groups based on food, detergents, personal products and speciality chemicals; the speciality chemicals business group has now been sold to ICI. Unilever has a relatively decentralised management style but the corporate centre has a co-ordinating role that ensures best practices are shared across the relevant business units. The group has also developed very strong skills in concept marketing to mass-market consumers, with the corporate centre focusing on marketing research, trade marketing, promotions and advertising, and fostering a company-wide marketing culture. However, the central marketing function is seen as a service organisation, working for the business groups and having to gain buy-in from each business group for any major new initiative. This has resulted in some excellent processes being implemented across the group as marketing knowledge is leveraged by the centre, but the 'independent' business units have used these common processes to develop their own tailored brand portfolios. Unilever therefore found itself with a world-wide portfolio totalling 1600 brands and has implemented a global 'Path to Growth' programme to rationalise this to a total of 400 brands. This is being achieved by more direct intervention from the corporate centre.

Conversely P & G never developed such a localised array of brands but it is also having to reconsider the role of its corporate centre, following its current failure to achieve its aggressive sales growth targets. It is actually moving to slightly more of a Unilever structure with seven global product category businesses replacing its previously geographically based businesses. The logic is that this is required to serve increasingly global retailers such as Wal-Mart, Carrefour and Tesco, but it will mean even less autonomy for the individual country-based business unit managers. This increased centralisation increases the risk that the corporate centre actually identifies inappropriate knowledge to leverage across the group.

The planning and control process

The identification of existing core competences that can be leveraged more widely within the group is the key source of added value by the consultant style of corporate centre. Therefore it should become the focus of the planning and control process for scope configuration groups. This requires a significantly increased level of debate between the corporate centre and its business units than was needed in either the scale or controls configurations.

The centre has to find out about new value-adding knowledge held in particular business units and to understand the issues and opportunities facing all its business units, so that it can identify any relevant knowledge that can be appropriately spread to other business units. As discussed above, the centre needs to create an environment in which the business units are happy both to receive these new ideas from the centre and to share with the centre any innovations of their own. This can be facilitated by the measures used within the group to assess the performance of the business units.

The level of independence of the business units clearly depends on the degree of intervention by the corporate centre and this needs to be allowed for in the managerial performance measures that are used. These measures do need to incorporate some indication of the utilisation that each business unit is making of the group-wide competences that the centre is trying to leverage. A low level of utilisation is not necessarily a criticism of the business unit managers. However, it should lead to a review by the group to identify the underlying causes, so that the utilisation measure can be improved in the future. It is important to remember that this leverage of knowledge is the principal economic rationale for the business units being part of the group.

Also, as is shown in Figure 6.5, the level of contribution to new group-wide competences should be measured as business units may respond to encouragement to share their value-adding knowledge across the group. This is a common problem in the scope configuration because the financial benefits from leveraging this knowledge are seen in the receiving business units, but the costs are incurred by the corporate centre and, in many cases, by the originating business unit that created the knowledge. A popular, but flawed, solution is to charge the receiving business units for implementing this centrally provided capability through some form of royalty (e.g. for brands or technologies) or licensing fee (e.g. for processes or systems).

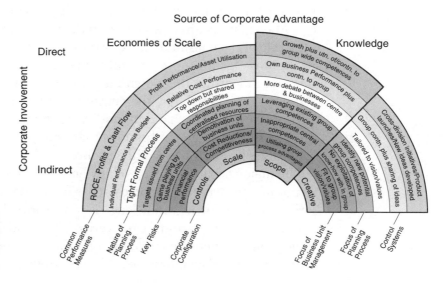

Figure 6.5
The Rainbow Diagram:
The planning & control
process.

This income stream can be used to offset the costs incurred by the corporate centre and to provide the originating business unit with a financial incentive to share its knowledge. Unfortunately this is not likely to lead to the group obtaining the maximum benefit from having a consultant style corporate centre. Once any leveragable knowledge has been identified it is clearly in the group's interests to have this knowledge applied wherever in the group that it is relevant. By introducing a charge for using this knowledge the centre is creating a financial disincentive for the other business units to do so. The potential receiving business unit may decide to invest to create the knowledge itself or it may find an external source of superficially similar knowledge that requires a lower charge. Obviously an internal transfer from one business unit to the corporate centre does not, of itself, create any shareholder value but if it decreases the exploitation of knowledge that already exists, it may significantly reduce the value that could have been created.

Further, providing the originating business unit with an income stream may not be such a good idea if it distorts the reported financial performance of this business unit. The focus of business unit performance assessment in the scope configuration should be the long-term financial performance of the business unit, so that investing for sustainable growth and profit improvement is more important than in the cost focused scale and controls configurations. However, the managerial performance of the business unit leaders must be assessed on only those areas that they can directly control. This should therefore exclude any 'windfall' type of royalty income if 'their' knowledge is more widely applied within the group. Otherwise there is a danger that business units start to consider the licensing potential of any development activity, rather than its direct potential in their own sphere of operations. It is the role of the consultant style corporate centre to identify and adapt such knowledge for more general application across the group. Where the centre identifies this potential prior to its full development by the originating business unit, the centre can reimburse the business unit for any extra costs incurred in modifying the development to incorporate any suggested generalisations that will ease the subsequent leverage process by other areas of the group.

The major negative impact of any licensing system is actually on the corporate centre itself. As stated earlier in the chapter, the value-adding period for any existing knowledge is quite short. The corporate centre adapts it if necessary and then leverages it as widely as is value adding to the group. It then needs to move on to identify the next potential area for more general exploitation. If it continues to receive an income stream from previously leveraged knowledge, it may appear that this corporate centre is still adding value. This is simply not true; *its* value adding role finishes when the knowledge is successfully passed to all the other business units.

There are many examples of corporate centres that have expanded dramatically on the back of a high continuing income stream that was generated by one highly value-adding opportunity to leverage existing knowledge. The problem is that most of this continuing added value is then dissipated by the higher level of costs incurred by the much larger corporate centre. As previously stated, the business units may continue to exploit this centrally provided knowledge for many years, but they no longer need the corporate centre in order to be able to do so. The centre only justifies its continuing existence by identifying new ways to add value. Even worse, this large corporate centre can become much more directly intervening in the operations of the business units and may seek to impose inappropriate central 'competences' on these business units.

Leveraging the product development process

Of course, the ideal sustainable consultant style corporate centre will identify and exploit a progressive series of competitive advantages that enable the group to establish a very strong corporate advantage. This may involve managing the group's exit from some businesses where the corporate advantage is no longer relevant. The Intel group is a good example of this.

Intel was founded in the 1960s to make memory chips and, based on this chip expertise, it launched the 4004 microprocessor in 1971. The group implemented an innovative strategy for its microprocessors in that it deliberately targeted the end user as its customer, rather than the Original Equipment Manufacturers (OEM) that most competitors were selling to. This strategy obviously took time to come to full fruition but the group emphasised new design wins (i.e. new customers) rather than sales volumes or even new products. In 1980, Intel had 2500 new design wins and then in 1981 it got Ford Motor Company as a customer. By 1983 150,000 Ford cars per month were being fitted with Intel microprocessors. Then, in 1984, Intel beat Motorola to win the IBM personal computer contract with its 8088 microprocessor.

During this period Intel had licensed its microprocessor designs to several other manufacturers for a number of reasons. It stopped these manufacturers investing in R & D directly and it gave Intel a more guaranteed demand for each new product innovation. These competitors were primarily selling to OEMs, which were not Intel's main targets, and this helped to make Intel's product architecture the industry standard. IBM also required a second source for its PC microprocessors.

However, Intel then stopped this licensing strategy and this forced previous licensees to reverse-engineer all of Intel's new products. This gave Intel about a one year time advantage on its new products and therefore refocused the corporate advantage to its product development process time scales. Intel now had to develop and market new generations of technology faster than competitors could copy them; it rapidly halved its product development time to well under one year, and keeps reducing it even though the technology gets more complex. The group moved to parallel generation development in three locations [California, Oregon and Israel] where completely new product ranges are started each year.

Intel's next move was into chip sets and then motherboards, which drastically reduced the entry barriers into the PC manufacturing industry. This gave it much greater competitive strength relative to the existing dominant computer companies, such as IBM, Compaq and Toshiba. Effectively Intel, with very strong help from Microsoft, was commoditising the actual PC industry. This was reinforced by the 'Intel Inside' marketing campaign aimed directly at consumers. This was launched in 1991, when direct consumer sales of PCs were still not that significant. Intel's market dominance meant that OEMs competed for the exclusive right to use the latest Intel design, because consumers would pay a premium to buy products incorporating these components. Once competitors were able to match this technology, Intel would drop its selling price significantly, but it would already have launched at least one, if not two new products, for which it could charge premium prices.

The development of Intel's microprocessor business had been funded by its early success in memory chips but this success did not continue. During the 1970s the Dynamic Random Access Memory (DRAM) chip market was growing dramatically and Intel was a profitable leading player. However, the dramatic growth attracted many large-scale Japanese competitors and the battle for cost leadership started. Matsushita, Mitsubishi, Toshiba, NEC, Fujitsu and Hitachi all built large-scale production facilities and forced down selling prices to levels at which Intel could not make a profit. In 1985 Intel decided that this had become a commodity business to which its speed of product development and group branding had no relevance. Thus it exited from memory chips and sacked 30 per cent of its workforce.

The key to sustaining such a strategy is clearly focusing on a limited number of things and ensuring that the knowledge gained in one part of the organisation can very rapidly be leveraged elsewhere in the group. This applies as much to new process innovations that will reduce the product development cycle as to the actual technology developments on which the group depends. A critical element for any such dominant technology group is avoiding 'shooting itself in the knee-cap' every time that it launches a new generation of products, that automatically reduces the value of its existing product range. So far, Intel has succeeded in this where IBM, as discussed in Chapter 7, did not to the same extent.

Sustainability issues

Intel has remained a highly focused group, with well-understood corporate advantages, an appropriately innovative culture and a strong central leadership role. However, as shown in Figure 6.6, scope configuration groups can comprise quite diverse businesses if the corporate centre is leveraging more general core competences. The problem is that these more general advantages are less difficult for competitors to copy and this can reduce the group's long-term sustainability. Interestingly it is possible to have a highly specific corporate advantage that binds together an otherwise wide range of businesses,

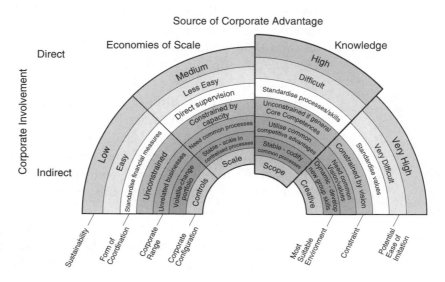

Figure 6.6
The Rainbow Diagram:
Sustainability issues.

but this can also limit the long-term value adding capability of the corporate centre. This can be illustrated by considering the Disney group's development under the leadership of Michael Eisner.

In the early 1980s Disney was in serious financial trouble after it raised a lot of debt to pay 'greenmail' to buy off a hostile corporate raider who had threatened to break up the group. The corporate centre had previously made several poor acquisitions and invested heavily in real estate and this management team was replaced in 1984. When Eisner took over, Disney basically produced movies, operated theme parks and licensed consumer products, but all these were operated as separate businesses. Also these separate businesses had problems. Attendances at the theme parks were falling and film production had experienced serious cost overruns that had led to a $30 million loss in 1983.

Eisner's initial focus therefore was to improve the core product performance; 14 of the first 15 films produced after he joined were profitable. The group also re-released several of its great animation films from the past and then developed some new blockbusters. However, the key move was to increase the value share that Disney captured from its intellectual content, and Eisner created a central corporate strategy team to focus on that. This started to transform Disney from a 'creator of content' to a 'creator and distributor of content'. The group moved directly into retail to create 'a different shopping experience' and build a more direct link with consumers. This sought to leverage the Disney brand and the specific service culture of the group, where customers are the 'audience' and employees are 'performers'.

Disney dramatically expanded its distribution capability with the acquisition of Buena Vista and then ABC/Capital Cities, which included ESPN and cable channels. This enabled the group to launch its own Disney channel. The year 1985 was the 30th anniversary of Disneyland's opening and the associated advertising campaign increased the number of visitors. However, the problem was that Disney captured too little of the total expenditure of these visitors. Thus Disney quadrupled its on-site hotel rooms and dramatically expanded the range of facilities, adding MGM studios, golf courses, conference facilities, the Disney Institute, etc. It became a complete vacations solutions company, having also expanded its theme parks internationally and moved into cruises as well as Broadway musicals.

Effectively all these businesses not only try to leverage the Disney characters but also comply with the fundamental positioning of the group as a 'family entertainment' company. Thus Disney has brought its specialised knowledge about entertaining kids and adults to a much wider range of businesses. For 15 years this created a large amount of shareholder value but, almost inevitably, there is a limit as to the leverage capability of such a specific corporate advantage. If the group tries to spread it too far, it can significantly, and possibly permanently, damage the critically important customer loyalty that has been built up over many years.

Another illustration of this stretch concept is the Virgin group, which relies heavily for its brand positioning on the highly irreverent and exciting lifestyle of its founder, Richard Branson. The group started life as a record label before moving into music retailing. It developed a strong brand image that appealed to young consumers and the group then applied this branding to air travel, financial services, mobile telephones and some consumer products. In each case, its positioning was significantly different to the established products on the market and reinforced the overall brand imagery. Also the Virgin group added value was focused on this brand positioning as the actual product delivery was either completely outsourced or achieved by bringing in a proven top management team with relevant industry expertise. However, the group then tried to apply its branding knowledge to the British railway industry following its privatisation. The relevance of the group's branding with its emphasis on 'fun plus a no-nonsense easily understood product offering' to this product group is much more difficult to understand.

Leveraging knowledge through franchising

The Virgin idea of increasing the potential for leveraging a group's specialist knowledge without losing focus is not new. Many groups have dramatically accelerated their rates of growth by exploiting their knowledge effectively through the efforts of others. As long as the group retains control over the key value-adding knowledge, it should also receive the vast majority of the resulting shareholder value that is created. A common way of implementing this type of corporate strategy is through franchising out the actual localised operations of the group, such as is done by fast food restaurant chains like McDonald's, and retail chains like Body Shop and Benetton. However, the earliest and best example is Coca-Cola, and it is interesting to see how the group has developed its corporate strategy over time, while always maintaining its focus on leveraging its control over its incredibly strong branding.

Coca-Cola Inc. was able to grow, initially in the USA, very rapidly by focusing on the manufacture of its syrup concentrate and the brand advertising for its soft drink product. The actual production of the finished consumer product was outsourced to over 1200 franchised bottlers spread across the USA. These bottlers were set up with territorial exclusivity, perpetual contracts and a fixed syrup price. The bottlers did very well during the market's rapid growth but the USA market matured in the 1970s with growth rates falling to 3 per cent per year. These franchisees then looked on Coke bottling and distribution as a good profit generator but no longer a high potential business.

Also Coke's bottlers were, by definition, locally based and therefore the group was not structured to do regional and national deals with the rapidly expanding retail chains. Pepsi-Cola could do this as it owned many of its larger bottlers and by 1977 Pepsi had an equal share to Coca-Cola in USA supermarkets. Coca-Cola needed to restructure its bottlers but the perpetual contracts and fixed price syrup made this potentially very expensive.

The new CEO, Robert Goizueta, used a significant product development to achieve this in 1981. The company had developed a high fructose corn syrup as an alternative to sugar in the syrup concentrate that reduced the cost by 20 per cent. Goizueta made the lower cost product available to bottlers on a condition of amending the original contracts. During the 1980s Coca-Cola then acquired many of its bottling franchisees and focused on developing the areas of other good bottlers. This significantly increased its asset base and reduced its return on equity, even though these bottlers were themselves highly profitable.

In 1986, therefore, Coca-Cola Enterprises was set up as a holding company for these owned bottlers and a majority stake was floated on the USA stock market. This meant that Coca-Cola no longer had to consolidate its remaining minority stake, so its return on equity rose back to its previous very high levels. Also the group generated over $1 billion in cash that could be spent on acquiring more bottlers. This model was replicated around the world as the group grew internationally with its large anchor bottlers that effectively controlled a country or region being partially owned by Coca-Cola Enterprises.

By the mid-1990s Coca-Cola had a dominant share in the soft drinks market outside the USA and this generated 80 per cent of its $4 billion operating profit. However, the growth rate in many of these markets is now slowing significantly and the group faces increased competitive pressures in many countries. This is being generated not only by its traditional competitors such as Pepsi-Cola, but also from new entrants such as Virgin Cola and retailer own brand Cola products which are sold at much lower prices. Coca-Cola has to date failed to leverage its consumer branding expertise and in-depth knowledge of production and distribution channels across into other product areas. It is therefore, in some senses, a victim of its own success and its stock market rating has inevitably fallen as investors and analysts lower their future growth expectations. The group could deliver continuing short-term growth in profits by reducing marketing support for the brand but obviously this would be at the expense of the company's longer-term future.

Conclusion

The scope configuration can sustain the value-creating role of its corporate centre as long as this consultant style centre can identify areas of knowledge that can be exploited more widely across the group. For many large groups this eventually becomes increasingly difficult. This can result in an excessive level of direct intervention by the centre as it either seeks to leverage inappropriate competences or becomes much too transactionally involved in the operations of the business units.

There are many examples of these directly intervening corporate centres then changing their focus from leveraging knowledge to directly reducing costs. In other words the transactional leadership emphasis and lack of knowledge advantage has changed the corporate centre to the manager style of the scale configuration. As discussed in Part I, this is particularly likely as the industry matures and the basis of competition becomes selling price rather than added value. Thus, if the latest knowledge that has been leveraged across the group was to do with 'how to reduce costs', it is easy to see how the corporate centre could decide to implement such cost reduction itself through centralising certain core processes or support activities.

A consultant style corporate centre should focus on its transformational leadership role so that its process expertise changes the way in which the business units themselves compete. However, once the centre has spread any specific knowledge and this is being applied by the business units, it ceases to add value until it identifies the next source of leveragable knowledge. In some cases this causes the corporate centre to try to stimulate the creation of new knowledge and this effectively means that it is trying to make the transition to the creative configuration. This creative configuration is considered in Chapter 7.

Chapter 7

The creative configuration

Introduction

Any corporate centre that seeks to create value through operating in the creative configuration has to overcome three significant challenges. First, it has to achieve a very high degree of buy-in from a wide range of people across the organisation to the key vision and associated set of values that the centre establishes as the core common elements of the group. Second, it has to achieve this while employing an indirect method of involvement in the underlying businesses. Third, even achieving this buy-in does not guarantee the creation of added value by the corporate centre, as the true added value reason for the creative configuration continuing as a group is generated by the business units working together to create new corporate know-how. This means that all creative configuration groups should be highly innovative, as they develop new know-how on a regular basis that can be exploited within the group, as is shown in Figure 7.1.

Thus the creative configuration corporate centre has to establish an environment across the group that motivates people from different business units to work together to create new value-adding ideas *for the group*. The corporate centre can facilitate this process by bringing different parts of the organisation together to work on group based projects and it can also encourage more informal contacts across the group. Both of these can be stimulated by more formal corporate centre-sponsored group-wide events such as conferences, training programmes, R & D exhibitions and a regular communication process covering all the business units.

The corporate centre is trying to create a strong group identity that subsumes the individual business unit cultures into a greater whole.

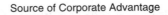

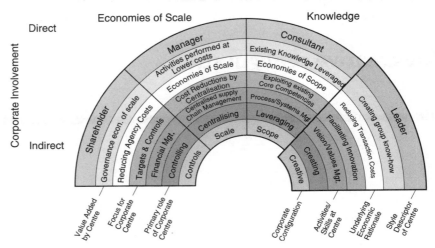

Figure 7.1
Corporate configurations:
The Rainbow Diagram.

This should mean that, although the separate businesses within a creative configuration group may operate in very different markets employing different technologies incorporated into dramatically different
products that are sold to different types of customers, all the business
units in the group have a common feel to them. Consequently
managers at various levels can be moved around the group by the
corporate centre. Such moves, particularly at very senior levels, are
often used as a way of reinforcing the group's vision and values.

The critical role of the centre in the creative configuration is the
development and communication of, and achieving commitment to,
this corporate vision and set of values. As a result, the real corporate
centre should be quite small and cohesive. However, in some creative
configuration groups, there may seem to be a quite large corporate
centre as some critical know-how creating processes, such as Research
and Development, appear to be centralised. As is discussed in depth
in this chapter, the key issue is where the control over these R & D
resources resides. In a creative configuration group, these resources
are actually controlled, and often provided, by the business units
rather than being directly controlled by the corporate centre.

If the leader style corporate centre is successful in stimulating the
creation of new corporate know-how, it faces a fourth challenge. The
centre now has to find a way of exploiting this new know-how without
destroying, or at least severely damaging, the very fabric of the group.
Leveraging existing knowledge across a group by direct intervention is
the domain of the scope configuration. The consultant style of corporate centre is very different from the leader style of centre in the creative

configuration. There are many examples of groups that start out in the creative configuration but, once they start to be successful, they rapidly make the transition to the scope configuration. Unfortunately this can often stop the generation of new corporate know-how as business unit managers increasingly focus on their own businesses and the exploitation of existing knowledge.

However if the corporate centre can find a mechanism to exploit the new know-how while maintaining the innovative corporate culture, it can continue to create value in the most sustainable way of any of the four corporate configurations. Unfortunately there is an obvious danger of continually creating new know-how but never managing to exploit any of it to create shareholder value. Such a group would undoubtedly be an intellectually stimulating and exciting place to work, until it went bankrupt!

A true leadership role

The creative configuration has the only corporate centre with a true leadership role, which is why its corporate centre style is described as leader, as is shown in Figure 7.2. This leadership role is critically important to the success of the group and should have a transformational, rather than transactional, focus. The corporate centre is seeking to change what the group does, rather than merely make it more efficient at doing what it already does.

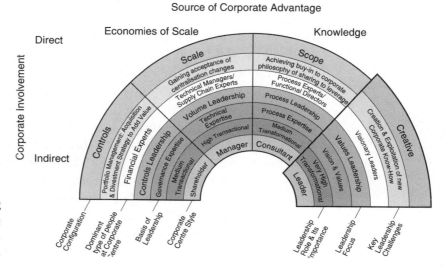

Figure 7.2
The Rainbow Diagram:
Leadership roles &
challenges.

Interestingly this is often achieved in a seemingly tangential way due to the indirect involvement of the centre in the day-to-day operations of the business units. However, although the involvement may be indirect, a leader style corporate centre can have a dramatic impact on the underlying businesses through the establishment of the group's vision and underpinning set of values. These can be established at such a challenging level that the business units have to revolutionise their ways of doing business if they are to have any chance of achieving the vision set by their corporate centre. This makes the business units much more likely to co-operate with each other to try to find new ways of working, or new products, etc., that may make the challenge achievable.

Of course, the leaders in this corporate centre must be able to win the total commitment of the business unit managers to the group's vision. This is the ultimate test of their leadership capabilities and a successful creative configuration group needs visionary leaders who can win the hearts and minds of most of the people in the group. In the controls configuration grudging acceptance of, and reluctant compliance with, the targets set by the shareholder style corporate centre is almost all that is required, but this would be completely unacceptable to a leader style corporate centre.

Indeed, if the group is to stay in the creative configuration success-fully, the corporate centre normally needs to develop even more challenging visions before the business units achieve the current one. It is now very common for companies to have a very general vision that can never actually be achieved and to motivate employees by establishing very stretching but just about achievable missions. These stretching missions must be measurable and should have a completion date, which makes it easier for the corporate centre to move the target as this completion date gets closer. Thus, although the leader style corporate centre emphasises the corporate vision and accompanying set of values, this leadership is not soft and fuzzy. In successful creative configuration groups the centre sets very demanding standards, both for itself and the business units within the group. This should be clear from the examples discussed in this chapter with GE being an excellent first illustration of a demanding leader style corporate centre.

GE, under Jack Welch, has been discussed in general earlier in the book but to really understand how the leader style corporate centre works we need to look in much more detail. Jack Welch took over a very successful company in 1981 that had already had a succession of very highly regarded Chairmen and Chief Executive Officers. Indeed a critical element in GE's continued success was the emphasis that the group put on developing the best general managers. For example, the selection process that ended with Welch becoming Chairman and CEO began in 1974 when a number of internal candidates for the job were identified. Virtually all the losing candidates went on to become CEOs of other major companies.

Jack Welch implemented the concept of 'integrated diversity' which meant: 'The drawing together of GE's different businesses by sharing ideas, by finding multiple applications for technological advancements, and by moving people across businesses to provide fresh perspectives and to develop broad based experience'. This constant focus on innovation across the group was brought into stark focus through a series of very challenging group-wide mission statements from the corporate centre.

The first of these was made in 1981 and was 'Be No. 1 or No. 2 in your industry, or Get Out'. This was done to refocus the group after a period of very diversified growth in the 1970s, and explains the high level of divestments and acquisitions very rapidly after Jack Welch took over that were mentioned in Part I of the book. In some cases the challenge to improve a business unit's industry ranking necessitated a dramatic change in its way of working and resulted in cross-divisional initiatives as radically new solutions were sought.

In the second half of the 1980s GE's corporate centre identified another group-wide challenge that was to cut through the bureaucracy within the group. A 'work-out' initiative was launched across the group that was literally designed 'to take work out of business processes', i.e. to re-engineer business processes in the business units. The key is that this initiative was stimulated by the corporate centre but implemented by the business units themselves. The process was started in 1988 and by 1992 over 200,000 employees in the group had been through work-out training. Each business unit's employees were able to propose 'bureaucracy busting' initiatives and the business unit's top management had to give an *immediate* 'Yes or No' response. This created a dramatic change in GE's organisational culture from its previously centre driven 'command and control' to a much more participative style that tries to realise the full potential of all employees. An important element in this mission was to transform the group internally so that it 'developed the sensitivity, the leanness, the simplicity and the agility of a small company'.

However, the biggest change was stimulated by Jack Welch's third major initiative. In order to avoid becoming forced to sell increasingly commodity style products to ever more powerful customers, GE sought to move into selling total solutions to a customer's problems. This involved building much closer relationships with many customers and understanding the 'total cost in use' to the customer rather than merely the selling price gained by GE as a supplier. As a result GE moved much more into the provision of services than it ever had before and this was only practical if its business divisions worked closely together. Thus GE Capital, which had previously focused almost exclusively on consumer finance, became involved in offering financing deals on many of GE's big-ticket technology products. For example, in 1993 GE Capital became the largest aeroplane leasing company in the world following its deal with the financially troubled GPA group. GE did not stop at financing and, in jet engines, the group manufactures, provides financing, performs maintenance for the airlines and sells spare parts. Following its acquisition of airline overhaul facilities, it also maintains jet engines produced by its competitors. The divisions still work in a highly decentralised way and develop their own competitive strategies that, in both GE Capital's and Aero-Engines' cases, can involve significant acquisitions. In addition they share ideas and work together to find new applications for technical innovations.

The next major initiative was in improving quality through its now famous 'Six Sigma' quality programme that aimed to eliminate defects by the year 2000. Once again, the visionary corporate centre specifies the scale of the challenge and the business units have to create the know-how to achieve the required improvement in quality. A critical element in this is sharing of ideas across the group so that the idea can be developed and improved by other divisions. This is greatly facilitated by the group's internal business school that uses ideas from within GE and both develops and disseminates them. The role of Crotonville, which is where the business school is located, is therefore to accelerate the process of spreading existing knowledge around the group, so that it can be improved and transformed into genuinely new know-how. The regular rotation of senior managers around the business units further reinforced this concept of redesigning the business before it is broken.

Yet GE also believes in delivering results in the short term as well as transforming itself to be more competitive in the future. Throughout Jack Welch's 20 years in charge of the group, its earnings per share grew in every year and indeed in every quarter of every year. Obviously there can occasionally be a conflict between 'delivering the numbers and sharing the group's values', particularly where the values are as clearly stated as they are for GE. The group states that it believes in 'honesty and integrity, individual responsibility and opportunity, and an interdependent balance between responsibility to customers, employees, society and shareholders'. As Jack Welch himself might have put it, 'If you make the numbers and share our values, that's great; share the values but miss the numbers and you get a second chance; miss the numbers and don't share the values and you leave. Those who make the numbers, but do not share the values cause the biggest problems to the centre as it agonises over whether they can be made to buy into the group's values'.

Continually creating new know-how

Of course the most obvious examples of creative configuration groups would appear to be those that are totally dependent upon the creation of new know-how for their survival, let-alone continued success, e.g. technology led groups. However, many of these have actually made the transition to the scope configuration because of an increasing level of direct intervention by the corporate centre in order to exploit the knowledge that has already been created by the group. As mentioned in the introduction to this chapter, it is in practice possible to maintain a position in the creative configuration even though the corporate centre appears to be quite large, as long as most of the resources located in this centre are actually controlled by the business units.

A brief consideration of the Canon group and the role of its 2000 strong corporate centre may make this clearer. Canon was founded in 1933 as the Precision Optical Research Laboratory, from which it developed its base in precision mechanics to fine optics. It has been producing lenses in-house since 1939 and developed an X-ray camera in 1940. From here, it moved into new technologies such as medical equipment, semiconductors and microelectronics producing calculators, copiers, word processors and computer peripherals. The group has always retained the manufacture of key value-adding components in-house.

The corporate centre sees its main role as the development and constant re-emphasising of the vision of the company. It believes that technological leadership is critical to its future success and that this depends upon innovation across both technologies and existing product groups. This explains the centralisation of basic technology research that may have relevance to more than one business group. Canon is organised into global product divisions with local sales units, so that its primary strategic drivers are the product groups with the geographic regions and functional disciplines playing a secondary role. Consequently the centralised Research & Development and Marketing

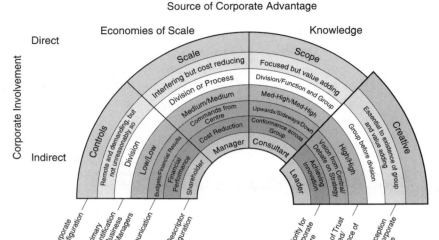

Figure 7.3
The Rainbow Diagram:
Implications for organisa-
tional culture.

resources are accountable to the individual product groups. This means that while *all resources* are seen as belonging to the group, they are effectively 'loaned out' to the business units to work on cross-functional projects. These task-forces have the authority to make their own decisions and have been responsible for several major new product innovations.

The creation of this large 'virtual' corporate centre allows most managers to pass through it at least once in their career and this creates a very strong identification with the group, rather than with their original business unit. As shown in Figure 7.3, this is very important to the organisational culture needed in the creative configuration, where employees should identify with the group before their own division. If most managers 'pass through the centre' and realise that they still retain a great deal of managerial discretion and authority when 'working there', there is likely to be the high level of trust between the centre and the business units that is also essential in the creative configuration.

However, this process also provides the corporate centre with the ability to challenge the performance of the business units, particularly with regard to innovation but also regarding cost structures. This should result in a healthy and constructive debate between the centre and the business units about the strategy that is required to deliver the centre's challenging vision. In a successful creative configuration group such as Canon, the business units should consequently view the corporate centre as being value adding and essential to the continued existence of the group.

The planning and control process

Of course this perception of the corporate centre as being value adding should be based on reality and this depends upon the critically important planning and control process that is implemented in this innovative type of group. As shown in Figure 7.4, the planning and control process for the group should emphasise the cross-divisional initiatives, new ideas developed and new products launched. This means that business units and individuals should be rewarded not just on the performance of their own businesses but on the contribution that they have made to the future of the group. The corporate centre is therefore trying to identify new group-wide competences that can be translated into shareholder value and, where necessary, to facilitate and accelerate the creation of the required underpinning know-how. At the same time it seeks to avoid the key risk that the group fails to exploit any of the new know-how that results from the exploration processes undertaken by the business units. This can be achieved by the use of appropriately tailored performance measures and by instilling a good financial evaluation and control culture within the business units.

History of 3M

A good way of illustrating this process is by considering 3M, as to many people it represents the archetypal innovative group. 3M was founded in 1902 as a corundum mine, but the quality of the output from the

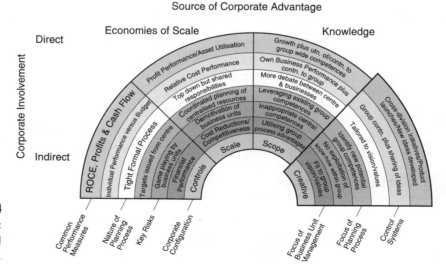

Figure 7.4
The Rainbow Diagram: The planning & control process.

mine was so poor that only one ton was ever sold to the original target customers. The company struggled for several years, using the poor quality abrasive output to make sandpaper before, in 1914, it developed its first innovative product, a cloth abrasive. The general manager, William McKnight, was an accountant who had become a sales manager but, fortunately for the group, he had an insatiable curiosity. Following the near immediate collapse of the originally single product dependent company, McKnight was also determined to build a diversified portfolio of products. Hence he encouraged experimentation, along with the associated learning failures. An early example of such a failure was a move into car wax and polish in 1924 that had to be abandoned. However the contact with automobile paint shops generated another opportunity that was to be spectacularly successful. There was a need for a foolproof masking tape for this market and 3M invented one. Later, when customers wanted a waterproof packaging tape, the group developed its masking tape technology to what ultimately became the Scotch tape range.

Similar stories abound in the history of 3M, including the world famous development of 3M's 'Post-it Notes', but the critical element is that 3M institutionalised the evolutionary process that resulted in these innovations very early in its lifecycle. From 1925 onwards, its technical manual specified that 'every idea should have a chance to prove its worth' so that the group had an ideas 'generating and testing' process. These ideas had to be genuinely new and they had to meet a demonstrable human need.

In order to generate new ideas the group has its 15 per cent rule, under which technical staff are allowed to spend 15 per cent of their time on projects of their own choice. Staff can also receive a technology sharing award when one of their ideas is shared with and taken up by another business unit. 3M has always kept the group broken up into small autonomous divisions with an ideal size of around 100 people and $250 million in sales revenues. This means that most new ideas will have a significant impact on the business unit, while this may not be true at the group level given that there are now over 40 product divisions and over 60,000 internally developed products ranging from roofing granules through various types of tapes to bioelectronic cars.

Group structure

Each business unit has its own laboratories that are essential to the future of the division and the group; thus there are nearly 200 laboratories working on well over 1000 new product developments at any point in time. These are co-ordinated by the central technical function which identifies and then disseminates new technologies. There is a very strong culture that products can belong to the business unit but the technology belongs to the group and should be shared. This is facilitated by regular technical forums to discuss new ideas and there is an annual technology fair where marketing and production staff can see what is being developed.

Indeed 3M's technical employees are heavily linked into the marketing process and many marketing managers started their careers in research and development. Sales and marketing are meant to understand in depth exactly how products are used by customers and to feed this back to their technical colleagues. Also the technical director at each business unit acts in a customer liaison role, as understanding specific customer problems has created many new product opportunities for the group.

Each product division is meant to fund its own growth by investing in R & D but the centre can get involved in particularly high profile projects. These are those identified to have both the potential to generate significant levels of shareholder value and to change the basis of competition in the specific marketplace; i.e. the new product should continue to produce super profits for several years as competitors will take time to catch up. For these projects, the corporate centre can provide ring fenced funding and a dedicated business team, including technical and financial support from the centre where necessary. It is quite possible that the new product may lead to the creation of a new business unit if it is very successful.

Thus the corporate strategy stresses new product development through a decentralised structure but with the emphasis on business unit performance.

Performance measures used

One way of keeping the emphasis on new products and technological innovation is to set targets regarding the proportion of sales revenues that must come from new product launches. In 3M the objective for all business units is that 30 per cent of sales revenues should be derived from products launched in the last four years. The group also looks for a 25 per cent rate of return on sales revenues, as its products should be in the early stages of their technology lifecycles when selling price is not the critical basis of competition.

The group has also been gradually introducing the concept of economic profit in order to get a more direct linkage into shareholder value at the business unit level. This financial discipline is achieved by having financial analysts integrated into every business team. Their role is to educate all the team members in the key financial risk and return relationships for this innovative group. In reality 3M is relatively risk averse in that it is very happy to experiment and have failures as long as these failures are on a small scale. It also emphasises acknowledging when something isn't working and closing it down, rather than keeping it going to see if it will somehow turn itself around. Also cost management is inbuilt into the culture and reinforced by the team based financial analysts. With this financial knowledge and culture spread throughout the business units, the centre can focus on stimulating the creation of new corporate know-how, confident that its business units have the competences and incentives to translate this know-how into shareholder value.

Embedding this financial focus within the business units enables the leader style corporate centre to concentrate on developing and communicating the critically important vision and set of values that bind the group together. In the other indirect method of involvement, the controls configuration, the shareholder style corporate centre focuses on the financial performance of the business units, and normally their short-term performance. It does this because there is no over-riding group vision or common set of values, other than making more money, that justifies the business units remaining as part of the group. As discussed in Chapter 4 this makes it much easier for a controls configuration company dramatically to change the portfolio of businesses comprising the group than it is for one in the creative configuration.

This eventually places a strain on the leader style corporate centre as the core business units compete in increasingly mature markets. In 3M's case, 75 per cent of the group's products use technologies that coat something with something else. The group has lots of patents and other forms of protectable technology and deliberately markets many niche products, although most are sold in office products, automotive and metalworking markets. Like GE, it prefers to be No. 1 or No. 2 in each market where it competes; if the niche market is quite small, 3M can dominate it while still keeping its business units small. However, as these markets mature, selling price is likely to become a more important factor and this will increase the pressure to realise economies of scale in manufacturing. If this happened 3M's smaller business units could become a disadvantage. To date, of course, the group has avoided this pressure for change by continuing to create innovative new products that do not compete primarily on selling price.

The risks of success

For many leader style corporate centres the major pressure for change actually results from the success of the organisation, as the overall group seeks to exploit its new competitive advantage in order to create the maximum possible shareholder value. This is particularly the case for single product groups, where the success of the main product can create an explosion in the opportunities available to the business. However, particularly in high technology industries, these opportunities can be quite short-lived and consequently need to be rapidly exploited before competitors can respond.

It is therefore not surprising to find corporate centres directly intervening to ensure the full potential is realised from the current competitive advantage, as shown in Figure 7.5. Unfortunately, by moving to intervene much more directly in the operations of the business units, the corporate centre may significantly adversely affect the continuing success of the group. The key to success in the creative configuration is the stimulation by the corporate centre of the creation of *new know-how* rather than leveraging the existing knowledge that exists within the group. The challenge therefore is to ensure that the business units are themselves motivated and incentivised to exploit the existing knowledge so that the corporate centre does not need to change its role to do this. An analysis of the development of Microsoft should help to illustrate the challenges that are involved.

The founding of Microsoft

Microsoft was founded in 1975 by Bill Gates and Paul Allen with an amazingly challenging vision, 'to make software that will permit there

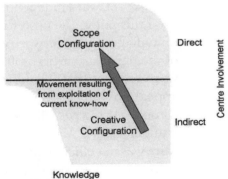

Figure 7.5
Increasing intervention from the centre.

to be a computer on every desk and in every home'. Initially they hired their brightest friends plus four experienced programmers and a key objective was to hire only the very best people even from the outset. Fundamental to their perception of the company's future was the ability of its people to think creatively, rather than the existing knowledge that they had when they were hired. Thus the new company rapidly developed an incredibly intensive recruitment process that involved up to ten interviews, tests of problem solving capabilities and thought processes, and the individual's work habits.

This was formalised after 1989 when Steve Ballmer joined Microsoft and took over the co-ordination of recruitment; he wanted 'people who are smart, who work hard and who get things done'. In the early years, these employees all worked very long hours and developed a very strong corporate culture. The company quite deliberately recruited fewer people than were really needed; what was known as the 'n − 1' factor. However, salaries and benefits were not excessive, but staff were motivated by getting shares in the company with the result that many become paper millionaires following the Initial Public Offering of Microsoft shares in 1986. This made Bill Gates a billionaire at the age of 31, and subsequently a number of other Microsoft employees have achieved this level of wealth as well.

However, the first major products of the company were very pragmatic solutions to major opportunities. The first personal computer kit product was launched in 1975, the Altair by MITS, and Microsoft adapted BASIC to create a condensed version called PCBASIC, for this new product. However, the licensing rights were owned by MITS so that Microsoft could not itself sell its PCBASIC product to any of the clones that rapidly appeared on the market. Eventually, after a legal battle, Microsoft regained its product rights and walked away from the Altair product.

This move was important as it signalled the start of Microsoft's drive to make software independent of specific computer manufacturers. Up until this point, the power in the industry had been with the hardware manufacturers as software was customised to optimise the performance of the hardware. Microsoft set out to create an industry standard software product that would run on anybody's hardware. This had great appeal to applications programmers as they would not have to completely rewrite all their applications software for all the different manufacturers. Achieving this common platform meant that the software was not efficient in its usage of computing resources, but hardware costs were now starting to fall rapidly and computing power was increasing exponentially. Thus Microsoft's timing was right. By 1979

Microsoft had contracts for PCBASIC from around 50 OEMs and annual sales revenues were over $1 million.

In 1980 IBM decided to enter the PC market and it was in a hurry. Consequently it outsourced the processor to Intel and wanted an external supplier for both the software languages and the new concept of an operating system for its PC. Microsoft offered both products to IBM within its one year launch time frame, even though it did not have an operating system. It bought a system called Q-DOS (Quick and Dirty Operating System) that was really a clone of Digital Research's market leading system, CPM. The redeveloped system was named MS-DOS but, this time, Microsoft retained the third-party licensing rights and made MS-DOS an 'open' system so that programming specifications were published. This was done to encourage applications developers to write MS-DOS based products. By the end of the 1980s Microsoft had locked in virtually all the major global players and had very high sales revenues from MS-DOS with incredibly strong gross margins.

Microsoft was therefore then able to implement in full its long-term corporate strategy for dominance of the software industry. A key element in building its initial leadership position was its emphasis on 'get the customer first, deliver the technology later', as shown by its first two major products. The next stage was that the product must deliver for all the potential customer groups, even though their requirements differ. Previously software providers had normally focused on only one group rather than embracing OEMs, application developers, systems integrators, distributors and end-users. If this total coverage could be achieved, then Microsoft's products could become the industry standard, around which all the other elements making up the industry would have to fit. This was helped by a very aggressive marketing strategy that included flat fee pricing to encourage OEMs to incorporate Microsoft's software in every machine that they shipped. Once established as the industry standard, the pricing was switched to a per machine rate!

With each new development in the industry, Microsoft has looked for ways to further strengthen its position as the industry standard; by linking its products, by linking with other leading players such as SAP, and by continuing to use its aggressive marketing strategies.

Potential problems

At the time of the group's flotation in 1986, Microsoft had around 1200 employees and it moved to its campus site in Redmond, 10 miles east of Seattle. Each employee had a standard small office that they could decorate as they wanted and the site had a subsidised cafeteria, free coffee, etc. as people still spent a lot of their time at work. Bill Gates kept reorganising the business into small work groups and he personally monitored 100 bi-weekly status reports from project and program development teams. He still had an immense personal impact on the business through his high energy, challenging involvement at many levels. He was a classic visionary leader of the group during this period. The management process during this period was therefore flexible and informal, although the company always used specific quantifiable objectives that were reviewed every six months: SMART objectives – **s**pecific, **m**easurable, **a**ttainable, **r**esults-based and **t**ime-bound. Reviews focused on learning from mistakes and the culture (fuelled by Bill Gates) was that the feedback was blunt and to the point.

By the mid-1990s, the company was scanning all 25,000 USA based computer science graduates to get 400 new hires, but it needed many more than this. It needed to hire several thousand people as the group continued to grow rapidly and it had 300 full-time recruiters to fulfil its aim of only hiring the best; this was restated as 'hiring better than they already had'. Inevitably, as the total employees grew to over 20,000 the organisation went through many changes and lost its original small company feel.

In 1996 Robert Herbold joined Microsoft as Chief Operating Officer after 26 years with Procter & Gamble. He defined recruitment as being Microsoft's No. 1 Core Competence, and made identifying future leaders into a more formal process. Thus the group moved to a key people review process that sought to achieve early identification and career planning. The objective was to create a group of better leaders and managers who would be capable of 'clearing the obstacles, making decisions quickly and defining clear goals'. This meant that Gates, Ballmer (he was made President in 1998), and Herbold would need to allow these new leaders to lead. Bill Gates then had 16 people in his Business Leadership Team and the process identified three waves of high potential future leaders.

However, this meant that the group had to review its employee feedback and development process. What about all the significant contributors to the company who were not identified as future leaders? How were these people to be developed, motivated and retained? To long-term employees, it was crystal clear what it took to succeed at Microsoft, but this was not true for the vast majority who had joined a much larger group in the more recent past. The Microsoft 'Competency Model' identified six success factors: taking a long-term approach to people and technology; getting results; individual excellence; a passion for products and technology; customer feedback; and teamwork. These factors were turned into 29 individual competences, with four levels of performance for each, so that performance reviews could be more formally compared across the organisation.

Unfortunately any such formality is not a full substitute for the much earlier 'meetings with Bill', which quite rapidly identified those employees who fully matched up to Microsoft's competency model! This problem was accepted by the group as it started to lose very good people. In-depth employee interviews highlighted complexity and bureaucracy as being major problems and the company sought to give its employees a new way of setting priorities, objectives and identifying what leadership in the group should mean. This was encapsulated in a new corporate vision that replaced the almost achieved 'a PC on every desk and in every home'. 'Giving people the power to do anything they want, anywhere they want, and on any device' should be a sufficiently stretching and challenging vision to motivate the business units to co-operate together to find completely new ways of moving forwards.

To facilitate this, Steve Ballmer has been appointed CEO and the group has been reorganised into eight new groups that are attuned to customers' needs rather than around technology issues. These new business units have more delegated authority with Ballmer acting as a 'leader of leaders'. The group is also seeking to influence the working culture, with Steve Ballmer publicly stating that he does not work weekends any more. This new structure has enabled Bill Gates to become exclusively Chairman of the group and has freed him to revert to the original visionary leader role that created the business initially. He can challenge the business unit leaders, and can also get involved in specific projects from time to time, but his main value-adding role is to be the embodiment of the vision and set of values that underpin Microsoft.

Reinventing the group

This refocusing of Bill Gates as the overall visionary leader of the group, but now supported by other senior executives who are also acknowledged as having significant leadership roles, should reinvigorate the long-term sustainability of its creative configuration positioning. The group is operating in a very dynamic environment and will need to develop new group skills to compete successfully once end-users no longer buy software but download it as and when they need it. As shown in Figure 7.6, the creative configuration is suited to such a dynamic environment while the scope configuration requires a more

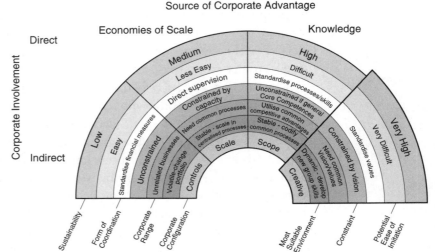

Figure 7.6
The Rainbow Diagram:
Sustainability issues.

stable environment so that the codified knowledge will still be relevant when it is applied more widely across the group.

As Microsoft grew ever larger there was a danger that the need to formalise the critically important people management processes would lead to the standardisation of processes and skills that is relevant to the scope configuration. When this is reinforced by an increased level of direct intervention from the corporate centre, the group has effectively made the transition to the scope configuration. The leader style corporate centre should focus on standardising values rather than processes, but bringing in senior managers from outside groups that are themselves very good examples of a different configuration can often create an unintentional transition to that configuration.

However, it is also possible for a large group to make these transitions when its management is completely home grown. Indeed, in the case of IBM, it took an external appointment to take the group back to its origins in the creative configuration.

The origins of IBM

In 1911 a merger of two small companies created the Computing, Tabulating, Recording Company but by 1914 the new company was in some trouble. It therefore recruited an outsider, Tom Watson Snr, to sort out its problems. He took over a business making mechanical devices for processing data and, from it, eventually created the modern IBM. The company had some further financial problems but, in 1924, Watson changed its name to International Business Machines and started to build the core values that were to be so important to IBM's later growth. He felt very strongly that beliefs come before policies, practices and goals, and he wanted to bring out the full energy and talent of the company's employees. In fact, Tom Watson openly admitted that he wanted to create an organisation of zealots, who would all totally buy-in to the vision of 'meeting the emerging needs of our customers' through 'selling service'. The company motto became 'Think', and everyone should 'go the last mile to do things right and seek superiority in all we undertake'.

The IBM culture was therefore built up in this period: well-groomed men wearing dark suits, no smoking, no alcohol, and marriage was encouraged. Watson instituted a 'promote from within' policy and liked IBMer's to socialise together to reinforce the culture. In the 1930s, by when IBM was market leader in tabulating machines, the company had its own 'schoolhouse' where employees sang IBM songs and stories about 'heroes' were told so that the company's beliefs were truly institutionalised.

A key element of this vision and set of values was that it was focused on the customer rather than being product centric. This made it easier for IBM, in the post-second world war period, to adapt to the rapid growth of the typewriter market. In the 1950s as a result, IBM had 72,000 employees and sales revenues of over $500 million.

Although IBM did not pioneer the computer revolution, it embraced it so emphatically that it rapidly came to dominate the new industry. Using its size, sales-force muscle, and marketing skills it had taken an 80 per cent share of the USA computer market by the end of the 1960s. IBM's customer focus led it to move internationally as its major customers did, and from this existing customer led strategy it then built leading market shares in many other countries as well.

The growth in sales revenues was very impressive (from $7bn in 1970 to $40bn in 1980), but the profits growth was even more impressive. In 1980, IBM had a 38 per cent share of the global computer industry's sales revenues but a 60 per cent share of its profits. This enabled the group to reinvest vast sums in Research and Development, massively outspending its competitors. At the end of the 1980s IBM was spending $9bn a year on R & D.

Problems set in

John Akers, a lifetime IBMer, took over as Chairman and CEO in 1985 and publicly predicted that IBM's sales revenues would grow in 10 years to $180bn from their $46bn level in 1984. This would still have been a slower annualised rate of growth than in the previous 10 years.

As a result of this growth expectation, IBM built an infrastructure capable of coping with this size of business so that the group had over 400,000 employees by the end of 1986.

Although IBM's sales were growing in several areas, its major source of profits was much more focused. As already discussed, IBM was late into the PC market but very quickly became market leader. Unfortunately even with $10bn of sales revenues this business unit was not shareholder value enhancing. Mainframe computers contributed the vast majority (60 per cent) of IBM's profits, due not only to their high share of total sales revenues but also to their very high gross profit margins (over 50 per cent). This was a market that IBM totally dominated, having a 44 per cent global market share and an 85 per cent share in the USA of the compatible mainframe market.

The problem for IBM was that this was one sector in the computer industry that was no longer growing. Increasingly computer systems were moving to client-server networks rather than the very large mainframes in which IBM excelled. This trend started in the mid-1980s but had grown dramatically as personal computing power and networking capability mushroomed. By 1994 client servers accounted for 50 per cent of total applications in the USA. What is particularly interesting is how closely IBM had been involved in these technological developments.

For example, Reduced Instruction Set Computing (RISC) is considered absolutely key to high performance work stations. RISC was invented by an IBMer, John Coske, but was initially exploited by Sun Microsystems and Hewlett Packard. In the early 1990s both these companies launched microprocessor based multiple parallel processor computers that were the equivalent of mainframes. This increased the competitive pressure that had been started by Digital Equipment Corporation (DEC) in 1989 with the launch of its first line of mainframe computers; these were priced at half the level of IBM's existing products. By 1993 it was estimated that traditional mainframe computing power was five to eight times more expensive than these newer technologies.

The financial impact of this was dramatic. IBM's hardware gross margins were slashed from 55 per cent to 38 per cent on sales revenues which fell 20 per cent in two years. This meant a $10bn fall in actual gross profits, from 1990 to 1992. The published financial results were also heavily impacted by the very large provisions that were made for headcount reductions ($6.7bn in 1991, $11.6bn in 1992); total headcount was back down to 300,000 by the end of 1992. The net results were that IBM reported losses for 1991 and 1992 of $2.8bn and $5.0bn after a profit of $6.0bn in 1990.

Not surprisingly the share price went into free-fall hitting around $40 early in 1993, having peaked at $175 in the mid-1980's. At the same time Standard & Poors, the credit rating agency, downgraded IBM from AAA (as good as it gets) to AA- (a significant fall). Indeed, there were several leading newspaper and magazine articles that openly discussed the possibility of IBM going bust.

A second outsider

On 1 April 1993, Lou Gerstner joined IBM as Chairman and Chief Executive. His impressive career had started at Harvard, followed by McKinsey. He then moved to American Express where he rose to President before he was, in 1989, hired by KKR to run RJR Nabisco following the leveraged buy-out. For the past four years, therefore, he had been reducing costs and generating net cash inflows to service and repay the $25bn of debt with which RJR Nabisco was burdened following the KKR deal. While at American Express, Gerstner had also become well-known for some aggressive cost-cutting strategies. However, he had never run a high technology products group.

In May 1993, Gerstner brought in Jerry York as Chief Financial Officer for the group. York had spent all of his career in the car industry, having been with Chrysler and before that with Ford and General Motors. [In August 1994, Gerstner brought in another complete outsider, Rick Thoman, to head up IBM's PC business. Thoman had a strong international marketing background and had worked with Gerstner for over 20 years at both American Express and RJR Nabisco.]

The 1993 financial results showed the scale of Gerstner's problems. Mainframe sales were down another 27 per cent, while PCs and services grew significantly. Unfortunately neither of these growth businesses made any real money, despite IBM gaining a 12 per cent share of the world PC market in 1993. Overall the group reported losses of $8.1bn, even though employee numbers were down to 255,000 by the end of the year. Lou Gerstner announced that his first priority was cost-cutting, with a target of $3bn savings in 1994 and another $1bn in 1995.

However, his next set of priorities started to reposition the group and significantly redefined the role of the corporate centre. This is particularly interesting as, in all his early pronouncements, he consistently stated that 'the last thing IBM needs now is a new vision, mission statement or strategy'. He then gave the group all of these and refocused everyone on creating shareholder value. He took IBM from being a product focused, technology driven company back to the 'global solutions' company that it had really been during its first period of success. He stated that 'IBM is too preoccupied with our own view of the world' and needed to get much closer to its customers; hence he formed specialist sales groups and consulting teams. He urged the business units to co-operate rather than compete, and refocused the group's software development on distributed networks.

Originally IBM's corporate centre allowed and effectively encouraged competition within the group, thus manufacturing business units could produce any products within the range and quote selling prices to any of the sales and marketing divisions. The logic was that if they were forced to compete internally, they should be very competitive externally, given that many of IBM's business units were bigger than its external competitors. Also this organisation structure continually re-emphasised the importance of mainframe computers to the current profitability of the group; 12 out of 13 major business groupings were highly dependent upon sales of mainframe computers. Not too surprisingly therefore, the proportion of R & D expenditure devoted to mainframe development actually increased in the period prior to Lou Gerstner's arrival.

Gerstner also made some seemingly minor, but symbolically important changes: he introduced casual dress to get away from the dark suit, white shirt and blue tie uniform that had previously made IBM employees so easy to spot. He opened up the company to buying technology if they hadn't got it, and to selling their technology to other companies, including competitors. He looked at strategic alliances and acquisitions as being valid to accelerate the rate of change of focus within the group. Thus IBM acquired Lotus Development for $3.5bn late in 1994 and also bought a large number of systems integration and consultancy businesses during the second half of the 1990s.

In 1997 this new focus was formally recognised with the creation of a Global Services Division. This new services business was competing directly against focused systems consultancies, such as Accenture, Cap Gemini Sogeti, Sema, EDS. These competitors applied a very different business model to that previously used by IBM. The consultancies made profits on the services that they provided and often supplied any required hardware at their cost. IBM's business model had been the reverse; the profit was made on supplying the computer hardware, and the software and consultancy was provided to gain the hardware sale. Interestingly IBM's internal financial planning and control system had emphasised product profitability analyses rather than highlighting the profitability of the group's major customers.

By the mid-1990s the stock market had started to regain its faith in IBM and the share price started to build towards its former levels. Indeed during the technology, media and telecoms frenzy at the end of the 1990s, the share price reached levels far above anything ever seen before. The shareholders believed in the reinvention of the group even though the major source of current profits was still mainframe computers, which had recovered much of their former sales revenues and profit margins, albeit possibly temporarily.

Summary

IBM's initial vision under Tom Watson Snr was to 'sell service' and to 'meet the emerging needs of our customers' and its initial dominance of the computer industry was achieved employing exactly those ideas. It was an expert at 'relationship marketing' before the term had been invented. Its sales force had unrivalled access to the key strategic decision-makers in the major USA corporations and they acted almost as strategic consultants rather than computer sales people. Not surprisingly, IBM focused primarily on the largest customers and these were the companies that needed big mainframe computers to process the mass of data that was critical to their businesses. Thus the product and the specific technology were driven by the customers' needs.

It should therefore have been relatively easy for IBM, with its very close relationship with these customers, to have identified 'their emerging need' for distributed processing and networking before its competitors. Given its huge R & D expenditure levels it should also have been quite possible for it to have developed the technology before anybody else. [Remember that, in fact, IBM did develop a lot of this technology but did not itself bring it to the marketplace.]

However, by this time, IBM's business units were being run by technologists and the corporate centre had seemingly lost sight of its key role within the group. In Lou Gerstner's words, 'It started to believe that it knew what was best for customers, rather than finding out what customers wanted and then giving it to them'. Also, unfortunately for IBM, at this time competitors were becoming much smarter and the external competitive environment was changing rapidly.

Competitors had gradually realised that they could not compete head on with a company as dominant as IBM. Therefore most existing competitors started to focus on specific segments of the IT industry, but equally specialist competitors were being attracted to enter the new very high growth areas. IBM was facing a 'death by a thousand cuts' rather than a knock-out blow by a single competitor.

Customers were also becoming more knowledgeable about the technology that had become so vital to the continued success of their own businesses. In the early years of the computer industry, IBM's brand name had stood for the low risk, reliable solution to your computing needs: it even used the maxim 'no-one ever got fired for buying IBM'. The strength of this reputation enabled IBM to obtain premium pricing even for 'me-too' technology. Yet its massive volume meant that its costs were the lowest in the industry, hence it generated incredibly high margins. Customers eventually became unwilling to pay a premium for the IBM name on the blue box. They were also much happier to have a range of computer suppliers, preferring to pick the best company for each particular element of its IT requirements.

Again IBM's dominant position in the industry should have given it forewarning of these changes but it had obviously stopped looking outside of itself to predict the future. As already discussed in this chapter, the creative configuration is most suitable for such a dramatically changing external environment. Unfortunately for IBM, its corporate centre was not operating in the leader style when its industry went through this dramatic upheaval. The good news is that the second coming of an outsider re-established the leader style corporate centre that enabled the group to recapture its previous focus on creating new know-how that is relevant to its customers, which nowadays like Microsoft includes everyone on the planet.

Conclusion

The creative configuration is the most sustainable way for a corporate centre to create shareholder value. The continuing creation of new know-how can enable a group effectively to re-invent itself as its external environment changes, so that there is no reason for the centre's value creation to cease.

Having said this, establishing and then maintaining a value-adding leader style corporate centre is also much more difficult than all the other styles of corporate centre. The need to get a high level of buy-in to the group's vision and values from the vast majority of people in the business creates a significant challenge for an indirectly involved corporate centre. This can be particularly difficult during a transitional period where the corporate centre is, of necessity, also having to force through other changes. Lou Gerstner's need to continue with the severe cost-cutting programmes made it even more problematical to establish a credible new vision for the group.

However, sending out tough messages should not be seen as being incompatible with creative leadership. Value adding corporate centres in the creative configuration are not vague and fuzzy, soft things. They are very demanding, set stretching visions with tough values standards that have to be lived up to, and they are totally focused on creating value.

PART III

Working with the model

Chapter 8

Changing configurations

Part II considered each of the corporate configurations in detail and, in this part of the book, we consider other aspects of applying the overall model in practice. This chapter focuses primarily on movements around the model and thus builds on the migrations and transitions that were discussed in earlier chapters.

Before considering major transitions that can be made from one side of the model to the other, the chapter deals with several other aspects of the configurations model that are important to applying the model successfully over time. Most corporate centres can be described as being congruent with the underlying businesses comprising the group, but this may not be the most value-adding option. A congruent, or coherent, corporate centre is one where the strategy of the centre is aligned with the strategy being implemented by the business units. Moreover this alignment of strategic intent should also apply to the organisational structures and processes that are applied within the group.

It is, however, possible to add value by applying an opposite approach in the corporate centre to that adopted in the business units, as has been illustrated in some of the case studies used in Part II. These issues are drawn together and developed in this chapter, but the majority of groups do still utilise a coherent approach to the selection of the style of their corporate centres. These corporate centres may cease to add value eventually and the group may then try a more radical approach which is to introduce a divergent corporate level strategy. This involves changing the corporate centre configuration without changing the focus or composition of the business units within the group. The objective is to generate positive creative tension between the centre and these business units as they adjust to the new role adopted by the centre. Obviously there is a risk that the corporate strategy becomes incoherent and consequently value destroying. This can happen when the change introduced by the corporate centre creates too much confusion within the group, or when the business units do not accept the changed role of the centre. Quite frequently this occurs when the corporate centre changes the configuration at the same time as it significantly changes the composition of the businesses comprising the group.

In order to understand the implications of these transitions from one configuration to another, some transitioning models are introduced and then applied to the more dramatic potential transitions around the model. Also a concept we have called 'swimming upstream' is discussed. This looks at ways in which corporate centres try to avoid the natural movement through the model that is suggested by the corporate lifecycle which was introduced in Chapter 3.

Opposites can attract

An important element in the corporate configurations model is the separation of the value-adding role of the corporate centre from that of the underlying business units. This means that it is not essential for the source of corporate advantage that is generated by the activities of the corporate centre to be the same as that employed by all the businesses comprising the group. Indeed a combination of opposites can represent a major way for corporate centres genuinely *to create* new sustainable shareholder value rather than, at best, *capturing* slightly more of the existing value-creation potential of their underlying businesses. This value creation can either result from an apparently counter-intuitive application of specific corporate centre skills to a radically different set of businesses or, as is discussed slightly later in this chapter, because the traditional congruence between corporate centres and their business units had reached the end of its value adding economic life.

Traditionally the corporate centre reinforces the shareholder value enhancing focus of the businesses within the group, i.e. it either assists in further cost reductions or in further value adding through the creation or dissemination of knowledge. There are many successful examples of each of these reinforcing corporate centre configurations, and several have already been discussed in Part II. In the controls configuration, Hanson epitomised the lean corporate centre that implemented the tight planning and control processes that enhanced the financial performance of its wide-ranging, but mature and cost competitive business units. Both the corporate centre and the underlying businesses concentrated on improving financial performance by cutting out unnecessary expenditure and increasing economies of scale. Growth was largely generated from acquisitions and the corporate centre was perfectly willing to sell any business unit if the price offered exceeded the internal assessment of its value.

At the other extreme, 3M is a good example of the creative configuration where the corporate centre seeks to facilitate the creation of new corporate know-how within the group. This results in innovative technology products, and the whole culture throughout the group is geared to organic growth from completely new products generated by sharing ideas with other business units. These new products should produce sufficiently high margins to more than compensate for the high costs involved in achieving the required level of innovation. Thus it can be said that these corporate centres reinforce the focus of the business units rather than challenging or changing it.

A more radical role for the corporate centre is one where its focus appears to be diametrically opposed to the underlying source of competitive advantage that is being applied in the group's business units. The possible combinations for the four corporate configurations are illustrated in Figure 8.1. In the controls configuration, there are many examples of groups of highly creative, knowledge-based businesses that have been successfully developed by the application from the corporate centre of very sound financial controls and governance practices. The corporate centre of WPP established the key financial

Figure 8.1
Opposites can attract.

management practices, such as managing working capital, and the resulting limited number of key performance indicators. This enabled it to control effectively the overall group, without unduly interfering with, or constraining, the creativity and client focus of the often high profile, charismatic leaders at the individual business unit level. [The developing role of WPP's corporate centre is discussed later in this chapter.]

The reverse position can be illustrated by GE where the very high profile, charismatic leadership of Jack Welch was applied to a large number of largely technically focused mature, business to business divisions. At first sight, a congruent corporate centre configuration would appear to be the controls configuration with its cost reducing, target setting focus and emphasis on financial performance. The leadership from the corporate centre of GE has consistently exerted a highly challenging but creative influence across the whole of the group. It has created a clear group vision and culture across this otherwise highly diversified collection of businesses, not least through the series of major group-wide initiatives. In fact one of the strengths of the GE type of approach is the total unreasonableness of the demands from the corporate centre. By requesting a 50 per cent cost reduction or a 0 per cent defects rate, the centre forces the business units to completely reinvent their business models; an incrementalist approach simply will not get close. This has also stimulated a significant level of value enhancing cross-divisional initiatives as business units work together to develop a radically new business model. Setting unreasonable goals in order to stimulate new really creative solutions can work provided that managers in the business units have a high level of trust in their corporate centre and identify primarily with the group, rather than with their current business unit. GE logically therefore moves senior managers across divisions and through the corporate centre in order to build this trust and group identity that generates the buy-in to the group vision.

In the example of WPP, the reverse is true in that it is critical to the credibility of the corporate centre that the targets which are set for the business units are stretching but attainable. The corporate centre is establishing itself as the expert in governance and controls, leaving the essential creative leadership to the heads of the business units. Hence the performance measures used must motivate business unit managers to perform appropriately – a clear illustration of the 'what you measure is what you get' school of motivation. Thus this type of controls configuration corporate centre may look quite similar to that of a Hanson type of group, despite the underlying businesses being very different. Equally the GE corporate centre will have greater similarities to that of 3M than Hanson, in spite of their more similar underlying businesses.

These successful examples of opposites combining to create sustainable value both have indirect methods of involvement in their business units, although neither could be described as remote and uninvolved. As indicated in Figure 8.1 it is quite possible for a directly intervening corporate centre to have an equally value adding but opposite focus. However, our research highlights that this becomes more difficult as the level of direct intervention increases.

In the scale configuration, the corporate centre adds value by centralising certain activities and processes in order to achieve economies of scale. If this centralisation only involves support activities, the business units may be more able to focus on their key value enhancing, knowledge-based core processes. However, once the centralisation starts to encompass these key value-adding processes, there is a strong possibility of conflict between the cost reducing focus of the corporate centre and the value-adding focus of each business unit. Thus the business units will be seeking appropriately tailored approaches to each specific market segment that they are addressing, while the corporate centre will require more standardisation across the group in order to increase the cost savings from centralisation.

There is a similar argument in the scope configuration where the knowledge leveraging corporate centre is seeking to add value to its cost focused business units. This can work if the knowledge that is being spread across the group relates to 'reducing costs', as this can accelerate the cost reductions in other business units. However, if the corporate centre adopts a very high level of direct intervention it will increase its own costs significantly and may try to force all business units to implement the complete range of cost-reducing initiatives that it has identified. Many of these may be inappropriate to the specific circumstances of some business units or be counterproductive given the cost-reducing measures that a particular business unit has already adopted. It is normally more value adding for a cost focused consultant style of corporate centre to codify cost-reducing knowledge and then make it generally available to all the business units within the group, while strongly recommending it to some specific business units, i.e. a medium level of direct intervention. Too high a level of direct intervention can destroy the value-adding attraction of apparent opposites.

Congruent, divergent and incoherent corporate level strategies

Whether the current role of the corporate centre is the traditional rein-forcing congruent one or the attraction of opposites, there is a very strong probability that eventually the law of diminishing returns will set in. For some configurations, as shown in Figure 8.2, this economic life can be extended through acquisitions and divestments which change the composition of the portfolio of businesses comprising the group. This enables the corporate centre to apply the same value-adding style to a new set of businesses and therefore can defer the need for the centre to consider changing its corporate configuration. Acqui-sition strategies are often important in the controls, scale and scope configurations but are less common in the creative configuration, although GE and, more recently, IBM have made significant use of acquisitions. Divestments can be used to maintain the size of the total group so that the corporate centre does not need to grow excessively as the portfolio changes. This is particularly relevant where the corporate centre is no longer adding value to the divested business units, which can be the case in the controls and scope configurations.

Notwithstanding this economic life extension through acquisitions and divestments, the value-adding potential from any specific style of corporate centre will eventually start to tail off. As discussed in Part II, the creative configuration is the most sustainable value-adding position for a corporate centre. However, even for a tremendously innovative group such as 3M, there may well come a time when the markets and products that its business units serve are so mature that cost competi-tiveness becomes critical even for new products launched into these markets. For the next most sustainable configuration, the benefits from leveraging existing knowledge across the group can generate long-term

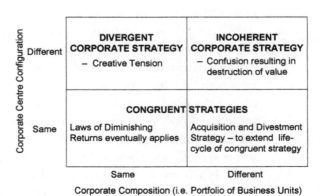

Figure 8.2
Congruent, divergent and
incoherent strategies.

sustainable competitive advantages for the business units. However, once all the existing knowledge has been codified and transferred across the group, the corporate centre itself is no longer adding value, but it may still be adding significant cost. Also, of course, eventually this existing knowledge will cease to be a competitive advantage as competitors catch up and the expectations of customers change.

Interestingly the scale configuration is one where the corporate centre appears to be required to continue to exist in order to sustain the delivery of the value created by its centralisation of support activities or core processes. Once all the economies of scale that can be generated by this centralisation are being fully realised, the operational management of these centralised facilities could in practice be transferred to an independent third party or to a new business unit set up specifically for this purpose, as was discussed in Chapter 5. Thus even though the cost reduction advantage may continue, there is no longer a true value-adding role for the manager style corporate centre.

Similarly in the case of the controls configuration, eventually all the business units in the group will have improved their financial performance as much as possible by implementing the leading edge financial planning and control processes developed by the shareholder style corporate centre. This level of performance should be maintainable in future, but the corporate centre is no longer adding further value to the group. This is where the possibility of divergent strategies emerges, as is shown in Figure 8.2.

In a divergent strategy the centre pursues a new value-adding strategy that appears to be at odds with the strategies being pursued within the business units. The original corporate strategy could have been the common reinforcing congruent strategy or it could have been applying the logic of opposites being attractive. Whichever was the previous case, the corporate centre now makes a conscious decision to make the transition to a different configuration in an attempt to restart the value-creation process. As shown in Figure 8.3, the new rate of value creation is likely to be lower than from the original configuration, as logically the corporate centre should select the most value-adding style first. However, this incremental value creation has to be compared against the flat and then declining level that would be produced if the original corporate strategy was continued. The danger is that the changes result in an incoherent value destroying strategy, which is also shown in Figures 8.2 and 8.3.

The divergent corporate strategy means that the corporate centre is challenging the business units in a very different way. This could be achieved simply by changing the performance measures used within

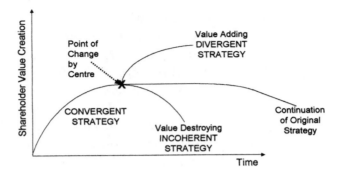

Figure 8.3
Shareholder value impact
of divergent and
incoherent strategies.

the group, without altering the nature or level of the involvement of the corporate centre. For example, in a group like GE that had been implementing a creative configuration strategy, the business unit performance measures would emphasise the adherence to corporate values, the degree of collaboration on new cross-divisional ventures and the sharing of complementary know-how with other business units. A divergent corporate strategy for the post Jack Welch era could be to move back to the controls configuration by changing the performance measures to emphasise exclusively the profitability of individual business units.

Such a change would probably result in a rapid movement towards internal transfer pricing and royalty agreements for any shared know-how or collaborative ventures, together with a much tougher financial evaluation of any cross-divisional initiatives, and rigorous questioning of the real value added by adhering to the corporate values of the group. In some creative configuration groups, where a lack of financial rigour and challenge has resulted in wasteful expenditures on group based projects, such a divergent corporate strategy may initially create substantial value. However, the sustainability of this type of divergent strategy can be questioned, as can the current corporate centre's capabilities to implement such a change successfully.

A potentially more sustainable divergent strategy can be where the corporate centre has been implementing a very tough financial controls regime across its range of businesses. The emphasis on the financial performance of individual business units normally results in a very limited degree of integration among these businesses and this may not be a problem. However, if the value created by this shareholder style of corporate centre is now diminishing, the corporate centre may wish to implement a divergent strategy.

This could take the form of seeking to leverage existing knowledge more widely across the group. The corporate centre now needs to intervene more directly in the operations of its business units and needs to identify what existing knowledge may have a wider application within the group. It then requires the systems and process skills to codify this knowledge so that it can actually be applied in the other business units. Clearly a potential constraint on the value creation from this transition to the scope configuration is the diversity of the business units within the group. Some rationalisation and regrouping may be required to avoid the spreading of inappropriate knowledge across business units where it clearly adds no value.

It is therefore not surprising that divergent corporate strategies often coincide with a change in the top management team at the corporate centre, although there are examples of these divergent strategies being implemented by existing management teams. The marketing services group, WPP, which was used as a main case study in Chapter 4 on the controls configuration, now appears to be moving to the more directly interventionist scope configuration. The term 'moving' is deliberate as the corporate centre still requires daily cash flow figures from the business units, but the move is an attempt to respond to the demands of its major multinational clients. Increasingly these multinationals, such as Procter & Gamble, IBM, Ford, Nestlé, Unilever and Kelloggs, want to have integrated marketing and communications strategies on a global scale. WPP is one of very few marketing services companies that can provide this, but it requires a much more integrated approach from its previously quite individual business units. More than 200 of WPP's largest clients now use at least four of the main services provided by the group. Accordingly WPP has appointed 'global leaders' to manage every aspect of these key multinational accounts, and individual country managers are responsible for integrating people and clients on a local basis. This process is co-ordinated at the corporate centre by a chief talent officer, whose role is to ensure that the group has the right people in the right jobs.

The challenge for the corporate centre is to maintain clarity as to what is its value-adding role within the group and to manage the inevitable tension that is caused as business unit managers adjust to the new roles and expectations within the group. If this transition is badly managed, it could degenerate into the value-destroying confusion of an incoherent strategy. The most dramatic opportunity for such major confusion is, as shown in Figure 8.2, when a group changes its corporate configuration at the same time as radically changing the composition of the group. This would appear to be at the heart of the problems at Marconi (GEC as was) that were discussed in Part I of the book, and to have contributed to the corporate problems at several other large groups. In practice, neither the corporate centre nor the business units have any relevant experience to rely on when everything changes, which results in an intolerable level of confusion across the group with a consequent destruction of shareholder value.

Of course, as discussed earlier, there are many reasons for a group deciding to move to a different corporate configuration. One which was considered in Chapter 3 was the concept of a corporate lifecycle, but many corporate centres seem to prefer to try to move the opposite way round the configurations model, i.e. they want to swim upstream.

Swimming upstream

The logic of the corporate lifecycle is that even corporate advantages have economic lives during which they can create real added value, when applied to any specific set of businesses. For example, as the industries in which the group is involved mature, the basis of competition tends to become selling price rather than product differentiation. Eventually therefore a consultant style corporate centre may need to become more focused on cost reduction than adding value through leveraging existing knowledge advantages across the group.

For the corporate centre, this would represent a fundamental change in its role and the skills required in its key personnel. At least the nature of involvement remains direct, so the centre is not attempting to change its focus of activity at the same time as it is changing its nature of involvement. However, once the focus changes from value adding to cost reduction, a forward looking manager style centre may realise that, in time, it will also need to reduce its direct level of intervention as it moves eventually to the controls corporate configuration.

To try to avoid this, we have seen a number of corporate centres attempt 'to swim upstream', by going back to a value-adding focus while retaining their direct method of intervention. This is diagrammatically illustrated in Figure 8.4.

There are two very different ways in which swimming upstream by such a corporate centre can create substantial added value for the group. As mentioned earlier, one way involves changing the portfolio of businesses that make up the group. If the corporate centre has highly developed, but very specific, process management skills, which are relevant to either branded products or high technology goods, it should ensure that the businesses within the group can make use of these value adding attributes. Thus, if the products sold by certain business units are now very price sensitive commodities, this corporate centre is no longer adding value to these businesses. However, it could

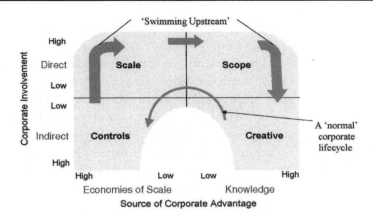

Figure 8.4
The corporate configurations model: Swimming upstream.

still add considerable value if other appropriate businesses were either started or acquired by the group.

Alternatively the corporate centre could adapt its value-adding skills somewhat so that they are still relevant to the existing businesses within the group. As already stated, the corporate advantage must be considered separately from the competitive advantages being employed at the business unit level. In the maturing business units, competition may be based on relative cost levels and selling prices. The corporate centre could try to reduce total group costs by centralising support and/or core activities, but alternatively it could seek to leverage the knowledge gained by these cost conscious businesses. In other words, the centre still focuses on leveraging knowledge across the group, but now the knowledge relates to those cost reduction ideas that have broader applications. If the corporate centre possesses broadly based systems and process management skills and has very extensive knowledge of the businesses in the group, it may be able to refocus its value adding role without needing to change its skills or personnel, or the businesses within the group.

Figure 8.4 shows that it is also possible for corporate centres to 'swim upstream' from the controls configuration and even the scope configuration, i.e. respectively to the scale and creative configurations. In both these cases the nature of the corporate advantage stays the same, while the nature of involvement of the centre changes.

However, these transitions are fundamentally different to the previous example. 'Swimming upstream' from scale to scope really involves a corporate centre avoiding the lifecycle change from scope to scale, so that its knowledge leveraging skills remain relevant to the group. It is less common to find such examples of stopping transitions from creative to scope and scale to controls. Thus these examples are genuinely cases of corporate centres changing their roles (i.e. their methods of involvement), rather than trying to preserve their existing one.

The less difficult transition is from the controls configuration to the scale configuration, particularly if the controls corporate centre has a low indirect form of involvement. As discussed in Chapter 3 there is relatively little perceived difference in direct and indirect involvement at the middle of the vertical axis; very low indirect involvement often means regular, almost daily, informal as well as formal contact between the centre and the businesses, while very low direct intervention could mean a small amount of centralised support activities.

If the controls corporate centre develops very strong governance skills and its managers are truly leaders in their fields, it may seem logical for them to centralise certain financial management processes (e.g. treasury and accounts payable). This would enable the centre to exert greater direct control (e.g. over cash flows), and could generate savings across the group. Of course it is then very common for the corporate centre to expand this centralisation initiative and this may result in the centre needing to expand the skills of its managers and change its leadership style.

Swimming upstream from the scope to the creative configuration is more challenging. The corporate centre in the scope configuration has a direct involvement in leveraging existing knowledge across the group, and it is trying to develop an indirect method of facilitating the creation of new corporate know-how. The easier element should be the change in the nature of involvement; but for most corporate centres becoming less involved is never easy! In the transition from controls to scale the centre of course becomes more involved.

The process and systems skills within the consultant style corporate centre may enable it to develop processes for cross-divisional collaboration. However, the centre now needs to create a commonly shared vision and set of values that will bind the businesses together, and create a strong group identity.

Deciding whether any of these alternatives is attractive to a particular group requires a precise positioning of the corporate centre within its current corporate configuration. This can be done by using the scaled axes in the model. However, a very clear understanding of the particular characteristics, and their relative strengths, of the current corporate centre and its managers is critical to this type of decision. It should hopefully also be clear that the best strategy for any corporate centre could be to avoid the necessity to swim upstream at all. This might be achieved by planning and then controlling any major changes either to the composition of the group or to the source of its corporate advantage. A rapid reaction to a shock may be preferable to no reaction; but avoiding, or at least predicting, the shock is even better still. This would also avoid the leadership challenges faced during any sudden and unexpected transition.

Transitioning models

In order to analyse the differing types of changes and attempts to avoid change in corporate configurations we have used a few analytical tools, which we find help in highlighting the key factors impacting on any particular type of transition. These transitioning models do not themselves predict the need for a change in the corporate configuration but they indicate whether a required change will be relatively easy or difficult.

The first of these useful analytical tools compares the level of control that can be exercised by the corporate centre with the degree of context there is across the group. By degree of context, we mean the level of similarity there is among the businesses comprising the group. This means much more than whether they are in the same industry, as it may be that a high degree of common processes across business units from very different industries will create a high context group. Conversely a common competitive advantage (such as low cost leadership) applied right across a group by a consultant style of corporate centre through the leveraging of corporate knowledge may still leave a low context group, because the businesses are, in all other respects, very different. This type of group could include both goods and services companies, industrial and consumer markets, high and low technologies, etc. and it would therefore appear, to the casual observer, as diverse as the most widely spread shareholder style group. [This transitioning model also builds on the framework introduced in Figures 2.7 and 2.8 of Chapter 2, which examined the degree of buy-in required and the number of managers involved.] This transitioning model indicates how the corporate centre can create any changes that it feels are needed in its relationship with its business units. The different corporate centre styles have very varying abilities to achieve their desired transitions from one corporate configuration to another.

One impact of the different levels of context in an organisation is the degree to which the group is constrained or not. Some groups find it relatively easy to continue growing, either organically or by acquisition, while others quite rapidly seem to run out of steam. As we are interested in corporate strategies and the role of corporate centres, the group's overall growth need not be totally determined by any single industrial economic lifecycle.

Indeed, some corporate centres may find it attractive to concentrate their business units within different industries that are each at a particular stage of development (e.g. creative configurations focus on industries during start-up and launch, scope on high growth industries, scale during consolidation and early maturity, and controls in later maturity and even gradual decline). However, a high degree of context within a group can act as a constraint on the long-term growth prospects of a group. The leader style of corporate centre normally has a relatively high degree of context in the group as all its companies must fit with the clearly stated vision and guiding principles. They must also be able to benefit substantially from the cross-fertilisation of ideas and the resulting generation of corporate know-how. Ultimately therefore this type of group should be constrained by the ability of the corporate centre to facilitate and add value to this process of sharing across the group. Thus it can take exceptional leadership qualities for any creative configuration to sustain itself if the group becomes highly diversified in terms of the industries in which it is involved; however, even this can be, and has been, achieved!

As previously stated we regard this is as the main achievement of Jack Welch (Chairman and Chief Executive Officer of General Electric). He transformed what was already regarded as a successful group through the policy of 'integrated diversity'. All business units within GE are expected to be either No. 1 or No. 2 in their own industry (but they are not too keen on being No. 2) but each is left to develop its own tailored competitive strategy to achieve this position. However, these diversified, decentralised business units are also expected to share ideas and to find new group-wide applications for technological innovations wherever they are developed. The corporate centre acts as far more than just the controlling shareholder in these businesses as senior managers are regularly moved around the group, and the centre preaches a remarkably consistent message of its vision and the values that must be applied by all the businesses in the group.

This does not mean that this style of corporate centre must be 'liked' by everyone in the group. Jack Welch's nickname was 'Neutron Jack'; this hard-nosed image was reinforced by GE's annual employee grading system that automatically ranks the bottom 10 per cent as unsatisfactory performers, who are either moved internally or out of the company. This image was also reinforced through his personal style and the candid way in which he expressed his vision for the group and the responsibilities that this vision forced on to managers and indeed,

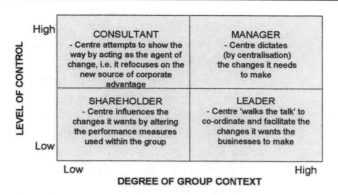

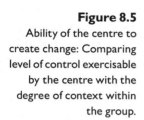

Figure 8.5
Ability of the centre to create change: Comparing level of control exercisable by the centre with the degree of context within the group.

all employees (e.g. 'Control your own destiny or someone else will'). Despite this image, or because of it, the group was tremendously successful over the 20 years of his tenure as CEO.

In order to do this, as explained in Chapter 2, it is essential that the corporate centre achieves a very high degree of buy-in from a very high proportion of the employees, not just very senior managers, within the group. As shown in Figure 8.5, this means that the leader style of corporate centre has to use this high degree of buy-in to overcome its lack of direct control, which is an inevitable result of its indirect involvement in the businesses within the group.

Similarly the centralising, scale configuration actually increases the degree of context within the group as it expands the level of centralisation. If only support services are centralised the level of context may be relatively low and the group is relatively unconstrained in its future growth. As centralisation incorporates more core processes, the businesses within the group start to become more similar and the future growth becomes more constrained. The centre may need to find new businesses that it can justify adding to the group, but these must be able to benefit from this increasingly specific set of centralised activities.

Conversely, as the scope configuration and the controls configuration expand, they are likely to reduce the level of context within their groups; i.e. they will probably become more diverse as they add new business units that can benefit from their particular corporate advantages. Thus they are both relatively unconstrained in their future growth prospects. However, the downside for these configurations is that they are also most likely to need to divest businesses from their groups, once their particular corporate advantage no longer has strategic relevance or value-adding capability.

The level of control exercisable by the corporate centre is clearly affected by the nature of the involvement (a more direct involvement normally resulting in a higher level of control), but this impact is increased if a low number of managers need to be involved as was shown by Figure 2.7 in Chapter 2.

As shown in Figure 8.5, the four style descriptors highlight important differences in the ways that corporate centres can, in practice, bring about any desired changes in their groups. The shareholder style has to influence the changes that it wants by altering the performance measures used within the group. The new performance measures should be designed to encourage the behaviour in the business units that is required to achieve the changes that the corporate centre wants.

In the scope configuration with its consultant style, the higher level of direct intervention means that the centre can attempt to show the way to the business units by refocusing its own attention on the new area of corporate advantage; i.e. it acts directly as the agent of change rather than trying to influence others to change.

For the manager style, the higher degree of group context (i.e. the shared activities) enables the corporate centre to dictate many of the changes that it wants to see by altering the balance of centralisation and decentralisation in these key activities. The leader style has to influence the businesses to change direction by modifying, or further clarifying, the vision of the group. If this corporate centre has previously established a very clear long-term vision and a well understood, agreed set of guiding principles, the creative configuration can be the most difficult to change significantly. It has a high degree of buy-in from a large number of managers across the group, and has to work indirectly to influence the business units to change from a corporate strategy they are quite happy with. Not surprisingly, this configuration often only changes in response to a crisis.

A key element in successful transitioning by any style of corporate centre is therefore the relationship between the 'ability and willingness to change' of the managers involved (both at the business units and at the corporate centre) and 'the clarity' with which both the need for, and the type of change required, are articulated by the corporate centre. This relationship not surprisingly therefore has been used as another transitioning model, as is shown in Figures 8.6 and Figure 8.7.

The clarity of change dimension refers to the articulation of both the need for change and the type of change that is required. An immediate issue is that this change is normally articulated and driven by the centre but the major impacts are on the business units. The key dimensions of these changes are the scale of change, the pace of change, the type of

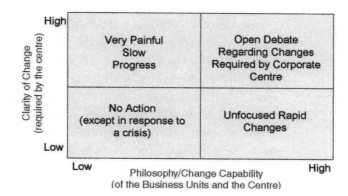

Figure 8.6
Transitioning models:
Clarity of change versus
change capability (I).

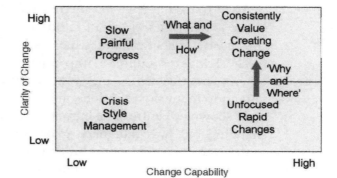

Figure 8.7
Transitioning models:
Clarity of change versus
change capability (2).

change, the impact of the change, the complexity of the change and the reason for the change. These multi-dimensions mean that the perception by the centre of any required change may not completely match with the perception of the business units. Indeed the perceptions of the business units within the group may differ and any such differences can impact the willingness to change.

In some cases the need for change may be identified by the business units themselves before the centre. This can cause frustration and resentment when the centre seeks to create change. Even worse is where the centre seeks to implement a different change to that identified by the business units. This often results in an unwillingness to implement the changes and some form of guerrilla warfare from the business units. Guerrilla warfare can also result if there is disagreement on the effects of the planned changes. If there is no real agreement between the centre and the business units on the original existing corporate strategy and configurational relationship, there can be no real clarity on the need for change to another configuration.

The ability and willingness to change can be referred to as the philosophy of the managers involved and with long-serving, senior managers, this philosophy can become very averse to almost any change. Not surprisingly, if the managers are unwilling to change or are actually incapable of change, even if the changes required are very clearly articulated by the centre, any progress achieved will be slow and relatively painful for all concerned. If the centre is not sure exactly what changes it wants, then the high resistance to change will ensure that the status quo is preserved. Where managers are quite willing to change but the corporate centre does not clearly and consistently articulate the required change, the result is a series of unfocused, often mutually inconsistent, rapid changes. The business units are responding very quickly to what they think the corporate centre wants, except they think that the corporate centre keeps changing its mind.

Any group that is facing the need to change obviously wants to be in the top right-hand box of Figure 8.6 because this leads to an open constructive debate about what changes should be made and how these changes should be implemented. The detailed processes of moving into this consistently value-creating box are obviously of great interest to many organisations, and can be developed from this model.

As shown in Figure 8.7, if business unit managers are quite capable of changing but have not been given the clarity they need from the centre, the corporate centre must work at improving its communication of the group's vision and long-term goals and objectives (the 'why and where' in Figure 8.7). If the existing corporate centre cannot provide greater 'visioning' clarity, the managers at the centre may need to be changed; but this means changing top management! Alternatively if divisional managers lack the ability to change, the corporate centre must help them with specific suggestions as to how the corporate strategy can be applied in their particular businesses (the 'what and how' in Figure 8.7). If these divisional managers are extremely unwilling, rather than unable, to change then, as an ultimate sanction, the centre may need to replace some of these managers in order to clear the blockage. However, these blocking divisional managers are probably very long serving, senior managers; the introduction of an early retirement programme is a common solution. Alternatively the centre may decide that it needs to adopt a more directly intervening method of involvement to stimulate the changes that it feels are necessary.

However, when applying this analysis with practising managers the start point can be in the bottom left-hand box of Figures 8.6 and 8.7. There is neither willingness to change nor clarity of the change required. In these cases we have found it very useful to change the descriptions on the two axes. It appears that management teams often see these issues as being the differences between agreeing on the interpretation of strategy (the causes) and agreeing about the

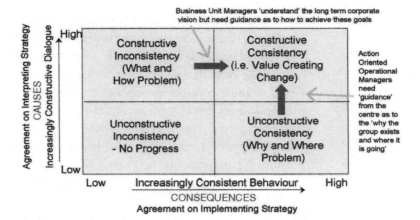

Figure 8.8
Corporate strategy:
Causes and consequences.

implementation of the strategy (the consequences), as shown in Figure 8.8. Restating the previous illustration, the business units could agree with the corporate centre about the over-riding corporate vision, its aims and overall objectives but disagree about how to achieve them. The result is that this business unit may have an apparently consistent long-term perspective but there is no relationship to their underlying competitive strategies. These business units need help with developing competitive strategies consistent with the overall group strategy (the what and how). Conversely, business unit managers may implement a rapidly changing array of very detailed competitive strategies but these have almost no relationship with the corporate vision; in other words there may be agreement on the implementation of the strategy but not on how the strategy is being interpreted with the result that there are too many initiatives. In this case, the centre needs to increase the agreement on the 'why and where' questions and can then leave the divisions to implement their own appropriately tailored competitive strategy.

The practical implementation of this process depends upon the degree of context in a particular group. In a 'low context' group, where there is limited commonality among the business units, the corporate centre can *impose* the required degree of agreement on the interpretation of the overall corporate strategy. There is normally the need for a much lower level of buy-in by divisional managers (e.g. the absence of overt hostility) and the centre must provide sufficient clarity on the vision and strategic objectives of the individual businesses within the group; there may be less need for great clarity on the group's overall vision. If there is no buy-in and agreement from divisional managers, the centre can restructure the portfolio of businesses through acquisitions and divestments. The key issue for such 'low context' groups is to obtain agreement on the 'what and how' of implementing strategy.

If this is not achieved, whatever performance measures are established for the divisions may result in dysfunctional behaviour by the divisions. This may be increased if there is a low level of trust within the group as can be the case in the controls configuration.

For a 'high context' group with its high level of similarity across its business units it is essential that there is great clarity on the interpretation of strategy (the 'why and where'). The high degree of context in the group requires a high degree of buy-in from divisional managers and, without agreement on the causes of success for the group, there can be no meaningful agreement on the 'what and how' of implementing the strategy. Once, and only once, there is agreement on interpreting strategy, the centre can seek to gain agreement on implementing this strategy. However, if necessary, this implementation can be delegated to the business units provided that there is total clarity and agreement on the interpretation of the strategy. This can be successful due to the high level of trust that exists between the corporate centre and the divisions, such as can be found in the creative configuration.

However, there may also be an inherent conflict between the type of change that is needed and the style of corporate centre that is best able to achieve it. Transitional styles may be needed just to facilitate the change, but this, of itself, creates the need for a subsequent further change.

Not surprisingly, we have found that organisations from the same corporate configurations have similar types of problems in terms of reaching the 'consistently value creating' status of high agreement on both interpreting and implementing strategy. These similar problems can have particularly significant consequences when these configurations need to stimulate a move to a different configuration. Some of these were discussed for each configuration in Chapters 4 to 7 and are briefly summarised for the creative configuration here.

Very few corporate centres in the creative configuration suffer from any substantial lack of understanding and agreement on the overall group vision; after all, communicating this is the main role for the corporate centre. However, this group vision and set of values may be the only common ground among the business units and the corporate centre has only an indirect 'facilitating and encouraging' role in these business units. Therefore it may not be too surprising if there is a lack of understanding and agreement on how this group vision is to be achieved. As has been stated earlier, the largest challenge for this corporate configuration is how does it ensure the full exploitation of any new corporate know-how that actually results from cross-divisional collaboration that it has 'facilitated and encouraged'.

In order to move from the top left-hand box of Figure 8.8 to the desirable top right, many creative configuration corporate centres may get much more directly involved in 'guiding' the business units; this may accelerate the exploitation of this new 'know-how' but may neither encourage nor facilitate the development of the next.

Major transitions

It seems logical to try to apply these transitioning models to some of the groups that have already been used as case studies in the book. In the major transition from the controls configuration to the creative configuration made by GE under Jack Welch's leadership, the key element from the corporate centre was providing clarity on the vision and values of the group. The previous role of the corporate centre had already developed a reasonable level of trust between the centre and the business units, but the business units were delivering the required level of financial performance in a wide variety of ways. This had resulted in a decade of diversification with the acquisition of many even more unrelated businesses but, equally important, many of these new business units were not leaders in their own industries. Thus the original shareholder style corporate centre 'influenced the change it wanted' by changing the performance measures used: 'Be No. 1 or No. 2, or Get Out'. Jack Welch increased the scale of this change by abandoning the group's previously highly structured planning and control process for his 'planful opportunism' concept.

The new leader style corporate centre then 'walked the talk' in the group by refining and developing the overall vision and set of values through establishing a series of challenging but quite specific missions for the business units. This was possible because the old style group had obtained a high level of buy-in to the previous role of the centre. Consequently Welch, who had risen to the top of the group under this previous regime, had the authority and credibility to retain this high buy-in to his newly defined role for the corporate centre. It is very interesting that this major transition was successfully implemented in a company that has such a low level of group context; as was shown in Figure 8.5 it is normal for creative configuration groups to have a high level of group context.

Equally interesting is the example of WPP because this shareholder style corporate centre has operated successfully with a high group context, that is not normally necessary for the controls configuration. Indeed the success of the group and the perceived planning and controls pre-eminence of the corporate centre should have created a good level of trust between the centre and its business units. This could make it possible for the corporate centre to make the transition to the creative configuration as was done by GE. To achieve this, the corporate centre would have to define a vision that would bind the group together and encourage the business units to work more closely together. This collaboration across the group should be driven by the business units rather than being orchestrated by the corporate centre, e.g. by setting up global account managers based at the centre. If the corporate centre takes a more directly intervening role it is moving to either the consultant or manager style, with very different consequences.

As already discussed it is much easier for a shareholder style corporate centre to make the move to the manager style, as the focus is still on reducing costs across the group. All that has changed is the method of involvement, as the centre intervenes more directly in the operations of the business units. This would be relatively straightforward for WPP's corporate centre as it already has very regular contacts with its business units and manages treasury and tax centrally. However, the key objective behind the new greater level of direct intervention by the corporate centre appears to be to add value rather than to reduce costs still further. Thus the centre is focusing on cross-selling services to major clients and getting the best business unit managers in the right jobs around the group. This effectively means that the group is seeking to move to the scope configuration where the leadership role is much more transformational than the previously transactional role of the current controls configuration. Both these configurations do have a lower emphasis on leadership from the corporate centre than the creative configuration, and this move also avoids the need for the centre to develop the critical group wide vision and set of values. The centre does, however, still need to provide clarity to the business units as to the need for the change and particularly of the need for a greater level of direct intervention by the corporate centre. Obviously this translates into a perceived reduction in operational independence at the business unit level.

Another issue that was raised in the section on transitioning models is the need for the corporate centre to make a temporary change in its style during a major transition. A very good example of this was IBM at the time of Lou Gerstner's arrival, when the group was facing a crisis. The corporate centre adopted a very directly intervening role in the short term to ensure that cost reductions were rapidly implemented, but it also drove the acquisition of Lotus Development as well.

This was done more as a very strong cultural change move to get rid of the 'Not Invented Here' syndrome that had become an issue within IBM. At the same time the corporate centre acted to send very clear signals as to its vision for the group and the values that should be applied by the business units in striving to achieve this vision.

Obviously there is a very real danger that the short-term actions will confuse the business units and detract from the longer-term re-positioning that the corporate centre is trying to achieve. This is why the temporary change of style of the corporate centre must be very specifically focused (e.g. implementing a major cost reduction initiative to rebase the cost levels of the group) so that once announced, the centre can move on to its new long-term role. Thus the responsibility for implementing the already announced cost reductions can be passed to the individual business units. The corporate centre can then revert to being indirectly involved but now focused on adding value through stimulating the creation of new group know-how. It can signal this new focus by changing the performance measures that are used across the group. The continuing use of now inappropriate performance measures is a very common feature of many of the mismatches in corporate configurations that have been highlighted in our development of this model.

Common mismatches

The simplest illustration of this is where a controls configuration has decided to make the transition to either the scope or creative configurations. As has been discussed neither of these transitions is easy to achieve, but they become impossible if the corporate centre insists on maintaining its previous tight budgeting system that had served it so well in the past. If the business units are still primarily held accountable for their individual short-term financial performance, this will remain their key focus. Therefore there will be very limited sharing of knowledge across the group or willing participation in cross-divisional projects unless, and until, some financial compensation has been agreed with the other business units. If the centre wishes to stimulate this 'group' ethos by moving the best managers around, it is not unheard of for business units to seek some 'transfer fee' in compensation for losing their star player!

Another common mismatch is where a scope configuration corporate centre finds that it has fully leveraged all the existing knowledge across the group. This consultant style centre can often seek to stimulate

innovation and the creation of new knowledge by its direct intervention. Interestingly, when this does not work, some such corporate
centres become even more directly interventionist by centralising
this process through the creation of 'innovation departments' located
at the centre!

A similar form of this inappropriate use of increasingly direct involvement by the corporate centre is sometimes seen in the scale configuration. The manager style corporate centre has added value by
centralising certain support activities and core processes but these
advantages have now been fully realised. In an attempt to create still
more value, the centre now attempts to leverage some existing knowledge across the group. This might be fine if the corporate centre
made the transition across to the scope configuration with all the associated changes in its focus and method of operating. However, to try
to do this while still maintaining its current cost reducing focus with
its operational management emphasis is very unlikely to prove value
adding.

Another illustration of a corporate centre failing either to identify
the need for a transition to another configuration, or at least to make
the required transition, is where the centre is still acting in the leader
style although the business units have progressed to the scope or even
the scale configuration. This means that the corporate centre is still
desperately trying to stimulate the creation of new know-how when
the business units do not know about the wealth of knowledge that
already exists across the group. Alternatively the basis of competition
for most of the business units has now become selling price so that they
are desperately looking for economies of scale from being part of the
group. Unfortunately the corporate centre is still locked into its now
redundant mind-set of creating a unifying group vision and underlying
set of values.

Conclusion

It is inevitable that any group will eventually need to move from its
current corporate configuration to a new more value-adding one.
Many of these transitions are difficult as they involve significant
changes to the nature of the corporate centre's involvement with its
business units or the source of the corporate advantage, or both.
However, if they are properly planned, which requires that the future
need for a change is predicted, these transitions can be successfully
implemented. If they are unsuccessfully implemented, they can create
a crisis for the group or, at least, the corporate centre's managers.

Even without prior planning there are many examples of successful transitions that have been made in response to some form of crisis in the group. However, most of these also involve some significant changes in the top management team. As this top management team is so important to the implementation of the corporate configurations model, the role of leadership is developed in the next chapter.

Chapter 9

Leading from the centre

Introduction

The corporation configurations model resulted from research into two related, major concerns of corporate strategy. First, the economic logic and justification of the multi-business corporation and, second, the organisational structure of this type of group, in particular the role of the centre. The main synthesis in this book therefore is the integration of economic and finance theory on the one side and organisation theory on the other.

Unfortunately these two communities rarely engage in dialogue, each discipline seeming to prefer to develop their own insights and then share them with like-minded colleagues; this is true for both academics and practitioners in these fields. However, as is the case with our creative configuration, significant value can be created by sharing across these functional boundaries and genuinely new know-how can be created, which really belongs to neither original functional discipline.

It is from this background that we seek to focus, in this chapter, on the key leadership issues that are raised by the corporate configurations model. This is obviously a critical area, not only as one dimension of the model represents the style of involvement of the corporate centre with its business units, but also because the resulting four corporate configurations raise such fundamentally differing leadership challenges for the top executive team at the centre of the corporation. Therefore this chapter starts by considering the different schools of thought regarding leadership. This identifies five critical leadership capabilities that are then developed and applied to each of the four corporate configurations. Not surprisingly this highlights that any leader may be successful in one configuration but fail miserably in another, as the requirements for true leadership are driven by the context in which the leadership is to be applied.

Redefining leadership

What makes for an outstanding leader has been the subject of inquiry from the start of ancient Mesopotamian civilisation onwards. Two schools of thought have vied with each other to provide the definitive response to the 'make up' of the inspiring, striving, successful leader. The 'born to lead' school champion the view of extraordinary attributes and qualities bestowed on the fortunate individual but denied to all those others around them. The alternative perspective is offered by the 'developmental' school, which emphasises that leadership is the result of individual tenacity and endeavour. Irrespective of who you are or where you come from, the 'developmental' school of leadership promotes the view that it is up to the person to rise to the occasion and overcome the challenges facing them. On this basis, the 'developmental' school, similar to that of 'born to lead', accepts that individuals display outstanding characteristics of leadership, but only for a time. As new challenges arise, new combatants come forward and the leaders of yesterday retire having successfully, or less than successfully, confronted the obstacles they faced.

By the last two decades of the 20th century, the 'born to lead' school of thought progressively fell into disrepute. Academics and practitioners alike could not definitively emerge with the universal attributes of the 'great leader'. The cost cutting and merger mania of the 1980s and 1990s critically showed that not all leaders would be successful in every challenge they faced. The Lord Simpson, Marconi, debacle, discussed earlier in the book, highlighted that brilliance displayed in one role can be balanced by dismal failure in the next job. Thus, the 'developmental' school of leadership began to take hold, as much championed by search consultants (head hunters) whose brief was, and is, to find the appropriate person for a job that is ever evolving in a dynamic and vibrant environment. Thus, the topsy-turvy dynamics of search allowed for an alternative perspective to emerge, namely that the leader's performance may not be consistent. Even in the same job, a highly successful individual may not be able to sustain the necessary effort over a prolonged period. As a result, a third school of leadership began to crystallise, namely one that focused on examining the changing shape and nature of the leadership role particularly in relation to the attributes, qualities and skills required for outstanding performance.

Thus, in order to understand what is required of our leaders, attention needs to be given to the tasks at hand. Certain tasks, such as setting clear goals, are evidently explicit, which in turn require the application of particular skills. In other circumstances, the clarity of goal setting becomes confused by market and internal organisational complexities or, even at times, people's egos. Hence, what is required of the organisation's leaders and what they, in turn, demand of their managers can emerge as a 'smorgasbord' of demands and requirements due to internal and external contextual idiosyncrasies.

The way to comprehensively appreciate the challenges facing leaders in organisations is through role analysis. Role analysis offers an additional benefit, namely that of differentiating the role of the leader from the role of the manager. The role of the manager is more prescribed, structured, leaving little room for the individual to use their personal judgement. Managers have jobs to do. They need to apply particular skills in order to accomplish the goals and tasks set on their behalf. In contrast, leaders are people who occupy roles that require them to truly think for themselves, exercise considerable judgement and be held to account for their actions even if clear direction is not given. On this basis, leaders need to take the lead and challenge the *status quo*. Leaders can emerge as the popular and successful hero, or villain who introduced unwelcome disruption. Leaders are required to use their initiative and stretch the discretions at their disposal. In this sense, the logic of leadership is that of peculiarity and idiosyncrasy. Certain individuals apply themselves in ways particular to them. One may wish to quickly make an impression. Another cannot tolerate their present circumstances. A third misreads the business dynamics of the context and becomes out-of-step with colleagues, or simply and genuinely holds a contrasting vision for the future, but is still out-of-step. In such circumstances, individuals may attempt to re-negotiate their role boundaries, areas of responsibility and even reporting relationships. In certain organisations such initiative is welcome and rewarded. In others, the person may be required to leave, irrespective of whether their actions are measurably successful or not.

Thus, the quality of leadership of any enterprise is the result of the values, actions and perspectives of those that hold the roles of leaders. The degree of cohesion and harmony amongst and between the leaders, their response to the changing nature of market, societal and political circumstances and their ability to effectively configure the organisation to enhance its performance, determine the future of the enterprise. In effect, how the organisation's leaders relate and work together or not, significantly determines the continued success or demise of the enterprise. Drawing together the three strands of leadership attributes, role requirements and contextual challenges, extensive research at Cranfield School of Management highlights that five critical leadership capabilities are required of today's top corporate managers, namely those of:

- crafting the future;
- handling paradox;
- engaging through dialogue;
- communicating for success;
- exhibiting staying power.

These five leadership capabilities are neither mutually exclusive nor sequential. Different leaders in different circumstances are called upon to apply themselves in differing ways in order to make a positive and powerful impact. In so doing, individuals may make all embracing transformational changes, or alternatively may be continuously attentive to detail, contributing through being transactional. Equally, any leader may switch from being transformational to transactional in the same day. It is the clarity of thinking, determining how to behave, for what purpose and to what effect that distinguishes the great leader from the mediocre. On this basis, attention is given here to both the five critical leadership capabilities as well as how they need to be applied in the four corporate configurational designs.

Crafting the future

Determining the future direction of the corporation is the leader's prime requirement. Once into the role of CEO, determining the current and future shape of the organisation and the manner in which to realign the enterprise's configuration are critical considerations for the survival of the organisation. Just because the CEO or Chairman believes that a particular pathway should be pursued, not all of the other leaders in the organisation may concur with the direction being promoted. Depending on the nature of the leader, the position they hold, or their exposure to contrasting external developments, it is not surprising that the vision, mission and strategy are viewed differently. Studies at Cranfield School of Management indicate that over one-third of the world's top directors and leaders, irrespective of country, location, sector or gender, hold contrasting views from their colleagues concerning the future nature, shape and positioning of the organisation. Such unresolved strain lends itself to unproductive tensions among the leaders. To not pursue a coherent and shared vision leads to organisational dysfunctionality, short termism and in fighting. The dissension and contradictory messages emanating from top management suppress others from taking initiatives. For the more inventive middle managers, the opportunity to further manipulate the present unproductive circumstances leads to even greater confusion through their paradoxical but undesired empowerment. Thus, taking the necessary steps to promoting quality visioning is a must, if the centre is to exhibit a level of contribution that is valued and respected. Whether the leaders of the enterprise hold genuinely different views or are driven by personal likes and dislikes of each other, overcoming such inherent tensions is critical.

It is incumbent on the leaders at the centre to display genuinely held strong conviction concerning where the organisation is now and where it should be in the future. Strength of conviction needs to encompass an organisational ambition, namely, a purpose that is carried way beyond personal considerations.

Establishing that the leaders care more for the enterprise than for themselves is prerequisite to moulding a shared vision. Within this more positive climate, enhancing the quality of dialogue amongst all of the top team is now possible. The question that remains is, who is in the top team? Critically, it is those managers who occupy the 'discretionary' leader roles in the hierarchy, which, in one organisation, could vary from a few, the 10 or 12 at the centre, to, in another organisation, the 60 or more scattered in both the centre and across the businesses. What can complicate membership of this senior elite is role title. Certain managers may hold the title of director but are not part of the group that crafts and moulds the organisation. Where financial controls, economies of scale and even economies of scope act as the sources of corporate advantage, more restrictive membership of the leadership cadre is likely. Not so many leaders are needed as the application of key *managerial* skills is required to power the organisation forward. The reverse is true where innovation and creativity are the focus for corporate advantage.

Once the leaders are identified, working towards a shared vision requires the involvement of all of the top team in both clarifying direction and emerging with a consistency of approach to make the vision work. The involvement of all leaders in both the generation and pursuit of the vision of the enterprise is likely to stimulate a deep sense of identity and ownership for the survival and prosperity of the organisation. Involvement equally nurtures a feeling of being treated with respect. As the key leaders feel themselves to be part of this greater whole, they are more likely to clearly distinguish between what is right for them as individuals and what is important to do for the organisation. Involvement equally encourages greater robustness for dialogue. Championing a particular viewpoint, offering feedback, providing counter-argument and responding positively to negative comment are the essential ingredients for full and frank discussion. In order to participate, each individual leader needs to exhibit the personal strength to listen to critique that they may not wish to acknowledge. Once the group of leaders feel themselves able to surface the tensions between them concerning longer-term strategic issues, operational challenges and personal animosities, then the team is 'ready' to address the diversities that face them. The top team has now established a platform for visioning. They have nurtured a supportive context for dialogue. They have built a common platform for experiencing change, whereby they can agree the critical milestones that they will adopt to measure the progress of change. Equally, through involvement, a common language between them is more likely to emerge. The leaders will not only agree on what they are doing and why, but will also express them-selves in ways that capture their understanding of the vision they wish to pursue and the steps needed to attain their aspirations. Grow-ing a shared language promotes confidence in each leader as well as promoting a confidence in the leadership of the organisation by the staff and management. We believe that by placing the role of the vision within the configurational framework we have set out critical issues, dilemmas and tensions can be surfaced and addressed.

Handling paradox

Additional to attaining a shared commitment and clarity of vision, attending to immediate, operational requirements is also necessary to ensure the continued success of the enterprise. However, pursuing a strategic direction whilst at the same time making the necessary tacti-cal choices can provoke dissonance. What can seem a very sensible operational decision may completely contradict strategy. The need to cut costs may be evident but the strategic message may be to improve service quality. Being caught between two contrasting forces, with no easy reconciliation between such tensions is an experience many top managers have repeatedly undergone.

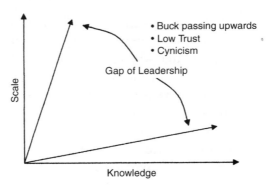

Figure 9.1
The paradox of leadership.

The paradox between focusing effort in a strategic direction that all agree is necessary while pragmatically accommodating daily necessities leaves senior management open to the accusation of being inconsistent. Rebuffing such critique with, 'Well, I had no other choice', rapidly wears thin. Alternatively, providing explanation of why such conflicts arise is more likely to induce a more understanding response. Nowhere is paradox more likely to arise than when scale synergies are being pursued simultaneously with knowledge synergies as shown in Figure 9.1.

Disciplined attention to costs is a necessity in order for any organisation to operate efficiently. Being economically well structured and clearly targeted, so indicative of a controls and volume leadership orientation, typifies a philosophy of sustaining competitive advantage through selling price and margin. The contrasting philosophies of process and values leadership require the generation and promulgation of unique knowledge as their prime basis to maintain a competitive edge. Promoting a sense of unique quality and being sympathetically responsive to the needs of clients and the market requires teamwork, consultation, openness of style, sharing of best practice and co-operation. A truism is that attention to costs whilst positively responding to the service needs of market and non-market stakeholders is an experience shared by organisations irrespective of whether they are economies of scale or knowledge driven. The question is one of degree, particularly as each enterprise could take different positions along the scale/knowledge dimensions in order to differentiate itself. Thus, two organisations, even sharing the same philosophy, experience tension in reconciling the demands of scale and knowledge in order to gain that extra step in the pursuit of competitive advantage.

Lacking any template for tension reconciliation, the leadership's balancing of attentiveness to cost, while encouraging openness, trust and co-operation, can make all the difference between realising the enterprise's vision and experiencing damaging and conspicuous strain, which undermines the credibility of the organisation. A top management that does not value all of the leaders in the strategic debate, a leadership that is not focused in its discussion of how to overcome differences and uncomfortable diversities, and a group of senior colleagues who do not promote the robustness necessary to 'eyeball' each other, can all unwittingly promote an undermining internal culture. Unable to face the strife and tensions, buck passing responsibility upwards, namely making the boss the scapegoat, becomes common practice. Feeling no sense of responsibility for the leadership actions that need to be taken, leads both middle and senior managers to abdicate their responsibilities. As a result, cynicism becomes rife. The trust that middle and junior management have in the leadership of the enterprise erodes. Allowing significant paradoxes to remain unresolved leads to the phenomenon of a leadership gap. The Cranfield studies conclude that two-thirds of the world's senior management of medium to large sized enterprises live with such continued tension, which slowly erodes the character of the organisation.

Not that such contrasts can be easily reconciled. Taking charge, providing clear and unambiguous direction, reducing head count, does not sit easily with being flexible, service oriented and encouraging others to speak openly. Irrespective of the dissonance any leader may face, only when exploration as to why issues remain unattended to and what it will take to improve personal and team performance will the vision for the organisation be more realistically pursued. The wisdom necessary to establish workable ways through organisational obstacles is a critical challenge that faces each leader.

Engaging through dialogue

Research evidence strongly suggests that the effective leadership of corporations is a team phenomenon that is so dependent on high quality dialogue. However, as seen in the section above, the Cranfield studies report that often sensitive issues remain unaddressed amongst the members of the top team. Yet, few top managers report that issues too sensitive to discuss are a 'critical threat'. Most organisations do not become bankrupt because top management did not effectively communicate with each other. What can be shown is that a clear relationship exists between poor quality dialogue and ever mounting opportunity costs. Not discussing and not confronting key issues leads to diminishing performance at the team, business unit and corporate centre levels.

Such inaction does not become obvious until some period of time has passed. Privately, top managers admit that they are aware of the damaging impact of allowing known problems to fester and can predict their consequential impact on the enterprise. But the will to confront critical concerns is low, largely because of the embarrassment and personal discomfort that is likely to be experienced. Therefore, the question remains, what is required for effective engagement among the leaders of the enterprise?

Clarifying who is and who is not a member of the senior forum is an important first step. Additionally, inviting comment from the general managers may stimulate that extra 'edge' to discussions, as these new 'top team' entrants will have experienced the frustration of being exposed to challenges that previously top management was reluctant to raise. Further, greater involvement in dialogue is likely to encourage attendance to neglected service and quality initiatives. Drafting a more representative meetings structure is an important step to enhancing strategic debate. Having attracted the 'right people to the right meetings', encouraging open discussion among managers who are unaccustomed to dialogue is the next hurdle. Penetrating debate can be an uncomfortable experience. Irrespective of the 'rightness' of the case, unacceptable levels of discomfort attract closure and act as a stop to further exploration. Achieving a balance between 'workable discomfort' and probing analysis requires profound skills of chairmanship. The style adopted by the leader of the meeting needs to be sensitive to contextual peculiarities. Encouraging open dialogue requires appropriate 'reading' of circumstances in order to capitalise on the sentiments that lead to effective engagement. Surfacing the appropriate dynamics that nurture more open conversation allows for penetrating examination of the topics at hand. Under more inviting circumstances, people open up irrespective of their reluctance to do so. Leaders masterful at unlocking conversations are more likely to continuously capitalise on opportunities.

Communicating for success

The will to succeed, the passion to achieve and the continuous display of enthusiasm can breathe new life into an organisation. Such powerful drivers are not just down to emotionality but owe as much to clearly thought through, logically sequential actions of organisational communication that cumulatively can have a profound influence on the enterprise.

Communication is a multi-fold concept. One perspective of communication lies at the personal and team levels, as has been discussed above. Additionally, communication refers to electronic bulletin boards, information sheets and presentations. Whatever the mechanism of transmission, communication involves a step-by-step process of cascade, whereby one or more important messages through a hierarchy of meetings, workshops and brainstorming sessions are pushed down the line. In effect, communication is a two-sided concept. Providing unambiguous direction through clarity of information has to be matched by symbolically powerful examples, namely the behaviour of senior management.

Providing direction is the more formal communication avenue. The mission of the enterprise, the corporate objectives, the operating business targets and the key areas of job related responsibilities have, traditionally, been the focus of communication initiatives. The effectiveness of communicating direction varies according to the discipline applied and the consistency of push of key messages. However, well organised, strategies of communication may still not have the desired effect. Past behaviours equally have an influence. A history of poor involvement of the senior managers at the centre with their counterparts and subordinates in the operating businesses can induce a climate where mission and vision statements are viewed as 'empty words'. A prolonged history of inappropriate 'living of the message' induces negativities. Thus, functional and operating business objectives are the only areas given 'real' attention. Short-term requirements are attended to and the broader goals and aspirations of the corporation progressively fall into neglect.

An alternative, impactful way of communicating is to personalise the message through providing the right example. The behaviours of the CEO and Chairman symbolise the aspirations and intentions key managers hold for the organisation. The Cranfield surveys asked leaders of corporations to identify those behaviours that promote critical messages to the rest of the organisation. An odd mixture of behaviours and personal qualities emerged, such as approachability, being open to comment, being understanding, being trustworthy, being disciplined in following through decisions made and exhibiting the capacity to be both visionary and disciplined in attending to details. Top managers consistently positively scored by their directors and general managers were the ones viewed as powerful communicators. Other top managers of comparable functional status and visionary skills who were not rated so highly were viewed as inconsistent between the words spoken and their actions. The contrast between what is said and what is done can undermine the motivation to succeed. Striving for success is as much a matter of passion and zest as it is a disciplined consistency of behaviour. There can be little worse than a well intended management at the centre unwittingly encouraging unproductive political behaviours that divert focus from the pathway to success.

Exhibiting staying power

How long does it take for any newly appointed director to fully appreciate the nature and intricacies of the challenges they may face in their newly appointed role? Evidence suggests that the transitional experience of finding your feet is likely to prolong to over 30 months before the senior manager in question can realistically determine the true competences of the organisation, its sales and marketing potential, the role the centre needs to play and the contribution it can make in steering the corporate enterprise to greater advantage. The 30 months transitional period may be characterised by pursuing inappropriate initiatives and even making, on reflection, unwise appointments to key roles. Hence, one element of staying power is to recognise the probable mistaken assumptions made early into a corporate centre appointment, and to display the willingness to rethink and remedy any errors of judgement.

At the other end of the scale, displaying the step-by-step determination to implement chosen strategies to successful fruition is likely to involve four considerations:

■ **Only think issues**   Life is dynamic. New opportunities as well as challenges, some of which may not be welcome, need to be faced. Attending meetings, reflecting on actions taken, confronting colleagues and reviewing the steps already taken, are common everyday experiences. Under pressure, it is all too easy to become defensive and project a 'this is my turf – keep off' message. It takes a particular level of robustness to emotionally stand back from the day-to-day experience and emerge with a rational perspective of the situation in order to attend to the issues at hand. Such maturity is particularly difficult to display when the issues that face senior managers involve a restructuring and a 'carving up' of their own territory. Particularly when well thought through change needs to be introduced, if the consistent example from the top is 'preserve one's own territory' that pattern of behaviour is likely to be replicated lower down the organisation.

- **Respect meetings** Assisting lower level management to accept greater responsibilities, including that of their own actions, is considerably assisted if senior management display respect towards their colleagues. Nowhere more so can such respect be exhibited than at crucial meetings. Executives do much of their work in meetings. Meetings are the forum where views are expressed, challenges are made and counter-arguments are presented. The backwards/forwards nature of meetings, so critical to clarifying how to proceed, can stretch the tolerance and patience of any manager. To make best use of colleagues' input at meetings requires that each person recognises the benefits that can be gained, irrespective of how irritated each can become with the behaviour and input of others. Respecting meetings is a prelude to learning how to appropriately conduct oneself at meetings. How should issues be raised without causing offence? How can a critical case be heard? How can colleagues be encouraged to enter into debate when they may feel they are being criticised? Whatever the levels of maturity of the managers attending meetings, respecting the processes of dialogue and debate assists considerably. Thinking issues and not responding emotionally is a necessity for executive meetings.

- **Promote cabinet responsibility** Due to the possible dispersed nature of the enterprise, not all 'top team' members may be able to attend all 'top team' meetings. But, irrespective of whether all top managers attend all senior management meetings, nurturing a sense of cabinet responsibility is the basis for ownership of key strategic and operational decisions. There is little value in behaving appropriately at meetings and then undermining the decisions made after the meeting by contradicting the decisions reached! Full cabinet responsibility requires implementing decisions in the manner agreed by the top team. Open dialogue at meetings is of true value when the top team members accept cabinet responsibility to do what they said they would do. Shared acceptance of cabinet responsibility provides the grit that makes for courageous actions as opposed to undermining, backroom behaviour.

- **Structuring to communicate** The message of structuring the job so as to 'walk the talk' is nothing new. The obvious benefit of getting out and about with the people in the organisation prevents the accusation of the 'invisible' leader. But why do so many leaders not 'walk the talk'? Because it is time consuming. What is often underestimated is the time needed to devote to effectively communicating the critical messages that the organisation and external stakeholders need to digest. As time needs to be devoted to the exercise of communication so does consideration need to be given to how other duties need to be re-allocated. Equally, assessing the capability and willingness of senior colleagues and the general managers to structure their roles to communicate needs to be considered. The message, the channels of communication, the time necessary to devote to their examination, and the job related implications of attending to the promotion of key messages require structural alignment as well as personal passion.

Positioning the leadership capabilities

Whether due to reasons of economic lifecycle maturity, or a management determined to break the mould and reposition their enterprise so as to gain greater corporate advantage, contrasting cultures differentiate one organisation from the other. From one organisation to the next, a variety of views exists concerning what is required to be successful as a leader. What effective performance may 'really' mean in one enterprise differs substantially in another.

On this basis, sensitively applying the five capabilities of leadership requires consideration of the attitudes, desires and accepted practices that prevail in each organisation. Attention to the finer nuances within each of the four configurations of creative, scope, scale and controls is an important consideration to gaining leadership versatility and ultimately mastery.

Leading the creative configuration

Before acting, the leadership needs to take into account the sentiments, dispositions and views of management in the creative corporation. A corporate centre powering its way through in order to realise its aspirations and objectives is likely to be met with substantial resistance or, more likely, the best people leaving, thus undermining the natural edge of the organisation over its competitors.

In order to craft a future in a manner that others will enthusiastically follow, promoting the grand vision by linking personal charisma with innovative ideas emphasising the unique know-how based values of the enterprise, is likely to make for a powerful impact, as shown in Table 9.1.

Table 9.1
Leading the creative corporation

Crafting the future	Promote grand vision; vision, values and mission linked to the individual; charisma and knowledge interwoven; focus on the creative heroes; best through innovation.
Handling paradox	Motivating; dependent on nature of challenge; formal processes interpreted as bureaucracy; need for freedom to act.
Engaging through dialogue	Display high regard for others; display respect; informal meetings; attention to networking; exposure to debate.
Communicating for success	Knowledge power; expression of professional expertise; creation of network loyalty.
Exhibiting staying power	Dependent on loyalty and teamwork; dependent on types of challenges to address; dependent on expression of creativity; acceptance in network is critical.

Benchmarking against past and present creative heroes and their capacity to emerge with innovative solutions to complex problems, is a particularly potent symbol. Paradoxes and unwelcome challenges need to be positioned as hurdles that are overcome through the energy and application of all in the organisation. Emphasis on the freedom to decide and the use of initiative motivates even more. Adopting formal processes to find ways through complex challenges is likely to be interpreted as an infringement of this freedom and as unwelcome bureaucracy.

Whatever the challenges faced by the organisation, fully engaging the staff and management is paramount. The creative enterprise is a highly personalised phenomenon. Displaying respect for others supported by intensive listening is likely to gain the attention of influential stakeholders. The more informal the meetings, the more likely it is that there will be a positive response. On this basis, attention to networking and being accepted in the network are also important considerations of leadership. As informality promotes more effective communication, informality of interaction is expected from top management. Any top manager who attempts to 'stage manage' communication events and does not expose themselves to the 'cut and thrust' of debate, is unlikely to be heard, irrespective of their skills of presentation.

Success is gained through the application of professional expertise and particular niche skills. The power of knowledge rather than dexterity with administration is likely to encourage others to strive for achievement. Similarly, the discipline to stay and see through the challenges confronting the enterprise is dependent on the continued exhibition of creativity and also acceptance by the extended peer group. Displaying loyalty towards others improves the levels of teamwork. Continuous attention to personal relationships is necessary as acceptance by the network is fundamental to continuity in a role of authority.

Leading the scope configuration

The catchphrase is 'best in class'! Within 'our field' we are the best! Irrespective of whether the word 'field' holds multiple connotations or not, as the organisation may have a variety of business interests stretching across different sectors, being seen as the best and being in a class of one's own are the essentials to visioning and strategy, as shown in Table 9.2. Dissecting 'best in class' into realisable components is how mission and strategic goal statements are drafted. An added incentive to crafting the future is attention to benchmarking against competitors. The need to prove 'best in class' must be promoted across the enterprise. Aspirational statements, without the backing of hard fact, undermine the philosophy of leveraging expertise across a configurational complexity of differing business interests.

Table 9.2
Leading the scope corporation

Crafting the future	Best in class; supportive of mission and goals; benchmarking according to best in class.
Handling paradox	Handled according to sourcing best practice; clarity of role relationships; explicit pathways through challenges.
Engaging through dialogue	Clarity of accountabilities, responsibilities; clear objectives.
Communicating for success	Reward; coercion; focus on best practice; work towards corporate goals; rapid promotion for results.
Exhibiting staying power	Loyalty to the enterprise; little loyalty to external networks.

The contrasting pulls and pushes of divergent interests are likely to make handling paradox a distinctly uncomfortable experience. The reaction of top management is to identify explicit pathways through such challenges. Individuals are likely to be given clear objectives and a specific mandate to 'iron out' the situation. Appropriate expertise is likely to be pulled together, some of which may be 'sourced' in from 'best in class' external suppliers.

Engaging the organisation is likely to be driven with equal discipline. Communicating effectively is viewed as any other business challenge. Individuals are given the responsibility to communicate and are held accountable for their performance. Undue personal panache and charisma are likely to be viewed as pretentious. Clear objectives, precise targeting and being up to date are the pillars of effective engagement.

Motivating staff and management to improve performance and be success driven is again dependent on clarity of goals – this is the target and this is what is expected of you! Rewards and coercion are likely to be utilised interchangeably. Successful individuals are earmarked for rapid promotion. Those less than successful are equally earmarked but more for an early exit out of the organisation. Yet, striving for success is not an unthinking process. Pursuing corporate goals without reflection is unlikely to attain 'best in class'. Challenging the goals set through a well prepared case whereby alternative considerations are brought into the equation adds to the perspective of 'we are the most successful and thus the best'!

As clearly thought through ways of achieving extraordinary levels of performance are indicative of a passion for success, the discipline to stay is shown by a loyalty to the organisation. Irrespective of the pressures placed on each individual, focusing on contributing to corporate achievement distinguishes the high performers from others equally professionally competent. Loyalty to external networks, no matter how relevant, is unlikely to position the individual as talent worth keeping; this type of group rates internal contributions not external reputations.

Leading the scale configuration

The focus of 'best in class', so prevalent to leading in a leverage focused organisation, is contrasted by the 'take note of the centre' message as the key driver to inform action, within the centralising enterprise as shown in Table 9.3. The leverage culture emphasises continuous responsiveness to external trends. The centralising

Table 9.3
Leading the scale corporation

Crafting the future	More internally driven; take lead from the centre; save where you can; leaders at the centre; managers in the business units.
Handling paradox	Clarify responsibilities; minimise contradiction; stick to the script.
Engaging through dialogue	Explicit; high engagement; making big thing of every little bit; challenge on tasks but not the strategy; charismatic presentations from top management.
Communicating for success	Transactional targeting; minimal discretion; improve existing efficiency measures.
Exhibiting staying power	Do what you are supposed to do; be attentive to costs; do not challenge the system; leave if you are disruptive; be politically astute.

organisation more highlights being internally driven; take the lead from the centre, with only the few true leaders at the centre scanning externalities. In order to craft the future, the centre knows best. The focus is on save where you can! Within such a configuration, it is clear that the true leaders of the enterprise are located in the centre. Managers, irrespective of their role title, are, in reality, positioned in the businesses and less so at the centre.

Similar to the leverage driven organisation, reconciling the uncomfortable paradoxes of being pulled in two different directions is addressed by clarifying goals, clarifying key managers' areas of responsibility and accountability in order to identify a clear way forward. However, unlike the leverage enterprise, the message that prevails is 'stick to the script'! Distinct challenge to the strategy, no matter how well thought through and prepared, is unwelcome.

Motivating staff and management through various approaches to communication follows a similar path. Be explicit, be clear, clarify who says what. Engaging the organisation to enter into greater dialogue is more an exercise in scripting. At communication events challenge is acceptable, as long as the focus is on tasks and how work should be undertaken. Part of the scripting process is to not threaten the centre. Exhibitions of charisma are acceptable as long as they emanate from the centre. Exhibitions of flair from the centre are viewed as a motivational experience in what could otherwise be a dull strategic message.

Communicating for success is achieved through emphasising efficiencies. The targeting process is transactional by nature. Improve what exists, continuous attention to economies of scale, good ideas are fine as long as they do not cost that much, are examples of the message the centre would promote. Being effective as an organisation is likely to involve inhibiting radical rethinking of the purpose and configuration of the enterprise. However, to give an upbeat note to the messages from the centre, the term effectiveness is likely to be adopted, but the underlying meaning is that of efficiency.

Whether striving for success or ensuring the survival of the organisation, not challenging the system remains. However, operating in any complex organisation, it is not always possible to stick to the remit of one's role. Challenges will arise that require general managers to use their discretion. The difference between making a contribution and at times being seen as disruptive is a fine line. Despite the 'stick to the script' message promoted from the centre to the operating businesses, being politically astute and forming relationships with the appropriate directors at the centre further ensures the continued survival and progress of the senior managers within the business units.

Leading the controls configuration

The visioning required for crafting a future is by nature opportunistic, as shown in Table 9.4. The theme promoted is 'sweat the assets until they can sweat no more'. The acquisition and disposal of enterprises is fundamental to the continual functioning of the corporate entity. Which business unit is acquired against what is discarded is dependent on the opportunities that arise in the market. The aim is to be 'one step ahead', sometimes not clearly of whom, but at least the impression promoted to shareholders is of continued success. In contrast to the centralising corporation, leaders exist in the operating businesses as well as at the centre. The freedom to act is fundamental to pursuing market driven opportunities.

Similar to so many organisations, paradox is undesired. Promoting clarity and minimising contradiction are achieved through focusing energy on clearly targeted goals. Goals emphasise profitability as much through revenue as through disciplined cost management. Once goals can no longer be realised, that enterprise is up for sale.

Table 9.4
Leading the controls corporation

Crafting the future	Opportunistic; next acquisition; sweat the assets; discard the assets; one step ahead; leaders at the centre; leaders in the businesses.
Handling paradox	Provide clarity; minimise contradiction; focus effort; freedom to act; goal driven.
Engaging through dialogue	Explicit; minimal engagement; insensitive to sentiments; low on loyalty; challenge is through goals achievement.
Communicating for success	Clear goals; clear stretching targets; discretion on actions; driven by results, judgemental on results; no excuses.
Exhibiting staying power	Only for the next target; as good as your last job; stay or leave; challenge the system but win; leave if you fail; disrupting the system works.

The overarching 'make money' theme equally drives the philosophy for communication. In fact, minimal engagement by the centre towards the rest of the organisation is the norm. The means to success become the mode of engagement with the rest of the enterprise. Setting clear goals and targets and being judged on results does not hamper people's opportunity to choose alternative modes of action. The message is that the targets are set – now it is up to you to achieve them. The more line management feel they are unclearly focused, the more they are likely to challenge the centre. However, the process of engagement holds little sentiment. Equally, loyalty means little. The most disliked general manager can be promoted to directorship on the basis of performance and results according to the goals set and achieved.

Many do not stay long in the organisation. Tenure is based on performance, which for many may mean a short-term future. The clarity of 'leave if you fail' is evident from first entering the controlling corporation. Equal speed of exit would be the norm in the centralising corporation if line management challenge the centre. Not so in an organisation embedded with a controlling culture. By all means, challenge the system, but win. Disrupting the system works as long as it makes sense within the shareholder oriented philosophy of cost focused management. Of course, to disrupt the system and have one's proposal rejected equally requires the departure of the offending executive.

Conclusion

Appropriate application of the five leadership capabilities varies from one organisation to the next. Reading the context accurately informs the manner in which leadership is to be applied. Awareness of the history of the enterprise, including its heroes of the past, the philosophy and orientation of the centre, the impact of market forces, the willingness of top management to face the reality of market demands and the brand strength of the group and/or its products, are the clues any new entrant into senior management should not ignore. The concept of leadership credibility is not just dependent on 'doing a good job', but also on acceptance by peers and immediate subordinates. Lack of attention to cultural clues is likely to mean ineffective performance as a leader. Any leader may make a powerful impact within one configurational context but emerge as incapable in another. Ironically, the person's skills may be of an equally high level in both contexts. Attentiveness to the prevalent sensitivities and norms promulgated by the centre determines whether one succeeds or fails.

However, it is possible to distinguish the leadership requirements of each corporate configuration in terms of the relative number of leaders required and their location within the group, as is shown in Figure 9.2.

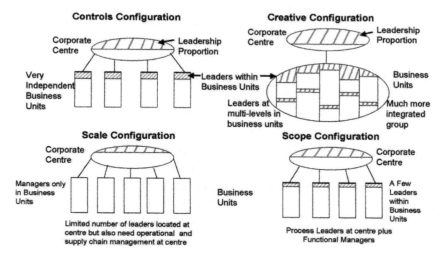

Figure 9.2
Contrasting leadership requirements in the four corporate configurations.

Chapter 10

Theoretical underpinnings

This chapter aims to put the corporate configurations model into the context of the academic theories and consultancy frameworks that exist in the area of corporate strategy. As stated at the beginning of the book, the reality is that most of the strategy research and literature focuses on the strategies of business units rather than the overall corporate level strategy. Indeed, even where the theory or framework states that it is considering corporate strategy, in many cases it merely regards the total organisation as a single entity without highlighting the specific role of the corporate centre.

Two main bodies of work, one by Henry Mintzberg and the other by Michael Goold and Andrew Campbell, do deal with the specific role of the corporate centre in multi-business groups and hence they are considered in some detail here. However, before comparing in detail our model with other existing work, this chapter briefly looks at the different types of corporate strategy so that the more detailed analysis is placed in an appropriate context.

The corporate configurations model is then analysed in terms of the fundamental theoretical building blocks of strategy theory, namely the Resource Based View of the firm with its related theory of Dynamic Capabilities, and Transaction Cost Economics. This is done because our model was, as already stated, developed from first principles rather than being deduced from studying a number of 'successful' multi-business groups. Hence the four corporate configurations should be capable of rational, economic justifications in terms of the value-adding potential of each style of corporate centre. These justifications were briefly discussed at the end of Chapter 1 but we now have the opportunity to deal with these issues more substantively. Several other popular strategic models are also discussed and compared to the conclusions of the configurations framework at the end of this chapter.

Types of corporate strategy

In the literature that was considered in writing this chapter, it is argued that there are eight basic logics behind corporate strategies. Some of these can equally be applied to the individual business units within larger groups, but they are still defended as being relevant to strategy at the overall corporate level. Obviously we are interested in how each of these types of corporate strategy can actually create shareholder value when applied in a multi-business group.

The first type can be categorised as the spreading of risk through diversification so that the corporation protects its own future by having a range of relatively unrelated business units. In developed capital markets, this justification for having a group has very largely been undermined. Shareholders can spread their risk by creating their own diversified portfolio of investments, and they can do it much more cost efficiently than any corporate centre can. Thus the corporate centre still needs to add value to the diversified businesses that it controls. In less developed financial markets or where the group is family controlled, there can still be a shareholder value enhancing logic for the risk reducing diversified group.

The second kind of corporate strategy is quite closely linked to the diversification theme as it is based on ensuring the survival of the organisation. This means that the group looks for new areas of activity once its existing business units have ceased growing or have already moved into long-term decline. In many cases this search results in a strategy of diversification that can take the group into new areas where it has little knowledge or relevant managerial expertise. This has led to the use of the term 'over-diversified'. This implies that some level of diversification may be value adding but, beyond a certain point, the group is destroying value rather than increasing or preserving it. Of course it is also true that the logic of 'preserving the group at all costs' is not appropriate from a shareholder's perspective. If the continued survival of a group will result in significant value destruction, economically rational shareholders would prefer the business to be wound up or sold now so that the current value could be paid out to them.

Portfolio management is the third type of corporate strategy and this can also be linked into the ideas of diversification and survival.

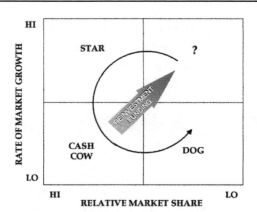

Figure 10.1
The growth share matrix
(product portfolio,
Boston Consulting
Group).

However, the most common philosophy behind portfolio management is for a group to have a relatively balanced portfolio of business units. This 'balance' can be achieved in several ways. The original, and still most common, usage of a balanced portfolio of businesses within a group, as opposed to the financial theory of an efficiently designed portfolio of investments, is to have some mature, cash generating business units that provide the funding for the high growth and start-up businesses that represent the longer-term future of the group. This was, of course, highly developed by the Boston Consulting Group through the use of short titles for each box (question mark, star, cash cow and dog) in its Directional Policy Matrix which is shown as Figure 10.1. The reinvestment of the high profits and cash flows generated by these successful mature businesses was designed to ensure not only the long-term survival of the group but also value-adding growth.

Unfortunately, once again, the reinvestment opportunities were often in industries that were unrelated to the group's original successful areas of operation. Also the risk associated with these newer, high growth industries was much greater than that of the now mature, normally more stable industries from which the group was generating its current stream of profits and cash flow. This meant that the group should have set a much higher required rate of return for any such re-investments than was required for its existing business units. Normally this financial adjustment was not made by the corporate centres which were often overly keen to find new investment opportunities.

These higher growth opportunities can be addressed organically by the group setting up new business units or by the acquisition of existing businesses in these new industries or sectors. If the acquisition route is followed, portfolio planning strategies can be regarded as a form of diversification through acquisition.

Not surprisingly, therefore, the fourth type of corporate strategy sought to reverse this trend towards diversification by emphasising that groups should focus on what they knew best. This was popularised by Peters and Waterman in their book, *In Search of Excellence* (Peters, 1982, 1985 and 1987) as 'Sticking to the Knitting'. The book was based on an analysis of 'at the time' successful American companies. The problems with models based on ex-post analyses of success are that it can be difficult to identify cause and effect in the relationships identified and the 'successful' companies have an annoying habit of becoming very much less successful shortly after the model is published. It is also quite often very difficult to generalise from these examples of success exactly what other groups should do in order to improve their own performance. However, the underlying generalisation of this type of corporate strategy is that groups should focus on specific industries, stages of development, or types of competitive environment.

A specific sub-set of this idea of focus has developed into the fifth type of corporate strategy and this involves groups focusing on restructuring businesses or even entire industries. The group seeks out industries on the threshold of major change or businesses that are already significantly under-performing or under threat. The corporate centre implements significant changes following its acquisition of these businesses in an attempt to improve the level of performance. In some cases, this restructuring strategy involves putting together several previously independent businesses in order to achieve critical mass so that potential economies of scale can be realised. If successful, this restructuring intervention can result in a strengthened company or even a transformed industry. However, the value-adding role of the group has now been completed so that there is a strong argument that the restructured business unit should be sold off once its performance has been enhanced. This would then allow the group to focus its attention, and its restructuring expertise, on another suitably under-performing target.

The sixth type of corporate strategy is quite closely aligned to this idea of focus but the group is supposed to focus on its core competences and skills, whatever these happen to be (Hamel and Prahalad, 1990, 1993 and 1994). The role of the corporate centre is therefore to identify these core competences and then to transfer them across the group so that they can be as fully exploited as possible. Obviously the core competences can take many forms and may involve reducing costs or exploiting specifically relevant knowledge. However, even if the core competence relates to cost reducing expertise, the value-adding role of the corporate centre is centred around its knowledge of this core competence and its ability to leverage it more generally within the group.

The seventh type of corporate strategy involves synergy where the group is worth more than the sum of its component parts. This means that the involvement of the corporate centre has somehow enhanced the overall performance of the portfolio of businesses comprising the group. This enhanced performance may be generated by lowering costs across the group or by increasing the level of differentiation that can be achieved by the individual business units. Alternatively the synergy may be produced by the business units working together in different ways to create completely new products or ways of competing.

The last type of corporate strategy is where the group's main aim is to grow, i.e. to become bigger and bigger. From the shareholder value perspective, this focus on growth should increase the rate of profits generated over time possibly through increased economies of scale or through increased market power. This growth based corporate strategy became popularised through the widespread use of the Ansoff Matrix, which is shown as Figure 10.2. The Ansoff Matrix highlights the four ways in which any business can grow; selling more existing products to existing customers, selling new products to existing customers, selling existing products to new customers, and selling new products to new customers. Selling more existing products to existing customers is normally described as a market penetration strategy, because any growth comes either from growth in the total market or by increasing market share. There is now much research that demonstrates that a market penetration strategy normally only creates shareholder value when the total market is still growing. This research, which has been carried out by analysing the PIMS database of the comparative results of over 3000 business units, shows that aggressive attempts to grow in a

Figure 10.2
Ansoff Matrix.

mature or declining industry often result in value destroying competitive reactions such as price wars that lead to less value in total being generated in the industry. These competitive reactions are stimulated by the inevitable loss in sales volumes that result from one business growing in an otherwise static market.

Selling new products to new customers can be restated as diversification but the Ansoff Matrix description highlights the risk increasing nature of such a strategic move. Rephrasing the description to be 'selling products that do not yet exist to customers which you have never previously dealt with' should show more clearly that diversification into completely new areas of activity is not necessarily a risk reducing strategy. However, it is the descriptions of the remaining two potential growth strategies that can create the greatest misunderstandings in practice. As shown in Figure 10.2, selling new products to existing customers is normally classified as a product development strategy but the real asset that is being leveraged in this growth strategy is the company's knowledge about its existing customers. This strategy is based around understanding the needs of these existing customers, identifying other products that they would be willing to buy from the company and then either developing or acquiring the capabilities needed to supply these products. Conversely, selling existing products to new customers is based on identifying those existing successful products that have greater sales potential, e.g. internationally, and then finding new markets in which to sell them. As shown in Figure 10.3, the strategic thrust builds on the existing product, which should be achieving a super profit in its existing market.

It should be clear that the corporate configurations model can cope with all these types of corporate strategy. The controls configuration is relevant for the spreading risk, survival, portfolio planning and

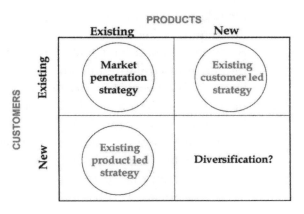

Figure 10.3
Potential strategic thrusts
of businesses (based on
Ansoff Matrix).

restructuring types of corporate strategy. The scale configuration is particularly applicable to some restructuring strategies and the 'sticking to the knitting' type of strategy. The leveraging of specific knowledge in the scope configuration covers the rest of the 'sticking to the knitting strategies' and the core competence classification. The creative configuration seeks to make the whole group worth more than the sum of the parts by creating new corporate know-how, thus also generating significant new growth opportunities. The other elements of the growth strategy fit into the scope, scale or controls configurations depending on the specific drivers of the growth.

Fundamental strategy building blocks

Transaction cost economics

Transaction cost economics (TCE) theory has developed from its origins in the 1930s (Coase, 1937) when it questioned the existence of frictionless, i.e. truly efficient, markets. It argued that there are costs incurred in using the market price mechanism, e.g. discovering what the relevant prices are. Thus these transaction costs can make it more efficient to carry out a specific activity within the firm rather than through the external market. This fundamental idea was developed to incorporate governance structures within the firm and to introduce the idea of asset specificity (Williamson, 1975, 1985).

Thus TCE sees firms and markets as alternative means of co-ordinating economic activities; firms co-ordinate through authority relations while markets use the price mechanism as their means of co-ordination. The costs of using the market pricing mechanism include negotiating, monitoring and enforcing contracts. These costs are required due to the risk of opportunistic behaviour by the other party to the contract. Opportunistic behaviour can be defined as self-interest utilised with guile and unconstrained by morality, and this is key to TCE theory. Opportunistic behaviour is therefore determined primarily by the expected economic benefits from such self-interested behaviour. This means that the risks associated with opportunistic behaviour increase as the assets involved in any transaction become more specific. These increasing risks result in greater governance costs being incurred related to safeguarding this type of external contract, i.e. costs associated with contracting, controls, monitoring, etc.

Consequently 'make' supplants 'buy' when contractual hazards and associated governance costs increase, which normally occurs as assets become more specific. A fundamental tenet of the original TCE theory is that common ownership of two activities (i.e. in-house activities) is economically beneficial only if such contractual hazards accrue. In other words, the market is assumed to be more efficient than the firm unless it can be proved otherwise.

Resource based view

An alternative theory emphasises the resources or capabilities of the firm, enabling firms to generate enduring sources of competitive advantage through distinctive ways of managing their resources and capabilities. This resource based view (RBV) of the firm (Wernerfelt, 1984 and 1994, and Barney, 1991) rejected the 'old way' of looking at the firm in terms of labour, capital and land (Penrose, 1959 and Rubin, 1973). Instead RBV regards a resource as a strength of a firm. Thus a firm's resources are both tangible and intangible assets which are tied semi-permanently to the firm, so that they include brands, knowledge, skilled personnel, customers and processes. Monopoly suppliers, monopsonies and substitute resources all depress the returns that can be generated from a specific resource.

Importantly however, a first mover advantage can create a resource position barrier that makes it economically unattractive for another resource holder to invest in order to exploit its competing resource, as the law of diminishing returns can apply. Thus resource position barriers are like entry barriers in product based strategies (Porter, 1980 and 1985) but they work against other resource holders, not just new entrants. In practice in order to achieve sustainable levels of super profits, firms need both resource position barriers and entry barriers. Some resource position barriers are particularly attractive because they can be self-reproducing through reinvesting part of the current super profits, e.g. customer loyalty, experience curve and technological superiority.

RBV considers diversified firms as portfolios of resources rather than portfolios of products. This means that a group can be exploiting one existing resource to deliver super profits while it develops the next, and so on. Both RBV and Industrial Organisation Economics (on which Porter's work is based) focus on explaining the achievement of super profits, i.e. the profits above the required rate of return that generate shareholder value. The source of this excess rate of return is located within the firm's transformation process, what Porter referred to as the value chain. RBV highlights the human or 'cultural' resources as being critical to this value creation process; i.e. inert resources cannot, by themselves, create value, they need human input.

This has led to the more recent development of the concept of the dynamic capabilities of the firm as being the processes by which resources are created and utilised (Teece *et al.*, 1997, and Eisenhardt and Martin, 2000). In this development of RBV, the term 'resources' is only used for inputs into the production process whereas, in normal resource based theory, 'resources' are used for both inputs (assets) and processes (Barney, 1991 and Dierickx and Cool, 1989). A key element of RBV is that it sees resources and dynamic capabilities as distinctive competences of firms, i.e. firms can be better than markets at carrying out certain activities. Inter-firm collaborations enable a firm to access complementary resources in order to overcome resource constraints. Then it can apply its specific dynamic capabilities to these resources in order to create value.

Application of TCE in corporate configurations model

TCE looks at why firms or markets are the optimal location for different transactions. The theory (Barney, 1999) has developed a hierarchy of governance levels for these transactions. Market governance is an arm's length exchange with market determined prices and these transactions often use commodity inputs. Intermediate governance applies to more complex, possibly long-term contracts that may involve strategic alliances or joint ventures. Hierarchical governance is used inside the firm where action and decision making is dictated by a line authority, such as the corporate centre. Logically the cost of governance is linked to its complexity and sophistication, thus market governance is cheapest. If minimising governance costs was the sole objective, then firms would draw their internal boundaries very narrowly. However, opportunistic behaviour can mean that the other party to the contract takes unfair advantage so that the higher governance costs of in-house activities may be worthwhile.

On the left-hand side of the corporate configurations model, where the source of corporate advantage is economies of scale, increasing direct involvement means more integration and less use of external markets. Business units may still 'buy in' activities, but these centralised activities are provided by the group. The justification is reduced total cost for the group even after allowing for the increased governance costs. In the controls configuration, the indirectly involved shareholder style corporate centre focuses on clear, unambiguous performance

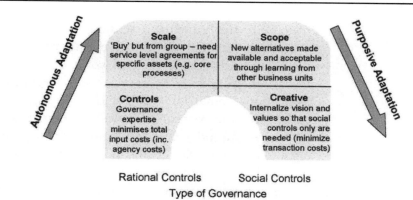

Figure 10.4

Transaction cost econom-
ics applied to corporate
configurations model.

measures, using its governance expertise to minimise the additional
control costs incurred by the group. It also seeks to have the minimum
possible constraining influence on the activities of the business units due
to its authority form of co-ordination. This centralised monitoring and
decision-making can be used to mitigate any measurement problems.
As stated in Chapter 1, the value added by the corporate centre is due
to the reduction in the level of agency costs that would be incurred if
all the business units were owned independently, i.e. only markets and
their associated pricing co-ordination role were utilised, as is shown in
Figure 10.4.

Movement up the vertical axis of the model, with a consequent
increase in direct intervention, results in increasing asset specificity for
the business units, particularly when core processes are centralised.
Under TCE, the increased production efficiency should be at least
partially offset by reductions in the governance efficiency due to the
removal of the market and its pricing mechanisms. However, as
discussed in Chapter 5, this should be replaced by the creation of an
internal market through the use of service level agreements and appropriately designed transfer pricing systems. This requires a relatively
stable environment for it to work properly, but this is exactly the same
if these activities were external market co-ordinated as the risk of
opportunistic behaviour is much greater in a volatile environment.

Applying TCE logic to the knowledge-based source of corporate
advantage is most easily done by incorporating other developments of
the theory. TCE and institutional theories can be combined to produce
a constrained efficiency framework that explains how organisations
seek to operate efficiently in an imperfect world under cognitive and
institutional frameworks (Roberts and Greenwood, 1997). The
constraints on organisational design are bounded rationality and both
pre-conscious and post-conscious institutional constraints. Bounded

rationality really means that the given organisation structure is only compared to available alternatives rather than to all theoretically possible alternatives. Also in the real world, decisions are made in an institutional environment, as well as a competitive environment. This institutional environment includes patterns of social relations and embedded interpretations as well as the fundamental political, social and legal ground rules. Institutional theory demonstrates how non-choice behaviour can occur and persist through the exercise of habit, convention, convenience or social obligation.

According to pre-conscious institutional theory, organisations operate and make choices in environments where much is taken for granted, thus shaping the decision-making process. Post-conscious institutionalisation argues that tangible forces divert decisions away from the proposed comparative efficiency framework of TCE toward the dynamic of legitimacy. This means that context is very important for organisational design decisions. Thus these constraints may restrict the alternative organisational designs that are considered to a smaller set than would be generated just by bounded rationality. Conversely, they may act as a source of information about alternatives that may be relevant to the organisation. We would argue that this learning from others through the leveraging of existing knowledge as is done in the scope configuration fits this theory well.

This constrained efficiency framework can clearly be applied to our multi-business groups with corporate centres and can explain the lags and delays in required changes in configurations. It can also explain the types of changes that are adopted, i.e. those legitimated by others in the industry. This development also argues that changes in the decision-making body (e.g. the CEO or board of directors) may change the institutionalised constraints significantly so that it is much easier to move to a new organisational design, i.e. make the transition to a different configuration. It further argues that the organisational design should be related to the transactions within the organisation, such as those between the corporate centre and its business units.

The next development of TCE theory verges on a refutation of the original logic in that it argues that organisations are not mere substitutes when markets fail (Ghoshal and Moran, 1996). The modern world is really an organisational economy not a market economy, where markets begin where organisations fail (Simon, 1991). This is the reverse of traditional TCE as firms replace markets when non-market means of co-ordination and commitment are superior (Rumelt *et al.*, 1991) whereas, as already stated, traditional TCE sees markets as the natural choice for activities. Opportunism as an attitude is also separated from opportunistic behaviour. According to the theory of reasoned action, volitional behaviour is caused by behavioural intentions which are determined by attitudes and subjective norms. This would make opportunistic behaviour positively influenced by opportunism.

However, opportunism itself has causal factors, one of which is opportunistic behaviour. The other two are feeling for the organisation and prior conditioning caused by both conscious and subliminal stimuli. Thus, feelings and prior conditioning could create a dissonance effect on opportunistic behaviour, particularly if such behaviour was accompanied by high commitment and freedom of choice. Strong governance may have a positive impact on the cost of opportunistic behaviour but it normally has a negative impact on the feeling for the organisation through the removal of trust. The dissonance effect could itself lead to modification in behaviour, without strong governance. In the corporate configurations model this can be seen in the differences between the controls and creative configurations. The controls configuration requires excellent governance because the business unit managers have no strong feelings for the group and are conditioned to deliver the stretch targets set for them by the corporate centre. Trust between the centre and the business units is not high but neither is it a critical issue.

In the creative configuration, the leader style centre has to achieve high identification with, and positive feelings for, the group from a wide range of business unit employees. Strong governance could erode any positive attitudes so that 'consummate co-operation' turns to 'perfunctory compliance'. There is also a distinction between rational control, the basis of TCE, and social control. Rational control is the normal, relatively formal governance process, whereas social control is based on people, their preferences, and informal mechanisms to build motivation and commitment. Social control can actually influence behaviour with or without a change in attitude. Its advocates seek to induce individuals to internalise the values and the goals of the organisation; such internalisation implies a change in attitude. Thus leader style corporate centres should use social control to win the hearts and minds of their groups' employees. Not surprisingly, rational controls work where performance can be objectively measured and evaluated (i.e. the controls configuration), while the vision and values must be totally compatible if social controls only are used.

This logic can also be applied to the development of organisations. Firms can adapt autonomously in response to external market signals but this 'autonomous adaptation' is directionless, so that it is biased towards static efficiency (Hayek, 1945). This is the transactional leadership of the left-hand side of the configurations model. However, firms are capable of 'purposive adaptation', i.e. co-ordinated but with a shared purpose. The shared purpose gives the adaptation direction and this has several advantages. It can work in the absence of prices and markets so that formal service level agreements and transfer pricing agreements are not essential. Firms can create new options and activities, and it can transform the institutional context in which relations are embedded. This represents the transformational leadership required on the right-hand side of the configurations model.

It is particularly relevant for innovative groups in the creative configuration, as innovative activities are often characterised by missing prices or markets, by strong uncertainty and high ambiguity. Groups may thus beat markets in this area of innovation, but they should do so from the creative configuration. In summary, shared purpose can play the vital role within organisations that price plays in markets.

Application of RBV in corporate configurations model

TCE emphasises friction in economic exchanges and the role of efficient governance while RBV focuses on friction in production and organisational advantage; the theories separate production skills from governance skills, but inter-firm collaborations blur the boundaries between production and exchange (Madhok, 2002). There needs to be alignment between the governance structure and both the transaction and the resource attributes. The vision and strategy of an organisation influence how its resources interact with any transaction and how the organisation chooses to govern it. This is the role of the configurations model. As discussed earlier in the book, we can distinguish between value creation and value capture but RBV theory enables us to be even more precise in analysing value capture. The transformation of input resources by an organisation produces a use value for the final output. This use value is, by definition, subjective as it is the use value 'perceived' by customers in relation to their specific needs. However, this can only be realised by producers through the exchange value paid by customers that actually buy this output; logically the customer's perceived use value of a purchase should exceed the exchange value paid. Indeed the concept of consumer surplus is exactly this gap between perceived use value and exchange value paid. The perceived use value can therefore also be thought of as the total monetary value of the output produced, but there will normally be a value gap between this total monetary value and the exchange value captured by the producing organisation.

This means that there are two potential sources of value capture for an organisation because most organisations act as both suppliers (receiving exchange value for their use value produced) and customers (paying exchange value for perceived use value supplied to them). One source of value capture for the firm is to focus on its role as customer and try to pay less exchange value for a given use value acquired, i.e. *increase* the value gap by reducing input costs. This is represented on the economies of scale side of the corporate configurations model. The cost reducing emphasis of these corporate centres does not affect the use values delivered to the external customers of the group's business units. These use values are simply produced for lower input costs. However, the other source of value capture does impact on the final customer because it focuses on the organisation's role as supplier. Here the supplier is trying to deliver the same (or something better) to the customer for a greater share of the total monetary value of the (changed) output. This is the value-adding, transformational role of the knowledge side of the corporate configurations model. Thus the two sides of the model utilise different sources of bargaining power within the total industry value chain.

The organisation can further seek to increase its value capture by creating 'intermediate' use values that exist outside of the people who created them, e.g. brands, reputation, software and other forms of relational capital. This knowledge can then be leveraged across the group. However, these 'differential' labour inputs can also create quite enduring human capital that leads to enhanced use values through the development of innovative products. Human use capital can take the form of informal networks, team working and communities of practice that often occur in an open, sharing culture such as should be found in the creative configuration.

The inert inputs of RBV can also be split into two categories; normal inputs (raw materials, generic labour) and the enduring inert capital (fixed assets) of the business. The scale configuration focuses mainly on the exploitation of the enduring inert use values within the group while the controls configuration tries to minimise expenditure on firm maintenance activities and minimise the exchange value paid to suppliers. Thus these cost reducing configurations concentrate on 'bought' inputs while the two knowledge-based configurations emphasise the inputs built by the group. These ideas are summarised in Figure 10.5.

As shown in Figure 10.5, it is also possible to identify distinct dynamic capabilities that are relevant to each configuration. Activities and

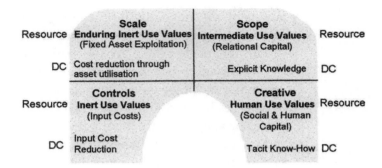

Figure 10.5
Resource based theory
applied to corporate
configurations model.

processes that are directed at the creation of future RBV resources can be regarded as dynamic capabilities. Governance processes in the controls configuration that result in very low levels of wastage on unproductive resources and minimal expenditure on firm maintenance activities are a dynamic capability that creates cost saving resources. In the scale configuration, the centralised management of activities and processes that maximise the utilisation of fixed assets are a dynamic capability that also creates a cost saving resource. The scope configuration takes existing group intermediate use values and codifies them so that their value creation capability across the group is optimised. The dynamic capability is the process by which the critical knowledge is made explicit so that other business units can utilise it. The capital stock creating activity of the creative configuration genuinely creates new value through the use of more tacit know-how rather than explicit knowledge. Tacit skills are a process because they are about how to do things and deeply ingrained tacit skills can be very difficult to communicate to outsiders. Therefore they are a dynamic capability of the leader style corporate centre and completely match the RBV definition of a valuable asset, i.e. Valuable, Rare, Inimitable and Non-substitutable. This is why the creative configuration is the most sustainable value-creating configuration.

Adopting a configurational approach

The idea of congruent configurations can be traced back to the early empirical studies of organisations conducted by, for example Chandler (1962), Burns and Stalker (1961), Lawrence and Lorsch (1967), and Miles and Snow (1978). However, Henry Mintzberg has developed the approach to provide many insights into the potential combinations of organisational structures and processes (Mintzberg, 1979 and 1981).

He argued that there are congruent combinations of structures and processes that match particular sets of contingent conditions; what he called configurations of situation as well as structure. 'The very notion of configuration is that all the elements interact in a system, with the central purpose of structure being to co-ordinate the work divided in a variety of ways'. These different methods of co-ordination have formed the basis of the standardisation classifications in our model. Mintzberg was analysing the total organisation and identified four configurations that are of particular relevance to our work on the role of the corporate centre. For example he also identified a simple entrepreneurial configuration which is one large business unit with a very small top management team that makes all the key decisions. For us this represents a single business without the need for a separate corporate centre.

The relevant configurations are therefore machine bureaucracy, professional bureaucracy, divisionalised form, and adhocracy. The machine bureaucracy emphasises the standardisation of work as the co-ordination mechanism, with the consequence of many low skilled specialised jobs within the organisation. These standardised work processes are designed by technical staff who have a lot of informal power but the formal power tends to be concentrated at the top of a very functionally structured organisation. Machine bureaucracies require a stable environment and high volumes to justify the investment in breaking down the overall workload into the much smaller, less complex, standardised roles. Hence it is most commonly seen in mass production companies.

The professional bureaucracy relies on the standardisation of skills as its method of co-ordination, because it is the skills of its employees that create value in this configuration. This results in a highly decentralised organisation as these skilled professionals need decision-making authority, irrespective of their formal level within the hierarchy. However, the skill holders often need a significant support structure so that they can focus on utilising their value adding skills. This support structure is normally much more centrally controlled as the jobs involved tend to be routine and repetitive, i.e. the roles that the professionals give up. This configuration also needs a stable environment as dramatic changes could make the standardised skills no longer value adding.

The adhocratic configuration is much better at coping with a dynamic, volatile external environment as it is made up of interdependent project teams. These businesses also require skilled experts, but these experts cannot work on their own simply exploiting their existing skills. They must work together with other experts to create new things or ideas, and these project teams will exist at various levels within the organisation. This makes co-ordination in this configuration more complex and businesses use matrix structures, task forces and managerial moves to try to achieve mutual adjustment. Power in an adhocracy is dispersed around the organisation depending upon the decisions that need to be taken and the relevant experts who can contribute to those decisions. However, these decisions are taken in the light of some shared understanding of where the organisation is trying to go. Adhocracies are often young organisations and they may either disappear, if unsuccessful, or migrate, as they mature, to one of the more bureaucratic configurations once their strategy and environment become more stable.

Hopefully readers can see some close parallels between these three configurations and, respectively, our scale, scope and creative configurations. However, it is Mintzberg's divisional configuration that is the main focus of our research into the value-adding role of corporate centres. The divisionalised form in Mintzberg's analysis is the only configuration that is focused on multi-business groups. As a result, he acknowledged that it is a partial structure, superimposed on other structures that exist in the divisions. However, in this divisional configuration, it is argued that the headquarters maintains a semblance of control through the standardisation of outputs, i.e. performance measures imposed on divisional managers. This results in these divisional managers retaining a high level of centralised control in their respective divisions in order to achieve these targets. Thus, in Mintzberg's configurational design, the multi-business group is restricted to operating only in our controls configuration. We believe that we have developed this configurational design to incorporate a more detailed view of the potential value-adding roles of corporate centres in multi-business groups.

As stated early in the book, our approach is rooted in the belief that strategy and structure should not be treated as separate phenomena. A strategy will have distinct and particular organisational requirements if it is to be realised. So, realised strategies and structures are inextricably linked. Organisational structures and processes should be regarded as partial descriptions of realised strategy, or, to put it another way, intended strategy is enacted through extant structures and processes. Therefore, although intended strategies (Mintzberg and Waters, 1985) can exist in an ideal form, realised strategies cannot. With intended strategies, we can detect likely mismatches between strategy and structure but, with realised strategies, structures and processes become part of the description of strategy. We have therefore attempted to establish feasible links between our four corporate configurations and distinct combinations of design parameters for both structures and processes. We have adapted Mintzberg's original set of parameters, and have focused on those most likely to vary by corporate strategy. The results are set out in Table 10.1, while Figure 10.6 depicts each corporate configuration in terms of Mintzberg's original 'logo'.

Henry Mintzberg has also focused on the many problems associated with strategic planning in large organisations (Mintzberg, 1994). We agree with his arguments about the disadvantages of having far too standardised, structured and formalised an approach to strategic planning. We hope that our corporate configurations model indicates a more tailored approach that shows the different value-adding roles which are possible for corporate centres. However he has, with others, (Mintzberg *et al.*, 1998) more recently analysed a comprehensive range of the strategy development processes used over the years, the last of which is called the configuration process.

The Design School regards strategy formation as a process of conception with the CEO as the chief strategic designer. The organisation starts by understanding its strengths and weaknesses, core competences or dynamic capabilities that should lead to the creation of strategic options. These are evaluated so that the best one is chosen and then implemented, even though this school says little about how to develop this best strategy.

The Planning School focuses on the formal process used to formulate the strategy of a business. A strategic planning model is designed with a detailed timetable and the process normally starts by setting overall objectives. The internal and external audits are more formalised than in the Design School but the result is similarly the selection of the business strategy, that is then implemented. Another difference from the Design School is that the process is now run by planning managers, with the result that the process often acquires a life of its own.

An even more analytical approach is taken by the Positioning School, which includes the military analogies of strategy as war. This considers that it is possible to identify the limited number of possible attractive positions within an industry and to develop the most desirable strategy based on a few key imperatives. Many popular forms of the Positioning School, which includes Porter's models, are consultancy based as they are empirical propositions. Thus oligopoly modelling and game theory based strategies fit in this school.

By way of contrast is the Entrepreneurial School of strategy formation. This sees the entrepreneur as the visionary leader who embodies

Table 10.1
Four configurations

	Controls	Scale	Scope	Creative
Dynamic capabilities	(Provided) Learning acquisition, resource allocation	Acquisitions, process and product development	Replication, transferring	Connecting, learning, collaborating
SBU strategy autonomy	Autonomy on means not ends	Constrained by process provision	Constrained by standard processes	Constrained by core values
SBU performance measures	Profitability	Mixed; e.g. cost reduction plus sales targets	Plural, including conformance to systems	Plural, including adherence to corporate values
Co-ordination across levels	Minimal	Strong, if core processes centralized	Required re: standard systems	Shared values
Co-ordination across SBUs	None required	Standard processes	Co-operation in knowledge transfer	Sharing ideas, collaborating on new ventures
SBU similarity	Can benefit from control regime	Same activities	Can benefit from same systems	Complementary knowledge
Role of centre	Operates financial control regime	Performs activities	Codifies and transfers know-how	Encourages creativity across SBUs
Predominant co-ordinating mechanism	Standardisation of financial outputs	Direct supervision of standardized activities by centre	Standardisation of systems and skills	Standardisation of values
Predominant part of the organization	Strategic apex	Centralised operating core and middle line	Technostructure	Culture/ideology
Location of created resources	SBUs	Centre	SBUs	SBUs

Design Parameters

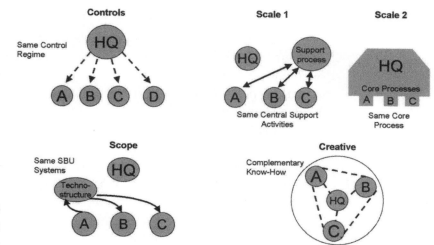

Figure 10.6
Four resource creating strategies.

the strategy that tends therefore to be intuitive. Often there is no real supporting process so that, if the strategy fails, the organisation simply finds a new leader, assuming that the organisation still exists.

The Cognitive School regards strategy formation as a mental process so that the personal cognitive styles of the strategists in the organisation will have a significant influence on the final strategy. There are two wings to this school which respectively emphasise objective and subjective views or interpretations of the world. The key argument of this school is that strategy formation may start out as a rational process but there is too much data to process. Hence strategies emerge as perspectives through the application of personal maps, schemas, frameworks, etc.

A more explicit acknowledgement of strategy development as an emergent process is given by the Learning School. Strategies are still being developed as they are being implemented so that the process becomes evolutionary. The organisation develops routines which evolve as the environment changes and learning takes place. Thus the organisation does not develop *the* deliberate strategy but a series of strategies *emerge*. Deliberate strategy emphasises control in the sense of making sure that management's intentions are realised. Emergent strategy emphasises learning so that the role of leadership is to manage the process of learning. It is, of course, also possible to distinguish between tacit know-how and explicit, transmittable knowledge and the learning process seeks to create usable knowledge and/or to exploit tacit know-how.

The Power School sees strategy formation as a process of negotiation through an overt use of power and politics to shape the final strategy. Power can be internal or external to the organisation but the process is based on exercising influence over key stakeholders, so that in-depth stakeholder analysis is an important element in this strategy process. The strategic manoeuvring that can take place can result in the creation of networks and alliances that attempt to make the strategy process more co-operative than direct conflict.

Another school that emphasises co-operation and participation is the Cultural School which sees strategy formation as a collective process. As already discussed, culture binds a group of individuals into an integrated entity and is, by definition, a collective and social process. Indeed, some would argue that businesses do not *have* a culture, the business *is* a culture, as culture represents the life force of the organisation. A true company ideology can therefore be described as a rich, passionately shared culture.

The ninth classification is the Environmental School which has strategy as a reactive process to the external environment. Thus the resulting strategy depends on which dimensions of the environment are most influential. There are different forms of the Environmental School. These range from contingency theory, which allows organisations to adapt to their particular environments, through the population ecology view, under which the basic character and structure of an organisation are fixed shortly after its formation, to institutional theory. Institutional theory, as part of the Environmental School, argues that there are pressures to conform that drive organisations operating in the same environment to adopt similar structures and processes. This is described as institutional isomorphism.

The final strategy school considered by Mintzberg *et al.*, (1998) is the Configurational School which, not surprisingly, includes all Mintzberg's organisational configurations. This school sees strategy formation as a process of transformation. Organisations normally exist in relatively stable states, i.e. configurations, with stable strategies but sometimes they require strategies that will move them to another stable state. The critical element of the strategy process therefore is to identify when such transformational strategies are needed. These strategic changes are consequently seen as revolutionary rather than incremental, as for example is the case with the Learning School. It is accepted that the strategists operating in the Configurational School may learn incrementally but they implement change strategies in a revolutionary way. Obviously there are differing degrees of complexity involved depending upon the nature of the transformation that is required.

Our corporate configurations model represents an expansion of one of Mintzberg's configurations, the multi-business divisional group. Consequently, groups require the ability to move from one of our configurations to another within the same overall model. This ability was discussed in our transitioning process, which can be seen as a sub-set of this transformation to another completely different configuration. Additionally, we believe that it is possible for a group to improve its position within the existing configuration and this we refer to as migrating within the configuration. In some cases, this migration may be done to facilitate an impending or predicted transition to a new configuration. As our model focuses on the value-adding role of the corporate centre and its involvement with its underlying business units, we believe that the corporate centre should be able to continue to add value to the group by staying within our model. However, this may require it to change the composition of the portfolio of businesses comprising the group or to change its style by transitioning to another configuration.

Other work on the role of the corporate centre

Henry Mintzberg has been a leading researcher and author in the field of organisational design and strategic management for over 30 years. Michael Goold and Andrew Campbell have also been at the forefront of their specialist field for 20 years but, with Marcus Alexander for some of this period, they have focused more on the specific role of the corporate centre in large groups. An early model (Goold and Campbell, 1987) identified eight strategic management styles based on the influence of the centre relative to the business units in the planning process and the type of control influence, which reflects the way that the centre reacts to actual performance. Control influences were categorised as tight financial control, tight strategic control, and flexible strategic control.

Of these eight styles, they focused on three main alternatives for centres in diversified (i.e. multi-business) groups: strategic planning, financial control, and strategic control. The strategic planning style combines flexible strategic control with a high level of corporate centre influence in the planning process. Thus the centre actively participates in formulating business unit strategies and may initiate new thrusts among interrelated businesses. As a result, the centre focuses on the long term and therefore is flexible in its attitude to short-term performance provided that the long-term strategy remains on track. Strategic planning groups ideally concentrate on a few core business areas. This style is particularly suited where there are potential synergies within the group and where progress requires large, high-risk decisions. The negatives of strategic planning are a tendency towards bureaucracy and an excessive level of involvement by the centre. This style overlaps our scale, scope and creative configurations depending on how the corporate centre actually seeks to add value and how directly intervening it is in the operations of the business units, as opposed to being involved in the planning process.

The financial control style has a much lower level of centre involvement in the planning process but a much tighter level of financial control. This style delegates strategic decisions to profit responsible business unit managers. The centre's role is to agree and monitor demanding, short-term financial targets for these business units. Financial control is most relevant in a group with a portfolio of stand-alone businesses. It is very closely aligned to our controls configuration and, indeed, some of the case study examples used are the same.

Strategic control requires a combination of tight strategic control with a relatively decentralised approach to short-term profit responsibility. These groups also have extensive strategic planning processes, through which the centre seeks to add value by reviewing, challenging and monitoring business unit strategies. However, in a later paper Goold and Campbell (1993 a,b) challenged the relevance of this style to diversified portfolios of businesses as it needs the corporate centre to have a good understanding of all the business units in the group.

In later publications, Goold, Campbell and Alexander developed this styles model into the concept of the parenting advantage of a corporate centre [Goold *et al.*, 1994 and Campbell *et al.*, 1995]. The idea of parenting advantage is that this corporate centre should be able to create more value from owning a particular business unit than any alternative parent, i.e. any other corporate centre or directly owning set of shareholders. The resulting model highlights key characteristics of both the corporate centres and the businesses with the identification of four sorts of corporate value creation: stand-alone influence; linkage influence; functional and services influence; and corporate development activities.

The stand-alone influence has the corporate centre as an informed but objective shareholder with a strong influence on senior management appointments and capital investment decisions. Its emphasis is on budgetary control and strategy reviews, but not strategy development. There are many similarities with the earlier financial control style and our shareholder style of corporate centre.

The linkage influence emphasises the enlightened self-interest of the business units and the corporate centre focuses on removing linkage blockages across the group. This means that the centre needs much better knowledge about the business units as it may provide linkages both geographically and across business groups. The centre can also channel resources into the potentially most value adding (i.e. incomplete) business units.

The functional and services influence is where the centre provides some services to, or functions for, the business units. These could be a centralised technical services function, as in 3M, or technical and functional expertise available at the centre, as in Shell. However Goold, Campbell and Alexander state that functional and services influence cannot, on its own, create parenting advantage. Indeed they believe that parenting advantage is normally achieved through a combination of stand-alone influence and linkage influence.

The corporate development influence involves the corporate centre affecting the businesses in the group's portfolio. This may be as directly as adding value by changing the portfolio through buying businesses cheaply, as with Hanson, or rearranging the existing portfolio by amalgamating or separating out businesses, as done by BTR and ABB. It could also involve creating new businesses through corporately sponsored new product development or collaboration across existing business units, as in Canon. A particularly interesting aspect is the idea of aligning the portfolio of businesses with the particular parenting approach of the corporate centre.

This parenting advantage model identifies four key inputs to the development of a corporate strategy. The first is understanding the characteristics of the parent: these include mental maps; the people and their unique skills; parenting structures, systems and processes; functions, central services and resources; and the decentralisation contracts. Next is understanding the characteristics of the businesses, particularly in terms of the critical success factors, any current areas of under performance and the resulting parenting opportunities. The third requirement is an assessment of the relative strengths and weaknesses of rival parents, in order to ensure that this centre will add more value than any other. This is followed by an analysis of how all these factors may change in the future.

The objective is to identify what are termed 'heartland' businesses for this parent where there is both a good fit between the parenting opportunities and parenting characteristics and between the business unit's critical success factors and the parenting characteristic. Apparently corporate centre managers make their biggest mistakes with what are described as 'value-trap' business units. These have a good fit in parenting terms but are a misfit in terms of critical success factors. Potentially the centre can see value to be added but the lack of understanding of the business unit's critical success factors can actually result in much value destruction.

More recently, Goold and Campbell have developed a new framework for assessing corporate design options (Goold and Campbell, 2002), in which parenting advantage is one of nine factors. They have identified four drivers of ensuring that an organisation is 'fit for purpose' and five good design principles. For each of these they have then developed in-depth tests that can indicate if the organisation design is contributing to, or detracting from, value creation.

The four fit drivers encompass product-market strategies, corporate strategy, people and constraints with related tests that question whether the organisation design takes each specific attribute appropriately into account. The good design principles and tests are more innovative and interesting. The principles cover specialisation, co-ordination, knowledge and competence, control and commitment, and innovation and adaptation. Specialisation and co-ordination both relate to how business units are set up: the specialisation principle encourages the development of specialist skills and cultures through concentration and focus while the co-ordination principle argues that co-ordination is easiest if similar activities are grouped together so that difficult linkages are avoided. The knowledge and competence principle is tested to ensure that all hierarchical levels actually add value, whereas the control and commitment principle has an accountability test for the appropriateness of performance measures used in each business unit. The innovation and adaptation principle has a flexibility test that checks how well the organisation design will cope with future changes.

We believe that our corporate configurations model is compatible with the ideas and frameworks developed by Goold and Campbell. Hopefully our ideas take their frameworks a little further but we do accept that we are being more prescriptive in our recommendations that corporate centres need to focus on being in *one* particular configuration as the source of their *own* value creation. However, the dimensions of our model do seek to take into account all nine of their corporate design principles, through the incorporation of specific, different corporate centre styles, cultures and identities, planning and control processes, co-ordination mechanisms, and degrees of sustainability for each configuration.

Other views of corporate strategy

Following on from his leading edge works on competitive strategy, Michael Porter then focused on corporate strategy in diversified groups (Porter, 1987). He regarded corporate strategy as being concerned with two key questions: what businesses should the group be in and how should the corporate centre manage this portfolio. His analysis of diversification records of major USA companies showed that most had destroyed rather than created shareholder value. He devised three essential tests that should indicate whether diversification would create shareholder value. These are: the attractiveness test, which indicates whether shareholder value can be created in this industry; the cost of entry test, which should not be so high that all future profits have already been paid for; and the better-off test, which says that the business unit and/or the group should be worth more with the business unit as part of the group.

This research also identified four practical concepts of corporate strategy. Each requires the corporate centre to interface with its business units in a different way. Portfolio management is in line with our controls configuration as it encompasses a range of highly decentralised business units controlled by a small corporate centre which focuses on acquisitions and divestments. Restructuring requires more active involvement from the corporate centre, at least initially when the centre makes significant changes to an under-performing new business unit. Once restructured, the now well-performing business unit should be sold as the corporate centre is no longer adding value. Thus, restructuring also fits in our controls configuration.

Transferring skills across the group is about leveraging existing knowledge, as the knowledge shared must represent a source of competitive advantage to the receiving business. If the centre runs out of opportunities to spread new knowledge to a business, or take new knowledge from it, the business unit should also be sold as the centre is no longer creating value. Therefore transferring skills is part of our scope configuration. Porter's fourth classification is sharing activities among business units which can create competitive advantage by reducing costs or increasing differentiation. Reducing costs through sharing is clearly about economies of scale and hence fits into our scale configuration. However, some forms of sharing in order to increase differentiation are really forms of leveraging knowledge and should be placed into our scope configuration.

Porter's four concepts do not therefore seem to encompass our most sustainable value-adding creative configuration even though his analysis included some of our case study examples of the leader style corporate centre, e.g. 3M and GE. He did propose the identification of a meaningful corporate theme to reinforce the value-adding interrelationships among the businesses within the group. This could be argued as similar to the establishment of the vision and set of values that are so critical to the continuing creation of new corporate know-how.

One team of eminent researchers who do focus on the creation of new knowledge by corporate centres is Hamel and Prahalad (Hamel and Prahalad, 1990, 1993 and 1994). Their initial framework considered groups as portfolios of core competences rather than portfolios of businesses. Core competences are regarded as the roots of competitive advantage as they *must* be competitively unique and make a disproportionate contribution to customer perceived value. These core competences represent the collective learning of the organisation and nourish the core products that are the embodiments of one or more core competences. Business units then incorporate these core products into the end products that they sell outside the group. The value-adding role of the corporate centre is first to consolidate corporate wide technologies and production skills into core competences; what we describe as leveraging existing knowledge across the group. One common problem is that particular business units may 'own' specific core competences, in that these are not seen as a corporate resource. Hamel and Prahalad refer to these as 'imprisoned resources', which may lead to 'bounded innovation' where the business unit only looks at their own close at hand opportunities for exploitation.

However, a second stage value-adding role for the corporate centre is to enunciate a strategic architecture that facilitates the building of core competences for the future. The strategic architecture establishes objectives for the type of core competences that will be needed by the group in the future competitive environment that is foreseen by the corporate centre. Thus the strategic architecture asks 'What do we as a group need to do now in order to be well positioned in the future?' Clearly no single business unit will automatically feel responsible to do this, so the role of setting the vision falls to the centre as does the task of creating an environment where the business units will collaborate in developing the capabilities required to deliver the vision. In terms of our corporate configurations model, this represents a creative configuration role for the centre.

Hamel and Prahalad then developed their views on strategy as resource leverage in order to fill the stretch gap that should be deliberately created between existing resources and the aspirations of the company. They identified a number of ways in which resources could be leveraged, but we would place some of these in different configurations. Leveraging resources by concentrating them on a few key strategic goals, by recovering them in the shortest possible time, and by conserving resources wherever possible are all examples of the role of our scope configuration. However, leveraging resources by accumulating them more efficiently can, in some instances, be seen as a scale configuration role, while complementing one kind of resource with another to create a higher order value resource is a creative configuration generating new corporate know-how.

These ideas were then all pulled together in a picture of how companies should be 'competing for the future'. This requires the group to have 'industry foresight' so that required changes can happen in a calm and considered manner. This means that the organisation's transformation can be revolutionary in result but evolutionary in execution. The transformation should aim to meet as yet unarticulated needs of as yet unserved customers through the development of new core competences. Such a group is aiming for intellectual leadership of its 'industry' by managing the migration paths taken to reach the future. Clearly this type of group needs visionary leadership from its corporate centre in a creative configuration.

Another body of corporate strategy research that highlights the truly creative leadership role of corporate centres in some groups is that of Jim Collins and others (Collins, 1992, 1994 and 2001). Collins identifies great leaders as requiring a paradoxical blend of personal humility and professional will; they do not need to be personally charismatic. The key function of these leaders is to create a clear vision that is both bought into and actively pursued by the employees of the company. This is greatly facilitated if the group has clearly identified what is critically important to it; what Collins calls the company's 'hedgehog concept'. The hedgehog concept represents the intersection of the company's core values, its core competences, and the key drivers of its super profits.

One of the very important elements in this framework of 'building and maintaining a great company' is that the vision not only incorporates the core values and beliefs together with the fundamental reason for the existence of the company (the core ideology) but also has a measurable mission statement. This mission should be challenging and compelling but have a measure of risk, if it is to create the stretch required for 'greatness'; what Collins and Porras called Big Hairy Audacious Goals (BHAGs). As one mission comes close to being achieved it needs to be replaced by a new BHAG so that the organisation is always stretching itself to reach new goals. Thus everything but the core ideology can and should change as required by the external environment. This is reflected in the standards applied by these companies. The values standards are very rigid and non-compliance should result in expulsion from the company. The performance standards are still very high, because great performers get very fed up if the organisation tolerates poor performance, but are less rigid. Indeed learning failures are encouraged, as long as the learnings are shared across the group. In our terms, the corporate centre in such groups should be acting in the leader style of the creative configuration.

Conclusion

Hopefully this chapter has demonstrated that we have reviewed and challenged our corporate configurations model against other corporate strategy models, frameworks and relevant theories. We have not found any irreconcilable issues arising from this review and indeed the corporate configurations model seems to provide a comprehensive understanding of the value-adding role of the corporate centre in a multi-business group. We sincerely hope therefore that it adds to the knowledge in this very important area for the large organisations that now dominate economic activity globally.

References

Barnard, C., 1938, *The Functions of the Executive*, Harvard University Press, Cambridge MA.

Barney, J.B., 1991, Firm resources and sustained competitive advantage, *Journal of Management*, 17 (1), 99–120.

Barney, J.B., 1999, How a firm's capabilities affect boundary decisions, *Sloan Management Review*, Spring, 137–145.

Burns, T. and Stalker, G.M., 1961, *The Management of Innovation*, Tavistock, London.

Campell, A., Goold, M. and Alexander, M., 1995, Corporate strategy: The quest for parenting advantage, *Harvard Business Review*, March/April.

Chandler, A.D., 1962, *Strategy and Structure*, MIT Press, Cambridge, MA.

Coase, R.E., 1937, The nature of the firm, *Economica*, 4, 386–405.

Collins, J.C. and Lazier, W.C., 1992, *Beyond Entrepreneurship*, Prentice-Hall, Englewood Cliffs, NJ.

Collins, J.C. and Porras, J.I., 1994, *Built to Last*, Random House, New York.

Collins, J.C., 2001, *Good to Great*, Random House, New York.

Dierickx, I. and Cool, K., 1989, Asset stock accumulation and sustainability of competitive advantage, *Management Science*, 35 (12), 1504–1511.

Eisenhardt, K.M. and Martin, J.A., 2000, Dynamic capabilities: What are they? *Strategic Management Journal*, 21 (10–11), 1105–1121.

Ghoshal, S. and Moran, P., 1996, Bad for practice: A critique of the transaction cost theory, *Academy of Management Review*, 21 (1), 13–47.

Goold, M. and Campbell, A., 1987, *Strategies and Styles – The Role of the Centre in Managing Diversified Corporations*, Blackwell, Oxford.

Goold, M. and Campbell, A., 1993a, Strategies and styles revisited: strategic planning and financial control, *Long Range Planning*, 26 (5), 49–60.

Goold, M. and Campbell, A., 1993b, Strategies and styles revisited: strategic control – is it tenable? *Long Range Planning*, 26 (6), 54–61.

Goold, M., Campbell, A. and Alexander, M., 1994, *Corporate Level Strategy*, Wiley, New York.

Goold, M. and Campbell, A., 2002, *Designing Effective Organisations*, Josey-Bass, San Francisco.

Hamel, G. and Prahalad, C.K., 1990, The core competence of the corporation, *Harvard Business Review*, May/June.

Hamel, G. and Prahalad, C.K., 1993, Strategy as stretch and leverage, *Harvard Business Review*, March/April.

Hamel, G. and Prahalad, C.K., 1994, *Competing for the future*, Harvard Business School Press, Boston.

Hayek, F., 1945, The use of knowledge in society, *American Economic Review*, 35 (4), 519–530.

Lawrence, P. and Lorsch, J., 1967, *Organisation and Environment*, Harvard University Press, Boston.

Madhok, A., 2002, Reassessing the fundamentals and beyond: Ronald Coase, The transaction cost and the resource based theories of the firm and the institutional structure of production, *Strategic Management Journal*, 23, 535–550.

Miles, R.E. and Snow, C.C., 1978, *Organisational Strategy, Structure and Process*, McGraw Hill, New York.

Mintzberg, H., 1979, *The Structuring of Organisations*, Prentice-Hall, Englewood Cliffs, NJ.

Mintzberg, H., 1981, Organisation design: fashion or fit?, *Harvard Business Review*, Jan/Feb.

Mintzberg, H. and Waters, J.A., 1985, Of strategies, deliberate and emergent, *Strategic Management Journal*, 6, 257–272.

Mintzberg, H., 1994, *The Rise and Fall of Strategic Planning*, Prentice-Hall, Englewood Cliffs, NJ.

Mintzberg, H., Ahlstand, B. and Lampel, J., 1998, *Strategy Safari*, Free Press, New York.

Penrose, E.G., 1959, *The Theory of the Growth of the Firm*, Wiley, New York.

Peters, T.J. and Waterman Jr, R.H., 1982, *In Search of Excellence*, Harper & Row, New York.

Peters, T.J. and Austin, N., 1985, *A Passion for Excellence*, Collins, London.

Peters, T.J., 1987, *Thriving on Chaos*, Alfred A. Knopf Inc. USA.

Porter, M.J., 1980, *Competitive Strategy*, Free Press, New York.

Porter, M.J., 1985, *Competitive Advantage*, Free Press, New York.

Porter, M.J., 1987, From competitive advantage to corporate strategy, *Harvard Business Review*, May/June.

Roberts, P.W. and Greenwood, R., 1997, Integrating tansaction cost and institutional theories: Towards a constrained-efficiency framework for understanding organisational design adoption, *Academy of Management Review*, 22(2), 346–373.

Rubin, P.H., 1973, The expansion of firms, *Journal of Political Economy*, 81, 936–949.

Rumelt, B.P., Schendel, D. and Teece, D.J., 1991, Strategic management and economics, *Strategic Management Journal*, 12, 5–29.

Simon, H.A., 1991, Organisations and markets, *Journal of Economic Perspectives*, 5(2), 25–44.

Teece, D.J., Pisano, G. and Skuen, A., 1997, Dynamic capabilities and strategic management, *Strategic Management Journal*, 18(7), 509–533.

Wernerfelt, B., 1984, A resource-based view of the firm, *Strategic Management Journal*, 5, 171–180.

Wernerfelt, B., 1994, The resource-based view of the firm – ten years after, *Strategic Management Journal*, 16, 171–174.

Williamson, O.E., 1975, *Markets and Hierarchies: Analysis and Antitrust Implications*, Free Press, New York.

Williamson, O.E., 1985, *The Economic Institutions of Capitalism*, Free Press, New York.

Williamson, O.E., 1996, Economics and organisation: A primer, *California Management Review*, 31 (2).

Index

Figures and tables are in *Italic*